Diplomatic Interventions

Also by K.M. Fierke

CHANGING GAMES, CHANGING STRATEGIES: Critical Investigations in Security (*1998*)

CONSTRUCTING INTERNATIONAL RELATIONS: The Next Generation (*co-editor with Knud Erik Jorgensen, 2001*)

Diplomatic Interventions

Conflict and Change in a Globalizing World

K.M. Fierke
Reader, School of Politics and International Studies,
Queen's University, Belfast

First published in 2005 by
PALGRAVE MACMILLAN
Houndmills, Basingstoke, Hampshire RG21 6XS and
175 Fifth Avenue, New York, N.Y. 10010
Companies and representatives throughout the world.

PALGRAVE MACMILLAN is the global academic imprint of the Palgrave Macmillan division of St. Martin's Press, LLC and of Palgrave Macmillan Ltd. Macmillan® is a registered trademark in the United States, United Kingdom and other countries. Palgrave is a registered trademark in the European Union and other countries.

ISBN-13: 978–1–4039–1540–5   hardback
ISBN-10: 1–4039–1540–7   hardback
ISBN-13: 978–1–4039–1541–2   paperback
ISBN-10: 1–4039–1541–5   paperback

This book is printed on paper suitable for recycling and made from fully managed and sustained forest sources.

A catalogue record for this book is available from the British Library.

Library of Congress Cataloging-in-Publication Data

Fierke, K. M. (Karin M.)
    Diplomatic interventions : conflict and change in a globalizing world /
K. M. Fierke.
        p. cm.
    Includes bibliographical references and index.
    ISBN 1–4039–1540–7 – ISBN 1–4039–1541–5 (pbk.)
        1. Intervention (International law) 2. Conflict management.
    3. Diplomacy. I. Title.

JZ6368. F54 2005
341.5'84—dc22   2005040544

10 9 8 7 6 5 4 3 2 1
14 13 12 11 10 09 08 07 06 05

Printed and bound in Great Britain by
Antony Rowe Ltd, Chippenham and Eastbourne.

To Michael Nicholson
In memorium

Contents

Preface

In international relations intervention is most often understood to be an act undertaken by states, usually involving some kind of coercion, that impacts on the territorial integrity or political independence of another state. These acts may be undertaken for a variety of ends, whether humanitarian or power political. L. Oppenheim referred to intervention as "dictatorial interference" in the internal or external affairs of a state.[1] R.J. Vincent defined intervention as activity undertaken by a state, a group within a state, a group of states, or an international organization which interferes coercively in the domestic affairs of another state.[2] Hedley Bull noted that international lawyers have traditionally viewed intervention as a dictatorial or coercive interference by an outside party or parties in the jurisdiction of a sovereign state or, more broadly, an independent political community.[3] Stanley Hoffman argued that in the widest sense, every act of a state constitutes an intervention.[4]

These definitions, and most contemporary uses of the word intervention, share a focus on the act of interference by one state in the affairs of another. They represent attempts to place boundaries on a potentially large and unwieldy concept.[5] The purpose of this book, by contrast, is to unsettle the definition of intervention by arguing that any particular border crossing or interference is constituted by a range of prior interventions. In this respect, intervention is a more general term that refers to that which through its presence modifies an existing state of affairs. I refer to these as "diplomatic" interventions in so far as they may involve some form of communication to avoid or limit recourse to force, as well as to realize it. The agents of intervention are not purely the traditional diplomat, however. Over the last century in particular the range of actors involved in some form of cross-border communication related to war has multiplied. Not only states, but international organizations, nongovernmental organizations, journalists, and others have shaped the experience of war.

There are two consequences of this act of unsettling. First, we shift emphasis from what one state does to another to the larger context of international rules and practices within which more specific acts are given meaning. An analysis of this kind focuses on the various background conditions that made a forceful intervention possible in, for instance,

Kosovo or Afghanistan, rather than an analysis of the use of force itself. Any particular act of interference is constituted or made possible by a larger set of assumptions, rules, and practices. These are interventions in and of themselves. For instance, human rights law or the Genocide Convention represent forms of legal intervention that provide a necessary background for justifying intervention for humanitarian ends. Or the Just War tradition represents a form of moral intervention to define the parameters of acceptable warfare.

Second, we shift attention from intervention as a specific type of act, with force, to intervention as part of a human attempt to mold and/or limit the experience of war. Intervention, in this respect, involves a form of agency that is larger than the decision to interfere in the affairs of another state. Agency resides in the attempt to alter the larger context within which war is defined and fought.

Realist International Relations theory has assumed that war is a natural and recurring feature of the international system, whether due to human nature or the inescapable condition of anarchy. Constructivists have argued that "anarchy is what states make of it" and that the shape of the system emerges out of interactions between states. On a theoretical level, this book is an attempt to explore the tension between these two statements, that is, that war is a recurring feature of international relations, and that it is a social construct, given form and meaning through human and state interactions. It is in the midst of this tension that the potential for conflict avoidance or transformation is to be identified. Each of the chapters explores this tension in relation to a specific type of intervention.

Chapter 1 examines the central tension underlying the book between realism and constructivism as it relates to questions of war. Several contrasts are explored: first, that between realist assumptions that war is an inescapable condition vs. war as a human and social construction; second, that between human nature or anarchy as a cause of international conflict and war vs. the idea that anarchy "is what states make it," that is, that conflict or peace are constituted through interactions in historically specific conditions. The analysis looks to the literature on causes of war, much of which grows out of the realist tradition, contrasting the assumptions of this genre with more recent arguments about the social constitution of conflict. The chapter analyzes what is at stake in this distinction, particularly as it relates to the potential for intervention to transform conflict.

In the realist tradition, war is considered to be endemic to the international system because there is no overarching global authority to adjudicate in cases of dispute. The Westphalian system, since 1648, has been organized around the principles of sovereignty and nonintervention, which presumes this absence. Yet, when approached historically, it is evident that the meaning and expression of war have taken contextually specific forms. Chapter 2 provides a historical overview of the changing structures of warfare, from the fragmented lines of authority during the medieval period, to the various balance of power logics within the Westphalian period, to the emerging web of state and institutional relationships against the background of globalization. The chapter argues that war, while a recurring feature, has always been constructed in the sense that it is given meaning and shape within particular historical and cultural contexts, defined by different technological and organizational forms to different ends.

One of the central themes of the realist framework is the tension between "is" and "ought." Realists claim to work with the world as it is, assuming power to be the determining factor in state interactions. Constructivists, by contrast, are more inclined to argue that normative and ethical concerns, that is, the "ought," are embedded in all actions. From this perspective, realism contains an "ought" like any other model, in that assumptions about the world give rise to conclusions about necessary action. Chapter 3 surveys different traditions of moral and ethical reasoning as they relate to questions of war. More specifically it looks at the historical evolution of Just War thinking, and related rules of war and humanitarian practice, as forms of moral intervention to shape and limit the destructiveness of war.

There exist several layers of international law, some growing out of the customary practices of states; others more explicitly represent the codification of moral principle. While the different types of law are sometimes in conflict, they are all part of a historical pattern, that is, legal codification has often been a response to problems arising from the increased destructiveness of war. Sovereignty and nonintervention were a response to the bloody Thirty Years' War. The Geneva Conventions were a response to the increasing destructiveness of war with the move toward forms of total warfare and the collapsing distinction between citizen and soldier. The Genocide Convention and Human Rights law were a response to the atrocities of the Holocaust. Chapter 4 grapples with the significance of the observation that legal codification has been a response to the increasing destructiveness of war and whether this strengthens or weakens realist claims regarding the supremacy of power and might.

The question of moral and legal constraints on war has played an important role in defining the parameters for military intervention.

Whether intervention is defined in terms of national interest or human rights, states have drawn on traditional moral and legal arguments to justify their actions. Chapter 5 looks at the relationship between different strategies of military intervention, related in particular to coercive diplomacy, humanitarian intervention, and pre-emptive strategies in the name of self-defense. Building on the discussion of the previous chapter, this chapter examines the relationship between strategic, legal, and moral criteria for military intervention, pointing to the increasing complexity of the social and institutional background against which states and other actors must shape and construct specific policy choices.

The economic corollary of the realist emphasis on military power is the arms trade. The arms trade is often viewed as a global logic in and of itself that reproduces conflict and war. However, arms transfers have historically been an instrument of policy, and thus intervention, to buttress allies and punish foes. Particularly during the latter part of the Cold War, arms transfers to ideological allies and "freedom fighters" were a potent tool in the conflict between East and West. During this period, another type of economic intervention, that is, economic sanctions, was not considered to be an effective policy choice. Since the end of the Cold War economic sanctions have been increasingly a tool for reinforcing global norms and influencing the policies of repressive states. The purpose of Chapter 6 is to explore the relationship between arms transfers and economic sanctions as forms of intervention. During the Cold War the superpowers flooded the globe with arms. In its aftermath, states have been forced to negotiate the complex tension between economic dependence on the arms trade, on the one hand, and, on the other, the need to re-establish control over "rogue states" and "terrorists," through economic sanctions, against the backdrop of widespread proliferation.

The previous chapters highlighted the delicate relationship between practices of war and attempts to limit or circumscribe its destructiveness, as well as the extent to which the current culture of international politics is woven in a complex tapestry of tensions. Realist theories have tended to ignore questions of culture, given assumptions that state action is a function of more generalized notions of human nature or anarchy. However, several trends since the end of the Cold War make it increasingly difficult to ignore the role of culture in constituting the possibility of war or its transformation. As the Cold War culture dissolved, the ideological conflict between East and West was supplanted by, on the one hand, nationalist conflicts, as in the Balkans, and, on the other hand, attempts to transform long-standing ethnic conflicts, previously subsumed by the superpower standoff. Chapter 7 explores the different ways in which culture plays a role in the constitution of war or its transformation. Culture has several expressions. It can refer to the increasing relevance of ethnic or other cultural lines for delineating conflicts. It refers more generally to meanings conveyed in language or visual image and how these constitute the possibility of war or peace. Propaganda has traditionally been an important medium for lending cultural meaning to conflict, albeit distorted, which has contributed to the construction of war. By contrast, dialogue has increasingly provided a context for actors to break down established assumptions and fixed categories of us and them, in order to re-describe the potential for new forms of identity and interaction and thus conflict transformation.

That individual and social trauma accompanies the destruction of war should be obvious. Yet trauma has only recently become a subject of serious study in the literature of international relations. Realists view patterns of recurring conflict as a natural feature of the international system. When approached from a more therapeutic angle, the repro-duction of conflict can be understood as the re-enactment of past trauma across generations in an attempt to seek vengeance. Politically this phenomenon can be observed in the important place given to past traumas and wars in the justification of contemporary action against new enemies. The year 1389 in the vocabulary of the Serbs or the Holocaust in the vocabulary of Israel and others have provided a frame-work for mobilizing public emotion and action. Interestingly, a "therapy" metaphor has provided a framework for practices such as dialogue, Truth and Reconciliation Commissions, or reparations. Each of these in different ways seeks to break the pattern of war by coming to terms with the past. The purpose of Chapter 8 is to explore the role of past trauma in reproducing patterns of war and different modes of conflict therapy which point to the possibility of moving beyond recurring cycles of violence toward some kind of healing.

The purpose of Chapter 9 is to revisit the various categories of interven-tion explored in this book from a critical perspective. Throughout the book emphasis is placed on efforts to limit the destructiveness of war. Each chapter reveals a tension between the reality of war and efforts to define boundaries around this reality. However, from a critical perspective, both sides of this tension are social constructions. For instance, the "reality" identified by realists is constructed on a range of assumed categories which have defined the international system, and not least the concept of sover-eignty. One goal of this chapter is to highlight the extent to which the book itself represents a critical intervention and how this requires that we look again from a new angle at international practices of intervention.

The other goal is to reach some conclusions about the overarching theme, that is, the relationship between realism and constructivism. First, as the chapters progress further layers of constructedness emerge until it becomes difficult to talk about a single unchanging reality in any meaningful sense. Instead, the range of conventions and practices that have defined or transformed war over time are bound up in an ever changing historical and cultural context. Second, the social construct-edness of war is in tension with the obvious element of destruction, including the deconstruction of civilization, which arises from this practice. Chapter 9 explores the paradox that war occupies a space on a spectrum spanning from social construction to deconstruction and examines the role of international intervention in situating a particular war along this spectrum.

Often the claim that the international system is constructed, and thus changeable, goes hand in hand with assumptions that we can move beyond the problem of war. Just as the human community once banned slavery, they will one day ban war. In this case the equation is much more complex, and does not add up simply to war or not war. Together a range of intersecting factors constitute any particular case of war or intervention. The field is not static, however. The constellation, including the background rules (morality and law) or policy choices (military and economic) and attempts to reconstitute meaning (culture, therapy) have changed from one historical era to another or one particular context to another. A tension, by definition, pulls in opposite directions, which can contribute to the reproduction of conflict, while transforming the historical constellation. Part of the usefulness of a constructivist analysis is that it provides a thicker understanding of how different patterns are interwoven and thus how they might be interrupted.

This book grew out of a postgraduate seminar taught for two years at Queen's University Belfast. Its contents have been enriched by my exchanges with students on the MA in International Politics. The class of 2001–02 engaged with the ideas before I began writing the chapters. Their insightful contributions (and the fact that many of them, much to my surprise, turned into die-hard realists) made me ask serious questions I may not have entertained on my own. I would like to thank Fiona Barr, Andrew Donnan (who also provided comments on Chapter 1), Karen O'Kane, Quentin Mayne, Neil McKintrick, Jerome Sherman, and Hung Jen Wang. The class of 2003–04 read early drafts of the chapters and provided useful feedback, as well as bringing a somewhat more optimistic take to the subject matter. This group included Agnes Cronin, Fiona Cullen, Louise Jones, Siobhan O'Leary, John Rogers, Taryn Sheppard,

Isil Ulguc, and Max Vogel. They are all in a small way contributing authors. My interactions with them have made me aware of exactly how important the link between teaching and research can be.

I would also like to thank Mary Jane Fox for her support and comments on some of the material in the text, particularly relating to the legal distinctions; the reader for Palgrave Press, for his or her encouraging and helpful reviews of the proposal and the book; Alison Howson, the editor at Palgrave, for her enthusiasm and support throughout the process of writing and producing the text; Charlotte McEvoy, for providing helpful comments on Chapter 7; William Cleere, Neta Crawford, Brian Frederking, Thomas Kehoe, Nicholas Onuf, and Nicholas Wheeler for taking time from their busy schedules to read through the almost final draft, and for providing very detailed and useful feedback; and Myles Courtney for reading through the completed text just before sending it off to Palgrave. I would also like to thank the Leverhulme Trust who granted me a research fellowship in 2002–03 for a project on the conceptualization of trauma and therapy as political concepts, which provided the basis for the argument in Chapter 8.

Last, but certainly not least, I would like to thank Michael Nicholson, to whom I have dedicated this book. His sudden and untimely death in October 2001 preceded both the conceptualization and writing of the manuscript. However, its two central concerns, conflict and methodology, are what brought us together in an academic project and later developed into a deep friendship and love. We agreed on very little, but that difference sustained and energized countless discussions on the beaches and in the forests of Northern Ireland during the two years preceding his death. His children, Jane, Carolyn, and Paul, and his grandchildren, Carmen, Mateo, Anna, and Sarah, have in the years since been a source of support, love, and laughter, and a continuing reminder that even in loss something is left over.

1
Cause or Constitution?

> Whereas aggression may be inherent (in human nature), war is
> learned behavior, and as such can be unlearned and ultimately
> selected out entirely. Humans have dispensed with other habits
> that previously seemed impossible to shed. For example, during
> the Ice Age, when people lived in caves, incest was perfectly
> acceptable, whereas today incest is almost universally taboo. ...
> Like slavery and cannibalism, war too can be eliminated from
> humankind's arsenal of horrors.
>
> John Stoessinger[1]

War is a reflection of the human condition. A few centuries ago, a similar
claim was made about slavery, which has since been formally abolished.
Slavery was once understood to be a timeless enterprise. It is now a historical phenomenon, for which US President George W. Bush, during a
visit to Africa in 2003, expressed regret. Forced enslavement is a prohibited
act in the statutes of the new International Criminal Court.

While an unequivocal moral rejection of war is more complicated
than that of slavery, the pattern is at best uneven. In the nineteenth century, during the Concert of Europe, there was a lengthy period without
major interstate war. The Kellogg–Briand Pact after the First World War
made aggressive war illegal. The European Union has been largely successful in creating the conditions for former enemies to cooperate. One
of the most popular contemporary theories of international relations
rests on the argument that democracies don't fight one another.[2]

The purpose of this chapter is to explore the tension between two
different claims about war. The first claim is that war is a timeless feature
of international relations. Whether due to evil human nature or the
anarchic international system, war is pervasive. At best, its worst effects

1

can be managed but not eliminated. The second claim relaxes the assumption about human nature and introduces more space for agency and reflexivity. War may be a recurring phenomenon. However, not all history is a history of war. Throughout history, actors have taken steps to limit, shape, or transform the nature of war. War, in this respect, is a social artifact, constructed by humans for specifically human ends, but potentially in conflict with other human ends. War is distinguished from violence more generally by its dependence on socially recognized rules. Indeed, as Adam Roberts and Richard Guelff note, "the idea that the conduct of armed hostilities is governed by rules appears to be found in almost all societies without geographical limitation."[3]

The tension between the essential quality of war, on the one hand, and the social construction of war interfaces with, but is distinct from, three further contrasts, which I explore in the rest of this chapter. The first section examines the contrast between the assumptions of realist and liberal theory. The second section relates this to a further contrast between positivism and constructivism as different methodologies.[4] The third section weaves these together in a further analysis of the distinction between the causes of war vs. the social constitution of war. These are elaborated in relation to specific arguments about the origins of war. Clarifying these distinctions, as they relate to the two claims above, will also clarify what is at stake in posing the problem in this way.

Realist and liberal theory

It is tempting to think about the contrast above in terms of the generalized claims of realist and liberal theories of international relations. From this perspective, the key issue is one of the potential for conflict as opposed to cooperation between states. However, while the conflict/cooperation dichotomy can incorporate elements of the larger tension, it is distinct. A closer look at these theoretical frameworks as generalizations about political life will clarify why. Both realist and liberal international relations theory have assumed the basic rationality of states as the central units of the international system. Both have assumed the condition of anarchy or the absence of an overarching authority at the international level. They have differed however in their conclusions about the origins of war or the potential for its elimination.

Realists, drawing on a long tradition of thought, spanning from Thucydides' *History of the Peloponnesian Wars* to Machiavelli's *The Prince* to Hobbes' *Leviathan*, have sought to describe and explain the world of international politics "as it is," rather than how it ought to be. Hobbes, for instance, depicted the state of nature as a condition prior to society where life was "nasty, brutish, and short."[5] People lived in constant fear of their neighbor because, in the absence of a common power "to keep them in awe,"[6] they were all equal in their freedom and vulnerability. Reason provided escape from perpetual war, but in the creation of the commonwealth, the problem of insecurity in the state of nature was transferred to the international level, where states "live in the condition of a perpetuall war, and upon the confines of battle, with their frontiers armed, and canons planted against their neighbours round about."[7]

The reality, in this depiction, is one of conflict and war. Traditional realists, who emphasize a pessimistic view of human nature, have been distinguished from neo-realists, who focus on the competitive logic of anarchy.[8] In both cases the conclusion is the same: states have to take care of themselves since there is no global authority to act on their behalf. This means that they must be continually prepared for war. The ultimate interest of states is to maximize their own power and self-interest. This tends to give rise to what has been referred to as the security dilemma.[9] The effort of each state to enhance its own security may be perceived as a potential threat by others, which generates a spiral of insecurity and conflict.

Liberal theories of international relations have also been influenced by a long tradition of political thought, including the ideas of Grotius and Kant, among others. Grotius, who established international law as an independent area of learning, claimed that laws would guarantee peaceful interactions among sovereign states that would benefit everyone.[10] Kant argued that republican forms of government would make rulers accountable to citizens and respect individual rights. This would lead to peaceful international relations in so far as the ultimate consent for war would rest with the citizens of a state.[11]

The liberal tradition more broadly has consisted of two strands, emphasizing, on the one hand, the maximization of individual utility, and, on the other hand, the possibility of progress and the realization of human potential.[12] These two are distinct and at times contradictory, but both have contributed to an emphasis on the importance of free trade, democracy, international law, and collective security, that is, the potential for states to cooperate in stopping any threat to the international system. Liberals have tended to assume that conflict or insecurity most often arise from misunderstanding or misperception. The creation of international institutions, laws and rules to facilitate communication and agreement can help to alleviate these misunderstandings and thus prevent war.[13] Further, the spread of liberal democratic principles to the international realm can create the conditions for a peaceful world order because "a world made up of liberal democracies would reciprocally recognize one another's legitimacy."[14]

The question is how these theories relate to the two claims above. As *theories*, realism and liberalism represent generalizations, which rest on assumptions about human or state nature, and conclusions that are derived from these. There is a clear affinity between claim one, that is, war is pervasive, and realist theory. Because power, greed, and conflict are endemic, war cannot be eliminated. At best it can be managed. The emphasis on managing conflict is reflected in the concept of the balance of power.[15] Indeed, communication regarding the balance of power was one of the central functions of diplomacy in the classical European system. If one state became too powerful and a threat to its neighbors, other states would join together to form an alliance to balance the power of the strong state. In the best case this balancing act in itself would re-establish equilibrium and prevent any war. In the worst case, war would have to be fought in order to stop an expanding power and restore equilibrium to the international system. In preventing any one state from achieving predominance over the system, the balance of power preserves the sovereignty of states and thus the international system.

The relationship between liberal theory and the second claim, that is, war is a social artifact, is less straightforward. On the one hand, liberal institutionalists emphasize the importance of rules, and the potential for states to create institutions that will ameliorate conflict, thereby highlighting the social nature of international relations in a way that realists do not.[16] Some realists would acknowledge the importance of the sovereignty and nonintervention rule, but stop there.[17] Liberals, by contrast, focus on the more complex array of rules that have over time emerged to shape multiple forms of interaction at the international level.

On the other hand, there may be a temptation to conflate the claim that "war is a social artifact" with liberal assumptions about the potential for progress and the perfectability of the human condition.[18] The argument of this book draws this conflation into question. A claim that war is socially constructed is not equivalent to a claim that we are progressing toward a more perfect world where war will be eliminated, however desirable that might be. At most, it suggests that human nature is not constant, and thus cannot be generalized as by nature good or bad. Rather, the multiple possibilities of human and social life are given meaning and substance in historically and socially specific conditions. In this respect, the argument of this book is more concerned with the process by which war as a social artifact is constructed than questions about the potential for conflict or cooperation. This relates to a further question about methodology.

Positivist and constructivist methodology

Realist and liberal theory make generalizations about the nature of international relations, which rest on differing assumptions about human nature and the potential for conflict or cooperation. There is a further tension between two methodological positions that is relevant to the initial claims. Methodology refers to a systematic way of doing, teaching, or studying something. Nicholson defines methodology as the "study of the methods by which one investigates the … social world."[19] Methodology rests on assumptions about how we know the world we study (*epistemology*) and the nature of being within that world (*ontology*). Positivism and constructivism approach these questions from two different angles.

The categories attached to methodological positions have themselves been a subject of debate.[20] For instance, many would confine the term positivism to the more narrow tradition of logical positivism, using the broader "social scientific approach" to refer to an emphasis on testable hypotheses and generalization. Likewise, some think of constructivism as a theory rather than an approach. I use these terms, recognizing the controversy concerning their use and, given the contrast, to avoid the impression that constructivism is contrary to the systematic and rigorous analysis associated with a scientific approach.[21]

Positivism begins with an assumption that "being," that is, objects, exist in the world independent of human interpretation or knowledge.[22] Being is thus separate from ways of knowing. Positivism places emphasis on observation and testing as the only way to justify claims to knowledge of the world. Like nature, the social world operates according to objective laws, which can be captured in law-like statements by the scientist, who is assumed to be an objective observer. From this perspective, the political world can be studied in much the same way as the scientist studies the natural world. The scientist fixes the meaning of the categories relevant to the subject matter she or he studies (e.g., states, balance of power, etc.), formulates hypotheses about the relationship between these categories, and conducts tests, to see whether the hypothesis corresponds with the world as it really is. In the philosophy of social science, this position would be referred to as broadly scientific, although it relates to various traditions of positivism. The end is to identify causal generalizations that provide the building blocs of a theory against which further tests can be conducted. The purpose of this procedure is to gain a clearer picture of the reality of the world. Theory provides a basis for extrapolating from the general to the specific, making it possible to predict the conditions under which certain outcomes will unfold or explain them when they do.

For instance, realist theory relies on concepts, such as national interest and balance of power, and general statements of cause that would provide the basis for formulating hypotheses related to particular cases. A realist might hypothesize that the end of the Cold War was brought about by the overwhelming military and economic superiority brought to bear by the United States of America (USA) on the Union of Soviet Socialist Republic (USSR), pressuring the superpower into submission.[23] Material power is a central feature of the explanation. This hypothesis would provide the basis for a test to see whether it corresponds with the facts. Ideally, through the process of testing, the theory would either be discarded, because it does not fit with the facts, or it would be strengthened. There is now a broad acceptance that theories can never be proven true or verified. Rather, good science will seek out the most difficult cases for testing, and deliberately try to falsify a theoretical claim.[24] If the theory passes the test, it will have been strengthened. The hope is to improve the power to predict future cases or, after the fact, to explain why a particular set of events occurred. The danger is that in setting out with a set of assumptions, based in theory, the observer from the outset excludes variables that may be significant and may see only what the theory already assumes.

The affinity between scientific assumptions about a real world existing "out there" and realist international relations theory is in part a function of the common assumption of a "real" world. However, it is also a function of how the latter emerged as a subject of academic study. Realist theory has been at the core of the effort, since the end of the Second World War, to make international relations into a science. Thus, within international relations, realism and positivism are sometimes used as if they were synonyms, although this is not accurate. Liberal theory has a different historical relationship to questions of methodology. Prior to the Second World War it was closely linked with the tradition of international law. During the Cold War, and in the climate of American social science, attempts were also made to codify liberal ideas into theories that would provide a competing explanation of the international system to that of realism. Liberals provided a different explanation for the occurrence of conflict but also sought to account for the possibility of cooperation between states. Interdependence theory, for instance, provided an explanation for the rise of regional economic integration in Europe,[25] which was inspired by a belief that the long history of conflict in Europe could be overcome by developing a common economic and political framework for the mutual benefit of states. For liberals such as Francis Fukayama, the end of the Cold War, and the collapse of the USSR were proof of the triumph of liberal democracy and capitalism.[26] Since that time, the idea that democracies don't fight one another, which is said to be the closest thing to a "law" in international relations,[27] has taken a central place in international relations theory. In sum, both realist and liberal theories of international relations build on a scientific methodology. They provide a set of assumptions about the world, which is the point of departure for generalization and theory testing.

Constructivism represents a different methodological position, which has been introduced into discussions of international relations since the late eighties, as the Cold War was coming to an end.[28] Since that time it has been at the center of scholarly debate and means different things to different people. As mentioned earlier, some want to make constructivism into a specific theory, like realism or liberalism, that is, a way of making causal generalizations about the world. Others argue that constructivism is an approach that at best sits uneasily with the formation of testable theory and at worst is in conflict with attempts to identify universal statements and causal patterns. For the sake of contrast, this argument focuses on the *contrast* between positivism and constructivism, rather than their potential compatibility.

If positivism assumes the world exists independent of human meaning, and that there are objective, causal mechanisms at work, constructivism assumes that the world is made and remade in the process of human and social interaction.[29] In this respect, the nature of being (*ontology*) cannot be separated from ways of knowing (*epistemology*). This does not deny the obvious point that the material world exists independent of or prior to human society. It does, however, presuppose that this material world has been dramatically altered by human interaction with it. A tree branch, aside from being a part of a tree, may be used as a weapon but it can also be formed into any number of human artifacts, from chairs, to baseball bats, to totem poles to a beam in the structure of a house. Once the material object, that is, the tree branch, is shaped into a specific form, it has a place within a particular type of social context where it has meaning in relation to other objects (e.g., chairs and living rooms or totem poles and religious rites), particular uses (to sit on or dance around, respectively) and is part of a language or grammar (of homes or religion). All of these are to some extent rule governed in that they rest on shared understandings about the nature of the object and how it is put to use. But, more to the point, it is not only that humans interact with nature, thereby transforming it; they also interact with each other. In the process they form different types of culturally and historically specific practices and institutions that are also rule governed.

From this perspective, we cannot assume that human nature is bad or good, or that states are by definition rational actors. States are also artifacts that have emerged out of historically specific conditions and are constituted out of shared understandings.[30] To be sovereign is to be recognized as sovereign by other states. The sovereign state is a historically specific phenomenon that can be distinguished from other historical forms of community, such as empires or tribes. Within the Westphalian period the nature of sovereignty has also changed from being invested in monarchs to being invested in parliaments or peoples. The diplomat has been the recognized representative of the sovereign in the international realm.

Given the "being" of the collective actor cannot be assumed, that is, that states, empires, tribes, or terrorist cells, are *constituted* in historically specific conditions, it becomes necessary to problematize the very process by which collective identity and agency are made or analyzed. Language from this perspective does not function as a mere label for objects in the world. Language, social being, and practice are intertwined. It is the difference between examining the thread with which a social fabric is woven, as contrasted with its more or less accurate reflection in a mirror. Rather than fixing the meaning of words, in order to compare them with the world, the analyst—him or herself a part of the world— is necessarily conscious of the relationship between a more scientific language and the language of the subjects of study. There are no universal meanings for any one word or practice, only family resemblances.

An unrelated example reveals the different way of knowing presumed by this approach. Suppose we want to create a theory of marriage, delineating the properties and internal structure marriage. In the scientific line of thought, this theory could be compared with the world to see whether they correspond. Proceeding in this way brings us to the positivist problem with definition: how do we distil the essence of marriage in such a way that we can capture all instances of it? Such a definition is necessary if the goal is comparison with the "real" world. We recognize a marriage when we see one, across cultures and across history; however, to construct a map of its properties we necessarily enter the realm of family resemblance rather than generalized theory. This requires that we "look and see" the types of relationship that fit within the parameters of marriage (master and harem, a hierarchy of dependency, an equal partnership, a man and a woman, partners of the same sex), the types of acts that constitute a marriage (saying "I do" or stamping on a piece of glass), and the overlapping frameworks within which these distinct but related practices and identities are given meaning across context. Only in this way could we develop an empirically sound taxonomy of the categories and practices that constitute marriage. As an investigation of *social* practices, an analysis of this kind necessarily takes the language of these practices seriously.

Causality and constitution

Causality and constitution are at the core of the difference between the two methodological positions.[31] Constructivist methodology does not preclude the possibility of a causal relationship. It does, however, raise questions about the distinction between causality and constitution. It problematizes the process by which "what is" is constructed or comes into being as the necessary condition for a causal relationship or indeed any other kind of relationship. While violence or conflict exists in nature, war does not. States or other kinds of agents, weapons or other kinds of material objects do not exist in nature. All of these have to be brought into being. They are social artifacts that rest on shared rules. They must become social artifacts before they can exist in causal relationship to other social artifacts. The next chapter explores this argument more specifically in regard to the history of diplomacy and warfare.

This raises a further question about how each works. A causal statement assumes two objects, one of which impacts on the other, transforming it in some way. To say that X caused Y is to say that without X, Y would have remained in some constant state. X thus made Y respond in a way it otherwise would not have. This relationship is captured in definitions of power by which X has power over Y if X is able to make Y do what it otherwise would not do. The identity of X and Y are assumed. The constant nature of X or Y, or their identity, is the necessary condition for a causal relationship. This is evident in a number of examples. To say that the teacher caused the student to take notes assumes the identity of the teacher as one who has power over the student and can impact on his or her behavior. To say that the threat from the USA caused the USSR to back down presumes a relationship between two distinct identities in which the latter's change of behavior is dependent on the action of the former. The cause of war has been a central question of international relations scholarship. Kenneth Waltz, in his classic, *Man, State and War* asked whether individuals, states, or the international system are the cause of war.[32] Each level of analysis has given rise to different explanations for the origin of war.

The levels of analysis problem was originally posed by David Singer.[33] The problem was whether to explain international behavior in terms of the units, that is, states, or in terms of the system of states or anarchy. Other formulations have included further levels, such as bureaucracies within states or individuals. For instance, a systems level analysis would see the behavior of states as a function of the larger structure of international anarchy and what survival in this situation rationally requires. An analysis at the level of bureaucracies might see the behavior of states as the outcome of bargains among bureaucratic agencies. The central question is the level at which causality and thus explanation is to be located.[34]

In regard to the cause of war, explanations at the individual level have focused on the personalities of leaders, their misperceptions or reduce causality to human nature. For classical realists, the existence of one evil man, such as Hitler or Saddam Hussein, is sufficient to cause war. Regardless of how peaceful others are, one bad apple can upset the apple cart. Hitler's effort to expand resulted in a spiral of insecurity and the Second World War. Other explanations of war at this level might focus on the personality traits of individuals and their tendency to misperceive or distort the actions of others, thereby escalating a conflict. For instance, it is often argued that the misperception of various European leaders led to a breakdown in the balance of power and the First World War.[35]

Another level of explanation focuses on the internal characteristics of states and whether some cultural or institutional qualities make certain states more war prone. For instance, liberal democratic peace theory argues that democratic states are less likely to go to war with one another. They are not necessarily less war prone, since they will go to war with authoritarian or totalitarian states. Nonetheless, the probability of war is not a function of individual leaders or the system of anarchy but the existence of a particular institutional culture.

Kenneth Waltz argued that theories focusing on individuals or the internal composition of states are reductionist, that is, they reduce the problem of war to the characteristics of the unit. Instead, he argues that the condition of anarchy, that is, the structure of the international system, is the permissive cause of war and the distribution of power is the key determinant of behavior. Given the absence of an overarching authority, anarchy makes all states insecure, isolated, and dependent on self-help. Out of their interactions, states are socialized into a system to which they have to conform in order to survive. Thus, in a system defined by a competitive logic and insecurity, arming will be the most rational course of action. The fact that insecurity is driven by a system of conformity wipes out any internal differences. Instead, the main cause of war at any point in time will be a change in the distribution of power. This may seem very similar to the individual level argument, that one bad apple, for example, Hitler, can make the whole system go pear shaped. In fact, it is quite different in so far as Hitler would be no less driven by balance of power considerations than any other state. All states, and Nazi Germany included, are primarily concerned about their own survival in a system where they must be permanently on guard. The systemic explanation isolates a change in the distribution of power as the key causal mechanism rather than any one individual or state.

Causal theories assume the nature of X, the antecedent condition to war, to be constant. For instance, at the level of the individual, if X (personality, misperception, etc.), then Y (war). At the level of the state, if X (a totalitarian state), then Y (war). At the level of the system, if X (a change in the distribution of power), then Y (war). While these do not exhaust the possible causes of war, they do provide a framework for thinking about these causes in terms of levels of analysis.

These statements can be arrived at through two different methods. The first is an *inductive* method, in which the scientist sets out to look at the raw facts and from these raw facts identifies patterns or correlations between variables.[36] Thus, by looking at numerous examples of war the hope is to identify correlations between variables, which may provide the basis for stipulating a causal relationship. The second method is more *deductive*. In this case, the scientist begins with a theory, such as realism, which builds on a general pattern or a *covering law*, and, on the basis of this theory formulates hypotheses that can be tested. The intent in both cases is to formulate theory and to test theory. The question is whether one moves from the facts to the theory or the theory to the facts. The argument for the latter is that the world is just too messy, there is too much going on to put facts together in the absence of general principles to focus the observation.[37] The formulation of theory helps to simplify and focus analysis. As already suggested, realist theories of international relations emerged in the context of the Cold War along with the desire to make international relations into a science. As a result, many theories tend to adopt realist assumptions regarding the causes of war, and the central role of material facts. Theories in the liberal tradition have been more inclined to emphasize misperception rather than power as the key factor or to include ideological or cultural factors, for instance, democracy or dictatorship, as causal. Others have stayed within the scientific tradition, but have questioned the distinction, acquired from positivism, between an empirical reality and a normative one. The idea that there is a real world of fact to be studied, which must be distinguished from normative statements about what "should be," has been central to the scientific enterprise.

The distinction between fact and value is at the core of the scientific project, but has increasingly been contested. For instance, David Welch argues that contrary to realist theory, leaders are often motivated by normative concerns that lead to behavior that may be inconsistent with material self-interest.[38] He analyzes the role of a justice motive in the outbreak of five Great Power wars and argues that justice is often an important reason for going to war, although each side is more sensitive to its own concerns about justice than those of the enemy. The question is whether in moving toward the causal power of normative concerns, such as justice, we not only upset the empirical-normative distinction, which is a building block of positivism, but also threaten the entire edifice.

Constitution

As the Cold War was coming to an end, many scholars became skeptical about the positivist approach to international relations.[39] First, the identities of the major players did not seem constant. After decades of engaging with one another as enemies, the USA and USSR suddenly began acting as friends and engaging in a process of disarmament. Second, given the emphasis on fixing meaning and fixing variables, the existing theories didn't seem to be equipped to explain a *change* like the end of the Cold War. For instance, realist theories tend to assume it is always more rational to arm than to disarm. Yet, Gorbachev and Reagan began disarming for the first time during the Cold War. Third, in so far as these theories did explain change, they tended to assume that this would happen through interstate war. However, the end of the Cold War came about peacefully as "Velvet Revolutions" shook Eastern Europe and Gorbachev, the leader of the Soviet Empire, stood by as the Eastern European regimes collapsed. The end of the Cold War called into question many timeless truths of international relations. Also, its advent came as a shock to observers, both academic and political, in the East and the West. Almost no one predicted its onset.

Against this background analysts began to look to more constitutive models for understanding change and thus war or its transformation. If the scientific model focuses on fixing variables and theory generation, a constitutive approach emphasizes how identities and outcomes are generated out of interactions between different actors. In this view, it would be counterproductive to start out by assuming actors have a particular nature or identity that is constant or that they necessarily respond in predictable ways. It may or may not be possible to predict that change will occur, that is, to formulate a theory of change or identify a cause of change, but it seems central to the concept that change may involve a transformation of units and their actions toward one another. In addition to the unpredicted change that Reagan and Gorbachev would begin acting as friends rather than enemies, there was a further change of the identities involved, as the USSR and East Germany disbanded, making way for a reconfiguration of the map of Europe.

At the heart of the social constructivist position is an argument that actors always have a choice. They are not determined in their response to others. In his seminal piece, "Anarchy is What States Make of It," Alexander Wendt uses the example of Alter and Ego, two space aliens who confront each other for the first time.[40] Through a process of signaling to one another, they generate a pattern of acting toward the other as a friend or enemy. Wendt argues that states in anarchy can in a similar way exercise a choice in responding to other states. Anarchy can generate different logics, which are more or less competitive or cooperative and this will depend on the specific choices states make vis à vis others. He takes the former Soviet leader Gorbachev as an example of a state actor who, against the background of changing conditions, rethought his rational interest and began acting toward the USA as a friend rather than an enemy.

This analysis gave rise to a widespread rethinking of the idea, made popular by Waltz, that the structure of anarchy overly determines the behavior of states, constraining their choices. In Wendt's argument, if there is a choice, that is, if others will respond differently to be treated as an enemy or a friend, then their identity is not fixed but changeable. Wendt has since been criticized for assuming the centrality of the state, failing to account for the role of other actors, such as NGOs or nationalist groups. Other constructivists have argued that the process by which the state itself is constructed must be drawn into the equation. They have further raised questions about the Alter and Ego example in so far as it suggests international actors could start with a clean slate, ignoring that they are always already embedded in a context of meaning, with a past, which constrains their room for maneuver.[41] Thus, given Gorbachev was situated in the competitive logic of the Cold War, it is necessary to problematize how it was possible for him to "act as if" cooperation with the USA was possible.[42] Answering this question requires looking to the broader social and political context in which Gorbachev could introduce the New Thinking as a meaningful alternative to balance of power politics.

The logic of constitution is thus different than the logic of causality. It does not assume that the identity of the actor is given, but rather assumes that this identity, along with the possibility of choice, is shaped by a historical context. In this respect, constitution can be understood in terms of an *abductive* logic, by which actors, in engaging with the other, "test" or try out different logics in an attempt to figure out who the other is and respond to them accordingly.[43] In a stable context this may look very similar to a causal relationship. In a classroom, the identity of the teacher and student are given. Thus the note-taking of the student can be situated in either framework. It would not be erroneous to say that the teacher, who lectures, causes the student to take notes, but we could also say that the relationship between teacher, student, and note-taking is constitutive of a particular kind of context, that is, the classroom. The identities of teacher and student are defined by the context of a classroom and note-taking is one of the things students do in this context. They together define identity and specific roles as part of the rules governing this type of interaction.

The distinction between the two is greater when the nature of the context is unclear, as is often the case at the international level. For instance, against the backdrop of the international debate over the invasion of Iraq in 2003, French President Jacques Chirac reprimanded leaders of the Central and East European countries (CEECs), soon to be members of the European Union, as if they were children, because they had backed the US position. If this were a causal relationship, we would have expected the CEECs to respond as if they were children, for example, accepting his reprimand and backing down, or whining, etc. Instead, they acted as if they were mature statespeople who had a right to their own views, even if these differed from one of the most powerful states in Europe. In "acting as if" they were mature statespeople they contributed to their constitution as this type of identity, thereby changing the shape of the context, and raising questions about Chirac's authoritarian tactics toward potential members of the European Union.

The abductive logic of constitution rests on a two-stage process rather than a single deduction. The first stage involves tending toward an Other "as if" they are of one type (children), as a form of testing the validity of the attribution. If the Other responds in kind (as children), the two together begin to converge on a common game (between powerful parental states and child states). If they respond on the basis of a different typification (mature statespeople), this represents a falsification of the original hypothesis and a realignment on a different game (between mature states, who respect one another). While using a similar language of hypothesis testing and falsification, this departs from a scientific approach. It is not the scientist who hypothesizes and tests theory, but the actors themselves, who are the subjects of analysis.

The discussion so far has focused on the end of the Cold War, and the transition out of a long-term conflict. There are several examples of more constitutive analyses of war.[44] A causal analysis might draw on realist theory to explain why war broke out in the former Yugoslavia after the end of the Cold War by pointing to the insecurity generated by the death of Tito. Once Tito was no longer there to mediate disputes between the different nationalities, ancient tribal hatreds between them gave rise to a spiral of insecurity. This assumes that Serbs, Croats, and Muslims living in the former Yugoslavia have a natural identity that goes back hundreds of years. However, given a high level of inter-marriage across these identity lines, particularly in the capital city Sarajevo, and a habit of living in relative peace over several decades, many have questioned how former neighbors were suddenly gripped by a hatred that degenerated into a vicious war. More constitutive analyses have looked at how leaders, such as Slobodan Milosevic mobilized Serb fears, drawing on stories of past defeat and trauma, to generate increasing insecurity and, in the process, magnified divisions between people, thereby making war possible.[45] In this view, the post–Cold War context contained the potential for either continuing cooperation or conflict. The role of Milosevic in inducing conflict, or encouraging Serbs to act as if Croats, Bosniacs, or Kosovars were enemies, can be contrasted with the role of a Vaclev Havel, the leader of another post-communist regime, who led the Czechs through a "Velvet Divorce" with the Slovaks and embarked on the process of joining the European Union.

Scientists, relying on positivist methodology, begin by fixing the meaning of terms, formulating hypotheses to be tested to see whether they correspond with the real world. These practices build on approaches to the natural sciences in which the scientist assumes an inanimate world and thus doesn't need to be terribly concerned with how the subjects of analysis give meaning to the world around them. From a constitutive perspective, the subjects necessarily become the focus of analysis. If political actors are always giving meaning to their world, which is the basis for their actions toward others, then more attention must be given to these practices of making meaning.

From this perspective, Welch's argument about the role of the justice motive could also be analyzed in constitutive terms, raising questions about the relationship between the meaning given to an experience of injustice and conclusions that the Other should be responded to in a war-like fashion. Some critical scholars have argued that realist claims about the predominance of power and insecurity can in and of themselves act as normative claims about who we are, who the other is and how we have to respond. David Campbell makes this kind of argument about the Gulf War in 1990–91.[46] Beginning with an observation that Saddam Hussein had been a client of the USA during the Iran–Iraq War, and had been armed by the superpower, he analyzes how Iraq's invasion of Kuwait was given meaning in terms of a "Hitler" invading a neighboring state. He argues that, given the history of the relationship, there were other possible narratives for situating Saddam's act. These alternatives were silenced in the construction of the Iraqi war. A narrative of a righteous "us" and an evil "them" made the Gulf War possible.

The language of causality asks a "why necessary" question. Why did X necessarily give rise to Y? Why did X, US military and economic pressure on the USSR, necessarily give rise to Y, the end of the Cold War and the USSR? Or why did X, the Iraqi invasion of Kuwait, necessarily give rise to the Gulf War? The language of constitution, by contrast, asks a "how possible" question.[47] How, given a logic of competitive arming that lasted decades, would it be possible for Gorbachev to act as if the USA were a friend, or to take unilateral steps to disarm in the hope of transforming the relationship? Or how, given the former Yugoslavia had been a multicultural society for decades, was it possible for a bloody war to break out? The two questions rest on different assumptions and focus attention in different ways. The causal question assumes X and Y exist in the empirical world, as constant features, which may impact on each other in predictable ways. X and Y are examples of a larger pattern, which can be drawn on to explain the particular case. The constitutive question assumes that human action is not determined, that actors do exercise choice, and they do so within a world shaped by widespread shared understandings. Any patterns to be found are less a function of natural law than social and intersubjective rules belonging to particular types of context. The one stands outside the world as a timeless entity to be observed. The other necessarily engages with a world that is constantly being remade.

Conclusion

This chapter has examined several distinctions. The first is a tension, which underlies the remaining chapters of this book, between a claim that war is a timeless phenomenon, which at best can be managed, as distinct from a claim that war is a social artifact that is subject to change and transformation. This was analyzed in relation to realist and liberal theories of international relations, which make different assumptions about the possibilities of conflict vs. cooperation. While there is a very close relationship between the claim that war is pervasive and realist theories of conflict, the relationship between liberal ideas about cooperation and the claim that war is a social artifact is more complex. The latter rests on methodological assumptions, associated with constructivism, that being in the world and knowledge about the world are intertwined, giving rise to historically and culturally distinct practices of war or change. This methodological position was contrasted with positivist assumptions, shared by realists and liberals, about a real world that can be studied with the same methods as the natural sciences, as if the subjects of study did not speak or bring meaning to their interactions. There has been a close association between social-scientific methodology and the evolution of realist and liberal theory, in particular since the end of the Second World War in the American context. This further relates to an emphasis on identifying the main cause of war as distinct from analyzing the practices by which war is constituted in historically specific circumstances.

In the introduction and the rest of the book, I have juxtaposed realism, a theory, and constructivism, a methodology, in relation to the two claims. This contrast cuts across the tensions explored in Chapter 1 and may seem counterintuitive. It has nonetheless been adopted for two reasons. First, realism brings together the idea that war is endemic to the international system with a methodology that assumes an objective world, themes that refer to the first claim in a way that a focus on positivism alone would not. Second, constructivism makes possible an understanding of war as a social artifact in a way that liberalism in and of itself does not. Liberal theories of international relations have often been married to a positivist methodology. A constructivist approach is not synonymous with either liberal ideas about cooperation or the assumption that humanity is moving toward a utopian end in which war will be eliminated. Constructivism thus seems to be the more appropriate category for referring to the process by which war is constructed as a social artifact.

In conclusion, two further clarifications are useful. First, a central point of the next chapter is to discuss war and diplomacy as social artifacts, that is, as rule-governed practices that have taken different shapes and forms in historically specific circumstances. A second point, elaborated in later chapters, is that recognizing war as a social construction, rather than an essential feature of human nature or anarchy, opens a space for greater reflexivity. The concept of reflexivity has been illustrated in the example of the person who at dusk stands before a window and simultaneously sees her reflection in the window and sees herself looking beyond the reflection to the world outside. Reflexivity means being able to stand back from the world and to see how one's actions are shaped and influenced by what is assumed about the world or by past conditioning. This does not necessarily contribute to the elimination of war. It does, however, increase the space within which actors at all levels of international society can make choices rather than acting as if war were the only option.

2
War and Diplomacy

> It is not what people do, the physical motions they go through, that are crucial but the institutions, practices, conventions that they make. Hence the social and historical conditions that "modify" war are not to be considered accidental or external to war itself for war is a social creation.
>
> Michael Walzer[1]

The last chapter raised questions about the cause or constitution of war, against the background of two alternative claims: war is a reflection of the human condition vs. war is a social artifact. At stake is whether war is determined by human nature or is a social product. Other animals, and not only human beings, are violent. Some, such as packs of wolves, engage in group violence. These activities would undoubtedly look the same whether a particular pack of wolves was located in twelfth-century Europe or twentieth-century Asia, assuming we are dealing with the same species of animal. War between human beings involves many more levels of organization and convention than violence between animals. Its reasons go beyond the need for food or protection to a range of more complex motives, ranging from glory to justice to economic gain. While war requires some level of group identity and conflict, this can take many different forms with consequences for how violence is organized. Wars between monarchs in the eighteenth century clearly differ in structure, intent, and forms of weaponry than the "War on Terrorism" at the beginning of the twenty-first.

War is a concept that shares a family resemblance with a range of other concepts. Conflict, fighting, violence, and intervention are all concepts that can overlap with or be used in conjunction with war. War is a form of conflict, for instance, but conflict is not by definition war.

War usually involves fighting between groups, but not all conflicts between groups are wars. Conflict also does not by definition involve a mutual contest of violence, as is evident in historical examples of non-violent conflict, such as Gandhi's India Campaign. The brute act of violence can also be distinguished from war. War involves a high degree of organization, through a system of socially sanctioned rules.[2] War has traditionally been declared formally between states, and has been shaped and circumscribed by various moral and legal principles, as we will examine in the next two chapters. Yet, we do refer to guerrilla wars or the War on Terrorism. In these cases, at least one of the actors is not a state, and thus it may be less than clear how the rules of war apply.

Forceful intervention may also be closely related to war. Saddam Hussein's invasion of Kuwait was an intervention, without consent, that was an act of war. The international community then intervened to uphold international principles of sovereignty and nonintervention. The former was considered belligerent and the latter was for the purpose of restoring international peace and order. In this respect, as Hall states, "although intervention often ends in war, and is sometimes really war from the commencement, it may be conveniently considered abstractedly from the pacific or belligerent character which it assumes in different cases."[3] The traditional definition of intervention overlaps with the concept of war, and the act may be constitutive of war. Intervention as developed in this book, by contrast, looks to the many layers of human agency that have shaped the experience of war or its transformation. In this respect, forceful intervention in and of itself is an act which is constituted by a range of other interventions.

The distinctions reveal the extent to which war, as distinct from other forms of conflict, is a social artifact, even while it may be given impetus by powerful human drives. Once war is understood to be a social artifact, the reality is more malleable and subject to interventions that alter its shape. The question then becomes whether intervention is understood to be an act that alters the "reality" of war or is part and parcel of the same social artifact. In the first case, war is a brutal reality and the various interventions to alter this objective condition are destined to fail precisely because they represent attempts to change the unchangeable. In the second, the relationship is less one of add and stir than of a maze of intersecting social constructs that are always in a process of transition and transformation, generated by the inevitable tensions between them. From this angle, war itself is no less a social construct than the various efforts presented in the rest of this book to limit or alter its course. The two have emerged and developed in tandem.

Diplomacy is among the oldest forms of intervention to limit recourse to war but it has also been its handmaiden. As Brian White States, "If world politics is simply characterized by the tension between conflict and cooperation, diplomacy together with war can be said to represent its two defining institutions."[4] The diplomat has been the representative of the state and its citizens abroad. During the last century of total war, this relationship has begun to change. As populations have become the main victims of war, with the breakdown of the distinction between civilian and combatant, their stake in diplomatic exchanges at the international level has increased. The formal diplomacy between states is now only one aspect of a system, involving multiple levels of intervention by multiple parties to alleviate or minimize the consequences of war. These parties are not necessarily identified by their allegiance to a state but may carry the card of an international governmental or nongovernmental organization. Diplomacy is an institution that has traditionally been defined by the estrangement and isolation of states.[5] Contemporary changes thus raise questions about its potential to survive globalization and the increasing interpenetration of states at all levels. Alternatively, there may be a need to rethink the meaning of the concept and the role of its practice.

The rest of the chapters in this book are devoted to analyzing a range of different types of intervention, raising questions about their role in diplomacy over questions of war. The purpose of this chapter is to look at a number of historical and contemporary distinctions that represent different ways of carving up a political and social landscape defined by war and diplomacy. This includes an examination of different forms of warfare, different reasons for fighting, and the significance of these for diplomatic intervention. The first section will look at the emergence of the contemporary state system and the evolution of warfare and diplomacy within it. The second section will raise questions about the changing nature of world politics and thus the changing nature of warfare and diplomacy, particularly in light of globalization. The third section will look more closely at contemporary forms of warfare, how the underlying assumptions differ from more traditional forms and the questions these raise about the meaning of diplomacy.

Diplomacy and war

Diplomacy is about communication with neighbors and the resolution of conflict by negotiation and dialogue.[6] Even the most primitive societies required some way of dealing with conflicts or communication with other societies. In this respect, diplomacy began when the first human societies decided it "was better to hear a message from outside than eat the messenger."[7] The oldest diplomatic document to be discovered is a letter inscribed on a tablet, dated around 2500 BC, which was sent by a kingdom called Ebla, on the Mediterranean coast of what is now referred to as the Middle East, to the kingdom of Hamazi, located in what is today Northern Iraq.[8] The first diplomatic system for which there is substantial evidence arose among the small city-states of ancient Greece. This system was necessitated by the absence of any single city powerful enough to impose an empire on others and gave rise to an etiquette of dealing with one another as equals.[9] Both of these early examples involved some kind of working relationship between communities, the use of emissaries to convey messages over a distance, rules and protocols, such as the mutual recognition of equality, some kind of common language and normative expectations about right and appropriate behavior.[10]

While a generic form of diplomacy goes back centuries, there is a more specific form of diplomacy that has emerged along with the modern state system. This form of diplomacy involves the management of relations between states. The state is a territorial entity. Within this territorial entity a government or people have sovereignty or are the ultimate decision-maker over what happens in that space. The world is carved up into these sovereign spaces. The need for diplomacy is a function of the absence of any kind of overarching authority to adjudicate disputes between them.

As in the case of ancient Greece, modern diplomacy arose in the absence of empire. Empires establish centralized authority over a large region. By contrast the international system is decentralized and characterized by multiple states and decision-making centers as well as economies that are relatively independent of the state. The state system emerged in Europe and its predominance is fairly recent. The Hapsburg and Ottoman empires, which covered a good portion of Europe, only disintegrated with the First World War. The model of sovereignty only became universal with decolonization since the Second World War. The global spread of the interstate system has thus been a gradual process.

From empire to states

Prior to the emergence of the state system, much of Europe was part of unified imperial structure orchestrated from Rome. In about the second century AD it began to crumble through a combination of internal corruption and paralysis and barbarian invasions from the East.[11] After its collapse, the Western portion was highly fragmented and distributed among a number of Germanic tribes. Charlemagne (742–814), who named himself emperor of the Holy Roman Empire in 800 AD, tried to reorganize the empire under his control. But after his death it once again came under attack from Vikings and Magyars. By 1000 AD there was nothing in Europe resembling the clear boundaries between states that exist today. The thirty million people who lived on the Western edge of the Eurasian landmass had no reason to think about themselves as Germans, Italians, or even Europeans. The memory of the greatness of the Roman Empire persisted.[12] The Catholic Church was the only institution providing any kind of common identity or unity. There were no boundaries between domestic and international politics and no states.

In contrast to the formal equality between states that exists today, medieval society was structured around a hierarchy of relations, with God at the top. St Augustine (354–430 AD), seen by many as the founder of theology, argued that God created princes to impose order on sinful humans.[13] His ideas reinforced a social structure in which monarchs were crowned by the Pope, lords and vassals were confirmed by religious oath, and the church had a monopoly on education and theorizing. Since the Pope was seen to be God's representative on earth, the monarch owed submission and obedience to Rome. This was a feudal system in which the King gave land to local military leaders in return for defending an area against his enemies. The result was a system of private warfare between lords and vassals. Sovereignty, and thus authority, was fragmented and there were several overlapping centers of power. The economy was localized and plagued by invasions.

Several changes beginning around 1000 AD encouraged individualism over universalism and thereby created the conditions for the emergence of the state system.[14] The first was the Crusades, which were undertaken by a group of knights, fighting on behalf of Christianity, who went to the Middle East to recapture the Holy Land from Muslim infidels. In the process, they discovered the classics of ancient Greece, including Aristotle, Plato, and Sophocles, and brought these back to monasteries in Europe. This represented the introduction of a more secular form of thought, including assumptions that humans possess reason, which contributed to the secularization of Church doctrine.

The second was an economic change as trade networks to the rest of the world, which had been destroyed by barbarian invasions, were re-established. The Crusades moved through southern Europe toward the Middle East at the same time as cities in Northern Italy were increasing trade with the near East. Technological innovations enhanced the possibility of creating surplus products for sale on the market, which lead to the creation of a separate merchant class. Merchants became wealthy from trade and finance, which established a source of wealth independent of the church or nobility. Cities in Northern Italy, at the center of the trading network, and on the crusader's path, began to grow. In the late fifteenth century, Venice, Florence, Genoa, Naples, and Milan became major cities and developed a diplomatic system of communication between them.

The third was a cultural revolution. The growth of the Italian city-states, and the creation of wealth, paved the way for the Renaissance, which was a flourishing of art, universities, and architecture in the fourteenth and fifteenth century. This eroded the Church's monopoly on learning and contributed to a secularization of thought. The rediscovery of Greek and Roman history, as well as the classics, gave rise to a new kind of more secular scholar, referred to as a Humanist. While Medieval scholarship was concentrated in the Church and focused on the interpretation of the Bible and holy texts, the new Renaissance scholarship emphasized the individual, historical self-consciousness and new literary forms, such as the autobiography. Religious stories of saints and sinners began to be replaced by stories of reasoning individuals who faced complex problems.[15]

The Reformation was a further change in the sixteenth century, which contributed to individualism and a focus on the state. The Reformation was a conflict between the Catholic Church and new Protestant groups who were redefining the nature of faith.[16] Prior to this time the Catholic Church had a monopoly on interpretation of the Bible, which was written in Latin and only known by a Church elite. The invention of the printing press about 1450 made it possible to print the Bible in a range of vernacular languages, which increased its circulation, as well as that of other reading materials and political pamphlets. As a variety of interpretations of Christianity spread across Europe, the illusion of Christian unity was broken.

A revolution in technology also transformed the possibilities for war.[17] The expansion of trading networks made possible the introduction of gunpowder from China, which increased the destructiveness of war. This gave rise to new forms of military organization such as the cavalry and drill. In contrast to the jousting between individual knights during the Medieval period, soldiers could now move in a synchronized pattern. As a result, it became more costly and complex to wage war. Knights and nobles could no longer afford to equip an army. Only the king had the taxes of the entire country at his disposal. This encouraged new forms of bureaucracy for the purpose of raising taxes and collecting them. The King's power was thus increased at the expense of the aristocracy. The King now needed merchants and bankers for taxes and loans more than he needed the landed aristocracy, which had previously provided military service.

Inventions relating to navigation, mapmaking and the compass made possible the building of more advanced ships and travel to distant lands, such as the Americas. The focus of trade thus shifted from the trading networks of the city-states in Italy to the Iberian monarchies and trading in sea vessels. The improvement in ships increased the possibility of exploiting far-off lands. The conquest of new lands provided revenues to consolidate the state and finance further conquest abroad.

The Westphalian system

By the sixteenth century it had become clear that the issue of whether Catholicism or Protestantism represented universal truth would remain undecided. The bloody Thirty Years' War (1618–48) ended with the Treaty of Westphalia in 1648, which is the date associated with the beginning of the interstate system. The treaty defined the nature of states, how they would interact, and thus established rules for the European state system. The treaty resolved that the King should decide whether his lands would be Protestant or Catholic, which further eroded the power of the Pope and led to bitter wars to resist the imposition of faith. The idea that Kings would be sovereign over a territory reflected an acceptance of *sovereignty* as a defining principle. While its meaning has since changed, at the time sovereignty was associated with the person of the monarch. Early theorists of sovereignty, such as Jean Bodin (1530–95), stressed the need for unconditional obedience to supreme authority.[18] The sovereign should have authority to settle religious differences. As a result more than 300 European states at the time would each have a single source of authority. The concept would later be broadened to refer to decision-making bodies, such as the Parliament in England or the United Provinces (the Netherlands) or to a people as a whole, with the American and French revolutions.

The concept of sovereignty helped to consolidate the absolute authority of the monarch, increasing the perception of his or her legitimacy, as the only unifying factor in an otherwise scattered territory. Sovereignty thus established the boundaries of a piece of land and clear authority over it. It was further an essential mark of independence. The territorial space of the state was to be free from interference by other states. Sovereigns did, however, have a right to enter into diplomatic relations. All states were to be formally equal, although they differed in capabilities and strength. There was to be no official hierarchy between them, which was an acknowledgment of anarchy as the structuring principle. This contrasts with the fragmented sovereignty of the medieval system, in which Kings did not have absolute power over their territories, and conceded a range of control to lords and vassals in return for military service. After 1648, the King or Queen became the center of the universe, and religion became less important.[19]

Sovereignty gave rise to a new structure of relations. Monarchs established standing armies, of which they would be the commander in chief. Sovereigns were closely bound by marriage ties. Marriage was a central part of diplomacy, which preserved royal rule. At the same time, they challenged one another over the rule of particular territories. Active diplomacy was a way to limit conflicts. War was less over religious issues than the glory of the monarch and the expansion of his or her influence and wealth. Wealth and military power were seen as reinforcing state power. This gave rise to the *mercantile state* and a growing emphasis on trade as a source of conflict.[20] Wealth strengthened naval power, which was necessary to protect trade, which created more wealth. Trading companies were established with official support. The Dutch and British East India companies established a monopoly on trade within particular regions of the globe. A monopoly for a company was a monopoly for the state.

The concept of sovereignty went hand in hand with a concept of balance of power, which guided the policy of states. The emphasis on balance, also evident in trade relations, emerged during the eighteenth-century enlightenment, along with science, and an obsession with a mechanical vision of the universe. Balance of power had not been part of the Thirty Years' War, but as the importance of religion diminished in the new system, this policy became a means of stopping any one power from dominating the continent. It thus preserved the system of sovereign states. In his book, *The Law of Nations* (1759), Emmerich de Vattel reflected this sentiment:

> Europe forms a political system, an integral body, closely connected by the relations and different interests of the nations inhabiting this part of the world. It is not, as formerly, a confused heap of detached pieces, each of which thought itself very little concerned with the fate of others. The continual attention of sovereigns to every occurrence,

the constant residence of ministers and the perpetual negotiations, make of modern Europe a kind of republic, of which the members, each independent but all mixed together by the tides of common interest can unite for the maintenance of order and liberty. [21]

When the system originated, in the seventeenth century, balance was a means to preserve the sovereignty of individual states, whose survival was dependent on preventing the dominance of strong states. In the eighteenth century, the emphasis shifted to long-term stability and equilibrium between states. There was, as a result, less emphasis on preserving the independence of smaller states and more on preserving balance between major powers. Poland, for example, was divided up several times, with parts going to Russia, Germany, and Austria, all in the name of balance of power.

The balance of power required flexibility, which meant there could be no permanent alliances. Friends had to become enemies and enemies friends if it was necessary to preserve a balance. This meant ideology or religion could not play a role in alliance formation. It also meant that states had to settle for less than total victory in war. If alliances were formed to balance the power of others, neither side could have total victory. The system gave rise to a rapid growth of diplomatic representation for the purpose of keeping one another informed of intentions and being ready to conclude new alliances if necessary. The system rested on a widespread assumption that the equilibrium between great powers should be maintained and that all should be ready to act to common advantage if the balance was disturbed.

Balance of power politics was not only internal to Europe but was played out in other parts of the world. The earlier competition between trading companies lead, over time, to the increased colonization of areas outside of Europe. Colonies were wanted for the products they supplied, which included gold and silver from South America, slaves from Africa, and spices from the East Indies. The colonies sent products to the mother country which were processed and sent back as exports. All trade with the colonies was regarded as a monopoly and they in the meantime weren't allowed to develop manufacturing industries that would allow them to compete. Indigenous people were subjected to a ruthless system of tribute and slavery. The colonies were there to support the interests of the European state. Because they were highly valued, the colonies became a source of major conflict. The English and Dutch came into conflict in America in the seventeenth century. France and England fought over territories controlling the fur trade in what is now the USA.

Increased wealth from the colonies contributed to the power of the state and therefore affected the balance of power. The European balance of power could be upset by helping to evict a rival power from the territories. France and Spain, for instance, helped the American colonies to expel Britain.

The Westphalian system had a tension at its heart. A system of communication was necessary because of the potential for conflict. On the one hand, states were all in some respect alienated and separate from one another,[22] and had no authority above them to decide in a dispute. On the other hand, they managed to cobble together a set of rules and shared understandings that would underpin their interactions. These rules became institutionalized to an extent that they had not been in earlier times. The monarch did not communicate directly with other foreign states. Rather he had emissaries to go between who were known as diplomats. This involved a process over time of constructing several institutions, including foreign ministries within states, and foreign embassies and ambassadors located in different countries and responsible for maintaining good relations and gathering information. The combination of expanded foreign ministries and the creation of embassies abroad led over time to the professionalization of diplomacy and the creation of an occupation.

Nation and empire

The eighteenth century was defined by the enlightenment. This included a progressive erosion of the influence of religion, an emphasis on science, balance, equilibrium and a mechanistic worldview, human reason, and the emergence of a state system based on these. If stasis and balance marked the eighteenth century, change and historical progress marked the nineteenth. With this came a shift away from state-building to nation-building, with consequences for the way war was defined and fought. Two revolutions marked the transition, which shook the old European order.[23]

The first was the political revolutions in America and France, from which a concept of popular sovereignty emerged, locating authority in institutions representing the people rather than the person of the monarch. The French Revolution presented a challenge to the absolute sovereignty of the king and was an attempt to dismantle this order, which changed the nature of war and international relations. War no longer focused on the glory of the king. It was no longer the business of the monarch but of citizens. War in defense of the nation was the basis for a call to arms. The idea of the nation as a popular social formation based on the interconnections between groups, sharing a culture and language, emerged at this time. Napolean mobilized the masses for war in the name of the French nation, to spread ideas of revolution to others. The mission was to propagate universal ideas of liberty, equality, and fraternity throughout Europe.

The second revolution was industrial and emerged in Britain. The Napoleonic wars strengthened this revolution, since Britain, unlike its counterparts on the Continent, was not devastated. Britain was also well endowed with coal and iron and well situated to benefit from Atlantic trade. The revolution, which spread slowly across the Continent, involved several factors. The first was a rapid advancement of technology. New means of mass production gave rise to rapid growth in the size of business and introduced new products for a mass consumer market. The second was the construction of huge factories, which required large numbers of workers, and caused a massive movement from countryside to city, rapid urbanization and thus urban squalor and poor working conditions. The third was a new wave of expansion abroad in search of markets for surplus goods and raw materials for factories.

Imperialism was a scramble by the great European powers for the earth's natural resources and markets.[24] It involved the penetration of the interior of different countries outside Europe, and not just coastal areas. Harbors, warehouses, railroads, and plantations were built and production was organized according to the needs of Europeans. The expansion was articulated in terms of historical progress. The progressive nation-states were there to help backward nations, bringing them Christianity, education, wealth, and European values.[25] The greater wealth of Europeans was seen as proof of their superiority and right to rule. By 1914, the European powers had annexed nine-tenths of Africa and a large part of Asia.

In sum the political and industrial revolutions of this era expanded the involvement of the masses, with the development of mass education, the extension of the vote, the emergence of a class of wage laborers, and armies made up of citizens. This gave rise to a shift away from an emphasis on war as the means to expand the state, fought by standing armies loyal to the king, to war fought by and on behalf of the nation. These developments coincided with the expansion of empire, as the major powers divided the globe between them.

The philosopher Jean-Jacques Rousseau (1712–78) wrote that war is a *social* activity and a product of civilization. It is the citizen who becomes soldier, not natural man. Rousseau argued that war was the job of a nation's citizens. Just war was not fought by professional soldiers in the pay of kings but by citizens of a republic. Rousseau's target was Thomas Hobbes and Hugo Grotius, whose theories, he argued, could be used in service of the imperial powers.[26] While the one provided a defense of absolute monarchy, and the old world of empire and slavery, the other endorsed principles of private war, conquest, and slavery.[27] In his *Principles du droit de la guerre*, Rousseau argued that war arises from unjust institutions. Political and civic virtue could be brought about through the struggle against the old world. Humans acted not by reason alone, but sentiments as well. They are driven by ambition to lay the basis for a just society.

The republican virtues provided the basis for a call to mass mobilization. The Napoleonic Wars were people's wars. Conscription was introduced in 1793 after which an army of 300,000 men was raised,[28] the largest military force ever to be found in Europe. Republicanism was an approach to war that focused on freeing the masses from the old oppressive order.

Both liberalism and republicanism were a reaction against the old royal order because it opposed progress and repudiated the equal rights of man.[29] These came to be pitted against a more conservative concept of nation, which provided a defense of the old order. A strong state in this view was necessary to provide stability and order. The Austrian statesman Metternich (1773–1859), for instance, was the architect of the Congress of Vienna (1814–15), which was a comprehensive peace treaty following Napolean's defeat that codified the rules of diplomacy and included a promise to "concert together" against any future threat to the system.[30] The Congress was the basis for the Concert of Europe, which managed post-war policies through a system of regular conferences between major powers to the end of preserving balance and preserving the Europe of the absolutist age of sovereign monarchs.[31] This required stopping the spread of revolution, which was eroding the power of the monarchs. They were not successful however. In 1848 a wave of revolutions spread through Eastern Europe, based on ideas of national self-determination and equality.

The conservative tradition also rested on a view of the nation as an hierarchical and organic community. Karl von Clauswitz (1780–1831), a Prussian general and writer of military strategy, analyzed Napolean's victory over Prussia in the Battle of Jena (1806) and argued that his success was a result of his ability to mobilize the French nation for war. Clauswitz was aware that total war was made possible by the total involvement of the population. In contrast to the Republican ideas that guided Napolean, Clauswitz had a vision of a spiritually unified nation based on the *volk*, which subordinated the individual to a nation led by a strong leader. War was conducted in the name of the state, on behalf of the nation and for its glory. Clauswitz conceptualized war as a rational activity, but one that involved the mobilization of emotions and sentiments to its service.[32] His strategy rested on two main theories of war. The first was that of attrition or wearing down the enemy by imposing a high casualty rate. This was a defensive strategy relying on a high concentration of force. The second was a theory of maneuver, involving surprise and pre-emption, which required mobility and dispersion to create uncertainty and achieve speed.

A number of developments in the nineteenth century brought this Clauswitzian version of modern war closer to reality.[33] The first was a dramatic advancement in technology, such as the railway and telegraph, which allowed for the greater and faster mobilization of arms and the mass production of guns. The second was the growing importance of alliances and the overwhelming force that was consolidated through alliances. By the time the First World War broke out the European powers had divided into two heavily armed and inflexible camps, which became locked in struggle. The First World War heralded both the breakdown of the balance of power system and the experience of total war.

Total war

By the end of the eighteenth century the pursuit of war was a highly organized activity that rested on a number of distinctions.[34] The state was the legitimate wielder of violence and the soldier the legitimate bearer of arms. Combatants were distinguished from noncombatants, who were excluded from war, and criminals, who used violence illegitimately. The internal territory of the state, characterized by peaceful civic politics, was distinguished from the external relations between states, which were characterized by violent struggle. The rise of capitalism further contributed to a separation between the private realm of economic activity and the public activities of the state.

The emergence of total war began to blur these distinctions. The Oxford English dictionary defines total war as "a war to which all resources and the whole population are committed; loosely, a war conducted without any scruples or limitations." As already suggested, Clauswitz regarded the Napoleonic Wars as total.[35] The First and Second World Wars involved a widespread mobilization of national energies for the production of supplies for fighting war. The involvement of society as a whole in preparations for war blurred the public/private distinction. Economic targets became legitimate military targets. Indiscriminate aerial bombing of cities resulted in a tremendous loss of human life and the breakdown of the distinction between combatant and noncombatant. The genocide of European Jews, among others, during the Second World War, made civilians an explicit target of the state. The development of nuclear weapons and the threat of nuclear war represented a further and ultimate breakdown of the distinctions that had characterized an earlier era of warfare.

Traditional diplomacy also broke down with the First World War. Many believed that the practices of secret diplomacy not only had failed to prevent the war, but were its cause in so far as they contributed to misperception and misunderstanding. This sentiment gave rise to a new diplomacy that revolved around several liberal ideas.[36] The first was that diplomacy should be much more open to public scrutiny and control. It wasn't so much that the public should be actively involved than the need for greater constraints on and accountability of a social elite, the European aristocracy, who had acted with excessive secrecy. The second was the idea that international institutions could improve communication and minimize misperceptions, and thus recourse to war. States remained the main actors and diplomacy still revolved around a well-established network of foreign offices and embassies.[37] But international organizations, such as the League of Nations and later the United Nations, emerged as actors in their own right. Nongovernment actors, such as private individuals and groups, began to play an increasing role.

After the end of the Second World War, with the complete breakdown of the European system, two superpowers emerged to fill the power vacuum. The Cold War between the USA and the USSR combined a mixture of the old and the new and brought a 40-year period of stasis following the dramatic upheavals of the first part of the century. Both the USA and the USSR were built on revolutions and critical of the old secretive practices of balance of power. The two presented different models of enlightenment and liberation. In this respect, the dissolution of the European empires and the decolonization of large parts of the world seemed to represent progress. On the other hand, the two superpowers became locked in a balance of terror involving nuclear weapons, which froze the map of Europe for half a century and held the world in fear of a nuclear holocaust. Despite the abhorrence of traditional practices of secret diplomacy, this period saw an unprecedented development of agencies for the purpose of collecting, collating, and evaluating intelligence, as well as the use of propaganda and psychological warfare vis à vis the public.[38]

The development of nuclear weapons changed the logic of balance of power as well as warfighting, given the tremendous costs attached to fighting with nuclear weapons. Nuclear deterrence, which underpinned nuclear diplomacy, was a strategy based on the idea that if the threat to use nuclear weapons was sufficiently credible no rational actor would consider making the first strike and thus peace would be preserved. The strategy of nuclear deterrence rested on mutually assured destruction or the ability to launch a devastating second strike with nuclear weapons after having absorbed an attack. The Cold War involved a steady build up of weapons by both sides and an increasing escalation of the threat, with revisions in strategy over time to enhance the threat's credibility. By the mid-eighties many critics argued that the increasing speed and destructiveness of weapons were contributing to the possibility of a first strike strategy or the probability of accidental nuclear war.

The Cold War was potentially the most total of wars. The main subjects were alliances, rather than nation-states. Entire societies were drawn into an ongoing process of preparation for war over several decades. Nuclear war, had it happened, would have made no distinction between combatants and noncombatants. The two sides possessed tens of thousands of these weapons, capable of being launched across continents or on the battlefield. Had it been unleashed, nuclear war would have made the world uninhabitable.[39] That it did not has been interpreted by some as a victory for the strategy of nuclear deterrence. Skeptics argue it was pure luck. War was not in any case eliminated by nuclear deterrence. While peace between states in Europe was preserved for close to fifty years, it continued, often by proxy, in other parts of the world.

When the Cold War suddenly came to an end, most scholars and politicians were caught by surprise. The way in which it happened did not fit with the assumptions of extant theories of international relations.[40] First, in contrast to assumptions that it was always more sensible to arm than to disarm, Reagan and Gorbachev agreed to disarm for the first time during the Cold War. Second, a few years later, Eastern Europe was shook by nonviolent "Velvet Revolutions," and the leader of the Soviet bloc stood by and let them to do it "their way." The change was not a function of war and balance of power politics but popular demand. In contrast to realist arguments about the centrality of states and military power, several scholars have demonstrated the important role of independent citizen's initiatives in both East and West in constituting the possibility of superpower disarmament as well as the Velvet Revolutions.[41] Third, the dismantling of the Soviet Empire and of the German Democratic Republic defied ideas that states would always act to maximize their interest in power. The sense of surprise extended to other areas of the world, such as Northern Ireland, South Africa, and the

Middle East where other seemingly intractable conflicts moved in the nineties away from violence toward more peaceful options. At the same time, new hot wars involving "ethnic cleansing" broke out in Rwanda and in the former Yugoslavia, on the periphery of Europe, after half a century of saying "never again."

The end of the Cold War, and the demise of the bloc system, gave rise to accelerated globalization.[42] Globalization involves complex processes of opening up barriers to trade and communication across the world along with greater localization. Regional integration, particularly in Europe, was given new impetus, as was increasing fragmentation and the phenomenon of "failed states" in the former Third World. Transnational and regional patterns of governance, which had emerged during the Cold War, were further developed. The explosion of international organizations, regimes, and regulatory agencies has given rise to greater cooperation across state boundaries and the growth of nongovernmental organizations. All of these increased the potential for international bodies to intervene for humanitarian ends in conflict areas of the world. Intervention, which had primarily been a practice of states communicating or crossing the boundaries of other states, came to be manifest in a variety of different types of practice, initiated by different types of organization, confronted with different types of warfare, which required different strategies for responding.

In so far as these interventions involved diplomacy, it was a diplomacy of a different kind than in the past. Both the old and the new diplomacy, after the First World War, primarily involved the representatives of one state communicating with representatives of other states. In the peace processes and emerging conflicts of the post–Cold War period, representatives of states, often in the context of multilateral institutions, intervened in conflicts that often involved non-state actors. As such, the diplomats were intervening on behalf of conflicts that may or may not have been directly relevant to their own interests. Many of these conflicts involved explicitly humanitarian goals or the intent to address massive violations of human rights.

Globalization has raised questions about the dominance of the state as the central actor. Globalization has corresponded with the erosion of state sovereignty and the proliferation of other types of actors, who are not necessarily defined by a territorial allegiance, from nongovernmental and multilateral organizations to the media. Later chapters will explore different forms of intervention in more depth. The purpose of this last section of the current chapter is to explore the different forms of conflict and war that have been the focus of these efforts. While these forms of warfare are not new, they have come to occupy a more prominent place in the international realm. Terrorism, for instance, was a feature of the Israeli/Palestinian conflict during the Cold War. With the attack on the US Twin Towers and Pentagon on September 11, 2001, and the Bush Administration's War on Terrorism, it became a defining feature of international politics. However, the distinctions below are not so clear-cut. The association of a violent act with terrorism, as distinct from guerrilla warfare, can involve a political act of naming. At stake is the meaning given by the observers or the perpetrators of violence to acts of violence. These new forms of warfare, unlike those of the past, do not focus on states or war between states, but on the relationship between states and different types of non-state actors. As will be explored in the next chapter, the legitimate use of violence has traditionally been associated with use by *states*. These new categories muddy the water, including the distinction between combatant and noncombatant that characterized traditional warfare.

War and non-state actors

Since the end of the Cold War the increasing role of non-state actors in warfare has grabbed international attention. Several features of this warfare distinguish it from the interstate wars of the past. These include the central role of ethnic conflict, as well as the use of nonviolent strategies, guerrilla warfare, and terrorism. In some respects, given overlaps as well as differences, these four categories make for an unwieldy comparison. Rather than distinct and separate strategies, they represent a mosaic of meanings.

Ethnic conflict first and foremost regards the identity of the unit in conflict, that is, it refers to conflict revolving around cultural differences relating to, for instance, religion, language, or nationality. The category says, in and of itself, little about how the conflict is fought, although it has acquired a connotation of brutal violence. Mary Kaldor argues that identity politics is one of the defining features of what she refers to as the "new wars."[43] In this respect, nonviolence, guerrilla warfare, or terrorism may be, but are not necessarily employed in ethnic conflict. Gandhi's nonviolent campaign to remove the British from India involved an element of identity politics, although it is not usually placed in the category of ethnic conflict. Part of the strategy was, for instance, weaving Indian cloth rather than buying British, which was understood as an act of resistance to British rule. Terrorism in Northern Ireland also had an element of identity politics in so far as the conflict was in part defined by identification with Ireland or the United Kingdom or with Catholic or Protestant identity. Both of these examples refer to earlier eras, rather than the post–Cold War period, which is Kaldor's focus.[44] Her main point is that identity was the defining feature of the wars fought in the Balkans or Rwanda, among others. It is arguably also a defining feature of the Bush Administration's War on Terrorism. Although officials have attempted to distance their rhetoric from categories of Christianity and Islam, some of their opponents define their acts in terms of Islamic Jihad.

Ethnic conflict did not begin with the end of the Cold War. In many cases, the ethnic dimension of conflict was foregrounded with the demise of the Cold War battle between socialist and capitalist ideology. But the end of the Cold War also brought the internationalization of conflicts. The war in the north of Ireland, previously treated as a civil conflict within the United Kingdom, became an explicit area of intervention by the USA, although not military intervention. The conflict in Yugoslavia mobilized ethnic divisions in the society, replacing the multiculturalism of Tito's Yugoslavia, with violent ethnic conflict between Croats, Serbs, and Muslims. From the beginning, the international community played a central role in the search for a solution, moving from intervention through negotiations toward the US intervention with force.

In principle, ethnic conflict may overlap with any of the three other categories, which are more strategic in nature. One further distinction is between nonviolent and violent conflict. The Velvet Revolutions that brought about the end of the Cold War were nonviolent. The Kosovar Albanians waged a lengthy nonviolent campaign in Serbia during the 1990s, prior to the formation of the terrorist campaign by the Kosovo Liberation Army (KLA). This nonviolent campaign involved establishing political and educational institutions for Kosovar Albanians in a situation where Kosovo had been stripped of its autonomous status, and the Kosovars of most of their rights. They were attempting to act as if Kosovo were a sovereign state.

A nonviolent strategy is far more than refusing to fight or remaining a pacifist. It is a strategy of those who play with a weak hand, because of their military inferiority or minority status, who would be unable to win by means of a violent strategy.[45] It is a form of resistance that follows occupation by a foreign power—as distinct from preventing it—or that is used by communities who have experienced long-term oppression.[46] Gene Sharp has documented numerous successful, although limited, cases of nonviolent resistance against occupation, including Nazi regimes during the Second World War.[47] The Civil Rights movement in the

American south was a campaign by the African-American minority, which attempted to bring the violence underlying segregation and racial discrimination to the light of day.

While involving a wide range of tactics, including forms of noncooperation as well as direct action, one commentator, referring to Solidarity's campaign in Poland, identified the overriding principle of the Polish strategy as "to be what you want to become."[48] By acting as if it was possible to establish a trade union in a worker's state, Solidarity presented a challenge to existing structures, exposing the discrepancy between words and deeds, and established the autonomy of the Polish people against the background of the old Soviet order. By acting as if Kosovo were a sovereign state, and establishing Kosovar institutions, the Kosovar Albanians defied the power of the Serb majority. By acting as if African Americans could sit in the front of the bus or at lunch counters for Whites only, they established their rights as free and equal citizens against the background of segregation. The concept of acting as if, discussed in Chapter 1, is most evident in nonviolent campaigns, where actors have refused to cooperate with the expectations of oppressors and have attempted to transform the context by acting as if they were free.[49] The tendency of the authorities to respond with violence raises important questions to the broader population about the moral legitimacy of the current order. The nonviolent and dignified stance of the weak, in response, establishes their entitlement to the rights they claim, while serving to further dissolve the power of existing structures.

Nonviolence tends to be viewed with skepticism or not to be taken seriously, as evidenced by the failure of the international community to engage seriously with Kosovo until the KLA emerged. However, the success of the nonviolent campaign in India in bringing an end to British rule suggests the untapped potential of this strategy. Like any other strategy, nonviolence can be employed more or less successfully and is dependent on certain conditions. The two remaining categories rely on strategies of violence, but can be distinguished by the degree of legitimacy attached to its use. Based on the traditional rules of war, guerrilla warfare and terrorism are illegitimate forms of struggle in so far as they represent acts of violence by non-state actors that blur the boundaries between combatants and noncombatants. However, since the Second World War in particular, there has been an increasing recognition of the right to resist occupation by means of guerrilla war.

Surprise has been an essential feature of guerrilla war and ambush a classic tactic. While also a tactic in conventional warfare, the guerrilla, unlike the conventional soldier, undertakes the act without the identifying uniform, often making him or her indistinguishable from ordinary civilians. French resistance fighters, during the Second World War, for instance, were often disguised as peaceful peasants. The problem arises because, in international law, a citizen of a state that has surrendered promises to stop fighting in exchange for a restoration of ordinary life and benevolent quarantine.[50] They are not allowed to resist the quarantine or occupation. In the past, if they did so, it was given the name "war treason," which was punishable like ordinary treason. This term has, however, largely disappeared, in part because the experience of the resistance fighters in the Second World War didn't seem to fit this category. There has since been a growing acceptance that even after occupation there may be a moral right to defend a homeland or political community. After national surrender there may still be values to be defended and no one to do so except ordinary citizens with no formal political or legal standing. The change presents new dilemmas, however. It creates a tension between the rules of war regarding occupation, and any commitment by states to follow them, and the requirements of governing in a situation where occupying authorities may be subject to attack at any time. This tension has been evident in Iraq following the invasion in 2003, where American and British soldiers have been subject to attack from a continuing resistance effort.

Because guerrilla fighters wear peasant clothes and hide among the population they challenge the fundamental principles of the rules for war, which draw a clear distinction between soldier and civilian and specify that each individual must fit only one of these categories. It is not the guerrillas that attack civilians or at least this is not a part of the strategy. Rather, by refusing to accept the distinction, they make it impossible for the enemy to distinguish soldiers from civilians and thus increase the likelihood that the occupier will kill civilians. Guerrilla war is "people's war." It is war from below, often seen as a war of liberation. The image of guerrilla war is of a whole people mobilized for war, rather than a solitary fighter. The oppressor is then not at war with an army but a nation. The implicit message is that if the oppressor is going to fight all, they will have to do so as barbarians, killing women and children. While guerrilla war may begin with the mobilization of a small part of the nation, it depends on counterattacks to mobilize the rest. The onus of indiscriminate warfare is placed on the opposing army.[51] In this respect, guerrilla strategy shares a family resemblance with nonviolence in so far as it places the powers that be in a position of having to choose whether to use violence against civilians, thus raising questions about the legitimacy of their rule. Guerrilla war differs however in the use of violent means of resistance to bring about this end.

Terrorism relies in some respects on an opposing logic.[52] While entire populations may be terrorized by both conventional and guerrilla war, for the purpose of destroying morale and undercutting solidarity, randomness is the central feature of terrorist activity. Terrorism is a much more indirect activity than the other two in that it avoids engagement with an enemy army and instead targets people, and primarily civilians, by chance.

As Bruce Thompson elaborates, the meaning of terrorism has changed over time.[53] When the term was first popularized during the French Revolution, it had a different and more positive connotation, in regard to a system for establishing order in the transition following revolution. Thus, rather than an antigovernment activity undertaken by non-state or subnational actors, as it is understood today, the French *regime de la terreur* was an instrument of governance established by a new revolutionary state. In the wake of the industrial revolution, with the emergence of new "universalist" ideologies, terrorism acquired many of its familiar connotations, prevalent today, of revolutionary, antistate activity. By the 1930s, it was used more to describe the practices of mass repression employed by totalitarian states against their own citizens and not least Fascist Italy, Nazi Germany, and Stalinist Russia. Following the Second World War, terrorism regained its revolutionary connotation. The term was primarily used in reference to violent revolts by nationalist/anti-colonialist groups in Asia, Africa, and the Middle East who opposed the continuation of European rule. In the 1990s some began to refer to it as a "gray area phenomenon," a term which highlights the fluid and variable nature of subnational conflict after the Cold War. The term thus came to be used to denote threats to the stability of nation-states by non-state actors and nongovernmental processes and organizations, such as Al-Qaida, to describe violence affecting regions where control had shifted from legitimate governments to new half-political, half-criminal powers, or simply to group into one category a range of conflicts that no longer fit within traditionally accepted definitions of war. Rather than the clash of armed forces from two or more states, these have involved one or more combatants from irregular forces.[54]

Today, terrorism is most often associated with non-state actors. In contrast to its contemporary portrayal as random and indiscriminate, it is often organized, deliberate, and systematic. While its goal and justification has often been the creation of a new and better society, replacing a corrupt and undemocratic system, terrorism nonetheless represents a clear violation of the prohibition against killing innocent civilians.

Ordinary citizens are killed, not for their individual activities, but simply to deliver a message of fear. Because the message is directed against entire peoples or classes, it can represent the most extreme and brutal of intentions. Terrorism can include the demand for unconditional surrender and tends to rule out any sort of compromise settlement.

Conclusion

War can be distinguished from other forms of violence or conflict by its dependence on organization and a system of rules. Diplomacy has been both its handmaiden and a form of intervention to limit recourse to violence. War may be fought between any range of identities, from empires to sovereign states to various forms of non-state actors. Throughout the Westphalian period, the rules of warfare and diplomacy focused on states and distinguished their acts of violence from those of illegitimate non-state actors, while providing some protection for noncombatants from the destruction of war. The locus of sovereignty has shifted from a focus on individual monarchs to bodies representing the people. The nature of warfare has shifted from a limited form, which recognized the importance of protecting the system as a whole, to forms of total warfare in the twentieth century.[55] With the emergence of total warfare, and with processes of globalization, the range of distinctions upon which the rules of warfare were based have begun to blur and populations have claimed a greater stake in diplomacy, questioning, in the period following the First World War, the practices of secret diplomacy by elites. Increasingly, since the end of the Cold War, warfare as well as intervention has involved a broad array of nongovernmental as well as governmental actors. The former have played a central role in the distribution of humanitarian aid and attempts to alleviate the suffering of victims of war. In addition, warfare since the end of the Cold War has tended to involve citizens directly in the execution of war while also claiming them as victims. In this respect, the changes accompanying processes of globalization increase both the stakes of diplomacy for civilian populations and open space for their increasing participation in interventions to limit recourse to violence or alleviate the consequent suffering. The next two chapters will look more specifically at the moral and legal principles that have shaped the rules of warfare. These rules represent interventions in and of themselves to shape the nature of warfare, limiting its destructiveness, while setting the stage for different forms of direct intervention in the wars of others.

3
Moral Interventions

Social science has assumed a distinction between empirical statements about reality as it is and normative statements about how the world ought to be. Realists who claim to work with the world as it is, also make this distinction. In this view, the empirical reality is one of power politics; thus neither moral principle, ethical action nor legal codification is ultimately important at the international level. In the absence of any overarching authority, states are guided by their national interest rather than moral principle. War is a brute reality and the attempt to introduce norms is a mere add on, growing out of a desire to alter the unalterable. However, if war is viewed as a social artifact, then its practice is no less permeated with moral and normative restrictions than more explicit moral or humanitarian efforts to limit it.[1]

Intervention is most often conceived as a practice involving the use of force and, in the realist conception, a practice of power politics, devoid of morality. Yet, the history of interventions to define the moral limits of war is older than the state system. Moral thinking often rests on an acceptance of the practice, as a necessary evil and a last resort, but one that must be kept within acceptable bounds. The objective is to limit the degree of human suffering and destruction. In this respect, moral interventions have given shape to the social artifact of war, even while recognizing—or even legitimizing—its persistence. The first section of this chapter will explore various approaches to the role of morality at the international level. The second section will look at the historical evolution of Just War theory, and early attempts to codify these in law. The third section will examine the attempt to outlaw war after the First World War.[2] The chapter ends with a brief overview of contemporary developments in the laws of war and new moral questions raised by more recent wars.

The next two chapters on legal interventions and military interventions are closely linked to this chapter. Indeed, it is difficult to make a clear separation between these categories. The Geneva Conventions, which are explored here, are fundamental documents of international law. Humanitarian intervention, which includes an obvious moral element, will not be addressed until the next chapter, in so far as it relates to fundamental questions and tensions at the heart of international law. While the two are clearly related, I have distinguished them in separate chapters, in order to highlight specific points. This chapter focuses on the complexity of applying a moral framework in a situation of war and the persistence of efforts to do so. The next chapter will analyze international attempts to judge and punish crimes of war and crimes against humanity. The chapter on military interventions examines the relationship between the strategic, moral, and legal criteria for intervention.

Moral reasoning and ethical action

Terry Nardin argues that to think ethically is to move back and forth between the general and the particular and to look at the wide range of considerations affecting choice and actions.[3] Morality is often more broadly conceived in terms of the background rules of proper conduct as distinct from the wide range of considerations affecting choice and action that is ethical. While legal codification in international law may represent a formalization of customary state practice, it can also involve the formalization of moral principle.

This raises a question about how we arrive at an understanding of what is moral. The answer is not straightforward and several traditions have formulated the problem in different ways. The deontological tradition, associated with the German philosopher Immanuel Kant, is "agent-centered" placing emphasis on moral motive and allowing principle and precept to override consideration of consequences.[4] The Categorical Imperative, which is familiar in its Christian form as "do unto others as you would have them do unto you," is one important expression of this reasoning. Others should be treated as having value in and of themselves. We should avoid treating other human beings solely as means to an end. The Ten Commandments were an expression of moral principle. Thou shall not kill is a moral principle to guide action.

Consequentialism, which is part of the utilitarian tradition in ethics, raises questions about the wisdom of this Kantian formulation, particularly in the political realm.[5] According to Anthony Ellis, consequentialism is based on the idea "that the only relevant factor in deciding whether any action or practice is morally right or wrong is it overall consequences viewed impersonally. The agent is morally obliged to perform any action, no matter what, if and only if it has the best consequences or, as it is also put, if and only if it maximizes the good."[6] The ethics of an action are to be judged by the outcome not by some universal notion of good. In this respect, ethical action is less a function of moral principle than a calculation of what means will bring about a desired end. Max Weber contrasted the saint who always acts according to good means, regardless of the outcome, with the politician who is sometimes required to use less than savory means to bring about a good end for his population.[7] He argued that acting for good ends was more moral than the good intention that may result in harmful consequences.

The question is what, if any, relevance these moral frameworks have for international relations. There is a long tradition of assuming that morality has little or no role at the international level. Realists have drawn on a variety of historical arguments to make this case. One lesson, drawn from Thucycides' *History of the Peloponnesian Wars*, is that fear, honor, and self-interest drive states with power to expand.[8] As a result, it has always been the rule that the weak should be subject to the strong. Machiavelli argued that moral action at the international level will not only lead to failure, but will also produce a greater measure of evil than a purely realist course.[9] Thomas Hobbes in the seventeenth century claimed that there is no just and unjust in the state of nature. Morality and justice require an authority who can step in to judge in cases of dispute and punish offenders. In the absence of a global authority, states are justified in defending their interests by any means they judge appropriate by the same right that existed in the original state of nature.[10] In the second half of the twentieth century the American theologian Reinhold Niebuhr, who has influenced contemporary realist thought, argued that, while individuals can be moral agents, states cannot be.[11] He referred to the "ethical paradox" of patriotism, which transforms individual unselfishness into national egoism.[12] While individuals can be altruistic, the national interest is likely to be pursued at the international level in a way that is at best self-interested, and at worst, brutal.

Most realists allow an instrumental political role for morality. As Nicholas Spykman argued, "Justice, fairness, and tolerance ... can be used instrumentally as moral justification for the power quest, but they must be discarded the moment their application brings weakness. The search for power is not made for the achievement of moral values; moral values are used to facilitate the attainment of power."[13] Moral arguments may be drawn on to justify state action, but these are likely to disguise other interests. Thus, while denying that morality is ultimately the reason for action, many realists, from Morgenthau to Kissinger, have recognized that conceptions of morality influence the beliefs and conduct of actors in world politics.[14] Military academies teach an ethical framework with respect to war, that is, Just War Theory, which is articulated in international law and in the US Uniform Code of Justice.[15] Just War theory influenced US conduct in the counterterror war waged in Afghanistan, amongst others.[16] As Michael Walzer argues, even though it is often misused, moral argument and Just War theory have always played a part in official arguments about war.[17]

The admission about moral argument raises a question about how morality contributes to the social construct of war. Here it is important to emphasize the distinction between realism, as a theory, and constructivism, as a methodological approach, as discussed in Chapter 1. A contrast between realist and liberal *theories* would revolve around the relationship between material interest and norms. Realists assume that the predominant role of objective material factors cancels out normative or moral considerations. Liberals, or more specifically, neoliberals have developed arguments about the causal role of norms in international relations. Most neoliberal arguments focus on the role of international regimes in enhancing cooperation, and thus provide little guidance for understanding how norms influence behavior in a context of war and one where moral issues, as distinct from purely instrumental or functional concerns are at stake.[18] Both extant forms of theory tend to rely on a positivist methodology and a separation between ideas and material reality. The key question regards the direction of causality.

As an *approach*, constructivism calls into question the distinction between "is" and "ought." If most human or societal interactions are dependent on contextually specific rules, it is difficult to make this distinction. Ethics and morality are assumed in our actions and therefore cannot be separated out from what is. Like the tree branch, which when altered through human intervention, may be formed into many different objects, appropriate to different types of context, moral argumentation and norms can be constitutive of different and changing realities. As Merryn Frost says, "Through their day-to-day participation in such practices, the actors in them uphold and endorse the ethics embodied in the practices in question. Participation in these practices requires adherence to the ethical code embedded in them."[19]

From this perspective the reality of the international system isn't a raw fact that exists independent of socially created structures of meaning.

As explored in the last chapter, the state system, and war and diplomacy within it, rely on intersubjective agreement about the nature of states as sovereign. Janice Thomson has argued that certain practices of diplomacy are so taken for granted that serious departure from them becomes unthinkable.[20] States should not intervene in the affairs of other states and balance of power is important for preserving sovereignty and the system of anarchy as a whole. This structure of rules is different from that of the Medieval period or that of empires. It is much different now, with the proliferation of international institutions, than it was in the eighteenth century. The dependence of sovereignty on recognition of sovereignty by others is a clear expression that the concept rests on an intersubjective agreement and one that is invested with normative power. This normative power has given agency to states, rather than individuals or other groups. It has legitimized the use of force by states, while defining other uses of force as illegitimate. In a pure sense, sovereignty elevates the ethical responsibility of a state toward its own citizens over ethical responsibility to others "outside." In this respect, the "is" of international society cannot be distinguished from a whole set of rules that define a corresponding "ought."

A constructivist approach to morality involves greater nuance than the simple acceptance or rejection of the importance of norms. Agents often claim that an action is ethical because it flows from moral reasoning about the "ought." But normative "oughts" are also part and parcel of the conceptual furniture of international politics. Also, far from being static or absolute, moral and ethical argument can be constitutive of change or, as a part of change, come to be embodied in international law and institutions.[21] The process of institutionalization does not necessarily lead to a uniformity of normative interpretation, however. As will be discussed in the next chapter, the normative structure surrounding human rights law often conflicts with that of sovereignty and nonintervention. Given norms or rules develop and change over time and place, the search for universal moral principles that would apply across history and context is, for many, problematic.

Limiting war

Despite claims that morality or justice is of little significance at the international level, Just War theory represents a long-standing tradition for applying moral principle to the practice of war. Neta Crawford presents Just War theory as a framework for debate and dialogue about the right causes and conduct of war:

> While the Just War tradition is not a theory in the sense of being a set of causal arguments based on observations of the social world of war—indeed, true causal arguments within the "theory" are generally lacking—it is a framework for ethical reasoning grounded on the belief in human dignity. In the view of Just War theorists, war is an interruption of potential human community, a disruption of peace. ... The Just War tradition is thus intended to be a framework for debate and dialogue about the right causes and conduct of war, with the underlying presumption that the burden of proof lies with those who want to wage war and who claim that their war is just.[22]

There is a very long history of trying to place moral limits on the use of force. These restrictions go back to biblical times, when recourse to force was only considered morally permissible if divinely ordained by God, that is, in the pursuit of Holy War. Within Christianity, the concept of a Holy War was replaced by that of Just War, shifting the source of legitimacy from the will of God to the justness of the cause.[23] Early Christian thinkers, such as Augustine, condemned war as well as excesses of cruelty or deliberate conquest. They saw war as a manifestation of the wicked and sinful nature of human beings. Nonetheless, some wars were understood to be just, for instance, the wars waged to maintain a traditional order, such as the Roman Empire, against barbarian invaders. It was far preferable for a Christian ruler to conquer a tyrant, particularly if heathen, than to be conquered.[24] Augustine stated that "A Just War ... is justified only by the injustice of the aggressor; and that injustice ought to be a source of grief to any good man because it is human injustice."[25]

One of the first attempts to develop systematic rules for determining when war is just was made by Thomas Aquinas (1225–74), a theologian during the Medieval Period. He was influenced by the classical Greek texts that the Crusaders brought back to Europe, particularly the work of Aristotle. These texts emphasized the capacity for human reason. Aquinas argued that God was the embodiment of perfect reason.[26] The key task of humans was to discover the rules of this perfect reasoning and to obey them. This relied on a concept of natural law or the idea that there is a divine order to the universe.[27] Politics is a part of this God-given rule-bound order. Once the rules of this order are discovered, again through reason, it is possible to distinguish good and just actions from unjust one. Aquinas set out to create rules for a Just War that would correspond with the perfect reasoning of God. Three of these rules had primacy over the others.[28] First, only sovereigns should declare war, not private persons. This argument, which was formulated well before the Westphalian system, was an early articulation of the principle of sovereignty. A second rule was that one had to have a just cause for war. For instance, it was only legitimate to attack others if they really deserve it, if a wrong or an injury has already been committed and needed to be set right. A third rule was that force should only be used with the right intentions, in order to ward off evil and advance good. The use of force was only justified for defensive purposes, not for revenge.

Secular philosophers as well as theologians have gradually developed the principles of Just War theory over several centuries. During that time, the conditions of war have changed dramatically, raising questions about the relationship of these ideas to nuclear weapons, to guerrilla warfare, humanitarian intervention, and, most recently, pre-emptive strategies. While its advocates, from Augustine to Hugo Grotius to the US Catholic Bishops have been faced with different problems and different questions, they have built on a body of theory with several key ideas at its core. The tradition of Just War, as it has developed historically has revolved around a distinction between *jus ad bellum* (just cause) and *jus in bello* (just use). The first has to do with the reasons a state has for fighting, that is, whether that reason is just or unjust. The second has to do with whether it is fought justly or unjustly. *Jus ad bellum* has revolved around seven principles.[29]

- *Just cause* in its classic expression related to the defense of innocents against armed attack, the retaking of persons, property, or other values that were wrongly taken and the punishment of evil.[30]
- *Authority to judge the justness of a cause* specifies that the person or body authorizing the use of force should be a representative of a sovereign political entity. The authority has to be able to control or halt the use of force, which means it must have a clear chain of command.[31]
- *Right intention*, that is, the authority should act with a just intent rather than for territorial advantage, intimidation, or coercion. This has implied that hatred of the enemy, "implacable animosity," "lust for vengeance," and a desire to dominate were to be avoided.
- *Proportionality of ends* means that the overall good achieved by the use of force should be greater than the harm done. The degree of force and means must be appropriate to the just ends that are sought.
- *War must be the last resort*. It has to be clear at the time a decision to use force is made that no other means will bring about the just end that

is sought. This is influenced by other *jus ad bellum* criteria regarding the level, type, and duration of the force to be used.

- *There should be reasonable likelihood of success.* Authorities are required to make a prudent calculation of the relationship between the means used and the justified ends that are sought. Again, other criteria relating to level, type, and duration of force are significant here.
- *The aim must be peace.* Authorities should seek to establish international stability and security, which includes disarmament and other measures to promote peace.

Two principles have defined *jus in bello* or the criteria for using force. While *jus ad bellum* includes proportionality of ends, the first principle of *jus in bello* is the proportionality of means. Unnecessary harm should be avoided, which means that torture is prohibited and that weapons, the days of fighting, and the number of soldiers should be limited. The second principle is noncombatant protection and immunity. People who are not involved in the prosecution of war should be spared from the harm of war.

The rules of war

Just War theory does not raise a question about whether war itself is an injustice. The tradition is rooted in an acceptance of human moral fallibility and the conviction that any moral pursuit will be more or less flawed. War is an imperfect instrument of justice.[32] The *jus ad bellum* criteria of Just War theory have provided a framework for judging whether a particular case of war is justified and, if so, the limits within which this war should be fought. The framework appropriates the right to make these judgments to states rather than to individuals. Indeed, as James Turner Johnson argues, competent authority should be the first criterion of consideration since only a competent authority can think through the determinants of Just War thinking.[33] Just Wars are by definition limited and they are based on rules that bar the use of violence or coercion against noncombatants, to the extent this is possible.

The term laws of war is usually used to refer to *jus in bello* or the rules governing the actual conduct of armed conflict. *Jus in bello* applies in cases of armed conflict regardless of whether the inception of conflict is lawful under *jus ad bellum*.[34] *Jus in bello* principles, and particularly those related to noncombatant protection and immunity, have in a more general sense been difficult to sustain in the face of technological developments that have altered the means of fighting wars.

Many of the rules of war, including noncombatant immunity, were traditionally accepted by the European military. However, the tension between the desire to limit war and the increasing destructiveness of war became evident in the nineteenth century, thereby complicating the application of these rules. Certain distinctions were blurred as entire societies were mobilized for war on behalf of the nation. The traditional dichotomy defined combatant soldiers in contrast to noncombatant citizens, presuming the innocence of the latter given their lack of involvement in the hostilities of war. The increasing destructiveness of weapons, and the development of artillery, made it possible for the first time to destroy the enemy at such distance that there would be no face to face contact. This paved the way for more indiscriminate forms of fighting. The development of aerial bombing in the First World War, and its strategic use in the Second World War, only exacerbated the problem.[35]

Unsurprisingly, the increasing destructiveness of war gave rise, particularly after the Napoleonic Wars, to more widespread demands from citizens that war be limited or banned all together. An international peace movement held up a critical mirror to governments regarding the institutions, habits, and consequences of war.[36] From the 1860s on efforts were made to codify and popularize new laws of war in order to show that war need not be as destructive as claimed by the peace movements and that noncombatants and private property could be spared.

Three strands of rules began to be codified at the end of the nineteenth century. These related to the rules of combat and the means of fighting war, the establishment of simple humanitarian arrangements, and the prohibition of new and dangerous weapons. The codification of the laws and customs of war began with the regulation of maritime commerce in wartime, a branch of law that, according to the Declaration of Paris (1856), had "long been the subject of deplorable disputes."[37] In the USA, the government (i.e., the Unionist side or North in the Civil War), asked the immigrant German jurist, Frances Lieber to provide a codification of the basic principles and accepted rules of war on land.[38] This request was made before it was known exactly how bloody and drawn out the Civil War would be.[39] International lawyers and soldiers in Europe, who were themselves seeking to codify the rules of war, drew on the example provided by Lieber's work.

The demand for laws of war went hand in hand with increasing attention to the victims of war. The Napoleonic campaigns introduced conscript armies and the use of artillery, which increased the numbers and suffering of the wounded on the battlefield. Somewhat later, in 1859 during the wars of Italian unification, 29,000 Austrians, French, and Piedmontese were killed or wounded within a 15-hour period in the Battle of Solferino.[40] Henry Dunant, a citizen of Geneva, observed the suffering on the battlefield and dedicated himself to humanitarian work on their behalf. In 1861, and again in 1863, he published a pamphlet, "A Memory of Solferino," which stated that each country should set up a relief society to aid the army medical services in times of war and that nations should enter into a convention acknowledging the statutes and function of national relief societies.[41] In 1863, a committee was set up in Geneva to study his proposals. Originally given the name the International Standing Committee for Aid to Wounded Soldiers, it became the International Committee for the Red Cross (ICRC) in 1880.

In 1864, an international congress was organized in Geneva, which established the first limited protection for the wounded under international law, the Convention for the Amelioration of the Condition of Soldiers wounded in Armed Forces in the Field.[42] Progress had been made on the improvement of military hospitals but the transport of the wounded to these hospitals remained problematic. There was some understanding that armies would respect the immunity of ambulance teams. In some cases local generals signed agreements in advance of battle, determining the signs by which teams and field hospitals could be identified. The Geneva Convention of 1864 produced an international agreement that established simple humanitarian arrangements that could be understood by everyone and applied everywhere. The St Petersburg Declaration of 1868 was a further codification whose proclaimed purpose was to ban the use of explosive and/or incendiary bullets, but also included an important summary of the law of war philosophy:

> On the proposition of the Imperial Cabinet of Russia, an International Military Commission having assembled at St. Petersburg [29 November/ 11 December 1868] in order to examine into the expediency of forbidding the use of certain projectiles in times of war between civilized nations, and that Commission, having by common agreement fixed the technical limits at which the necessities of war should yield to the requirements of humanity, the Undersigned are authorized by the orders of their Governments to declare as follows:
>
> Considering that the progress of civilization should have the effect of alleviating as much as possible the calamities of war;
>
> That the only legitimate object which States should endeavor to accomplish during war is to weaken the military forces of the enemy;
>
> That for this purpose it is sufficient to disable the greatest possible number of men;

That this object would be exceeded by the employmer
which uselessly aggravate the sufferings of disabled men, or r
death inevitable;

That the employment of such arms would, therefore, be contrary to
the laws of humanity; ...

The Contracting or Acceding Parties reserve to themselves to come
hereafter to an understanding whenever a precise proposition shall
be drawn up in view of future improvements which science may
effect in the armament of troops, in order to maintain the principles
which they have established, and to conciliate the necessities of war
with the laws of humanity.[43]

The text did not explicitly mention noncombatants, although it
accepted that the only legitimate objective of war was to weaken the
military forces of the other and that the necessities of war must, to the
extent possible, "yield to the requirements of humanity."[44]

The international peace conferences in The Hague in 1899 were the
culmination of an organized effort, involving a series of congresses, by
European and American peace societies.[45] Instigated by the Russian Tsar
Nicholas II, the conferences codified provisions for the treatment of
prisoners of war. These provisions reflected the idea that they should be
treated in a manner consistent with that of the detaining power's troops.
At the second Hague Peace Conference of 1907, this was revised and
became the Hague Convention No. IV, which remained in operation
until replaced by the Geneva Prisoners of War Convention in 1929.
Conventions on the treatment of the wounded and sick, originating
with the first Hague Conference, were also updated during this time and
continued to be effective until replaced by the 1929 Geneva Convention.
The latter was heavily influenced by the experience of the First World
War.[46] The Hague conventions included, among others, limits on the
use of asphyxiating gases, provisions that non-belligerents be notified of
minefields and that these be swept away after their military purpose had
been served, technical standards for weapons, confirmation that direct
attacks on civilians and "undefended" places were unlawful, and
a respect for civilian and cultural property.

Eliminating war

The laws of war were put to the test in the First World War which broke
out in August 1914 after the assassination of the Austrian crown Prince
Franz Ferdinand in Sarajevo. The assassination sparked off a series of

events that escalated quickly to war. The European powers were already divided into two heavily armed camps. The major states became locked in a struggle between two inflexible and roughly equal alliances. The Great War became a bloody stalemate that led to the breakdown of the European balance of power system.

Rules developed for limited war were severely strained in a context of total war. The mobilization of entire societies in the name of national defense, involving the entire teenage and adult workforce to serve the war effort, and arming all adult males from 16 to 60, made it more difficult to clearly distinguish the civilian by the principle of noncombatant immunity. New weaponry, and bombardment from the air, made questions of the distinction between combatant and noncombatant, as well as proportionality, more relevant than ever before, and provided opportunities for attacking civilian sectors and industrial centers far away from coasts and war zones as never before.[47] The fundamental humanitarian principles of protecting the sick and wounded and treating prisoners decently did survive the war intact, however.[48] The codification of *jus in bello* principles in law corresponded with a dramatic increase in the problem. Technological developments, which made war far more destructive—themselves the product of human thinking and agency—had outstripped the attempt to limit war. The war lasted more than four and a quarter years, during which nine million died, at an average rate of more than 6000 a day.[49] The delegates who met at the Paris Peace Conference of 1919, at the end of the war, had one primary concern: to ensure that such a war would never happen again.[50]

The American President Woodrow Wilson was one of the main figures behind this movement to develop procedures to avoid war. He formulated his famous Fourteen Points, which included a call for an end to secret diplomacy. In his view, if people were informed of the military actions of their governments, diplomats would be less able to lie and enter into alliances that would lead to war. He called for a peace founded on the full freedom of travel and trade and for the right of all nations to self-determination. He also proposed the establishment of the League of Nations.

The League of Nations was to be a global institution, including all states as members. Its main objective was to prevent a recurrence of a world war. There was a clear consensus in public opinion and among leaders about the need to avoid another war. The League was to replace the balance of power system with a system based on collective security.[51] Collective security begins with an assumption that it would be possible for each state to identify a permanent common interest with every other state. Because all states wanted to avoid war and because they all wanted to preserve the system, they would join together to stop any emerging power that would threaten the system as a whole. When, through miscalculation or misinterpretation, tensions began to mount, it was in everyone's interests to join together and bring them to an end. The League created institutional procedures for restricting recourse to war. For instance, efforts were made to impose a cooling-off period for conflicts that had the potential to disrupt into war. Parties to a potential conflict would have to submit to some kind of arbitration or judicial settlement.[52]

In June 1927, the French foreign minister Aristide Briand approached the US government with a treaty that would outlaw war between the two countries. The US Secretary of State, Frank B. Kellogg, returned a proposal for a general pact against war, which after prolonged negotiations was signed by 15 nations and ultimately was ratified by 62. The Kellogg–Briand Pact of 1928, commonly known as the Pact of Paris, condemned "recourse to war for the solution of international controversies" (Article 1). The contracting parties agreed that war should be renounced as an instrument of national policy and that pacific means should be sought for the resolution of all conflicts, regardless of their origin or nature. While the treaty was surrounded by public celebration, the signatories had allowed considerable space for its qualification and interpretation. Kellogg–Briand did not, for instance, prohibit wars of self-defense, nor did it provide a clear interpretation of the meaning of self-defense. It also did not outlaw resort to force short of war. These, together with the failure to establish a means of enforcement, made the agreement ineffective in the face of developments, detailed below, in the 1930s.

In the aftermath of the First World War, international institutions such as the League tried to develop procedures that would improve communication between states and minimize the likelihood of error. General public education was also seen as an important instrument in limiting war.[53] As E.H. Carr wrote, the whole conception of the League of Nations was from the first closely bound up with the twin belief that public opinion was bound to prevail and that public opinion was the voice of reason.[54] The birth of international relations as an area of academic study came in response to public demand after the First World War. The First World War represented an end to the idea that decisions about war should be left in the hands of professional diplomats.

The new discipline sought ways to minimize the likelihood of war and had the task of educating the public. These educational efforts and the attempt to mobilize public opinion on behalf of the League assumed the primacy of ideas. "Idealists" believed that progress at the international level was possible if the right ideas were pursued in the right way. Further, public opinion could be relied on to judge correctly on any question that was presented to it rationally, and would use reason to pursue the good.

The problem in this case was that states did not always reason rightly or with moral concerns in mind and this contributed to the eventual downfall of the League. By 1930 almost all states in the League had ratified or declared their intention to comply with the Pact of Paris.[55] It was thought to be irrevocable. There was a popular picture of an aroused internationalist populace demanding that their governments renounce war. The success of the treaty seemed to demonstrate the primacy of ideas over tradition and the triumph of a long-term common international interest over parochial national interest.

But the sense of victory didn't last long. In 1931 Japan invaded Manchuria. This act was followed by nearly two years of diplomatic maneuvering which led only to getting Japan to withdraw from the League. In October 1934 Nazi Germany also withdrew. The gravest blow to the prestige of the League of Nations came in 1935 when Mussolini's Italy invaded Abyssinia, or what is today Ethiopia.

The League did not respond effectively to these crises. It took more than eleven months to adopt economic sanctions against Italy. Also, while declaring public support for the League, the British and French governments were involved in secret dealings with Mussolini. Against this background a whole series of acts led to a deterioration of the legitimacy of the League and any hope of it acting effectively. In this crisis situation, states were clearly acting in their own self-interest rather than in the interest of international law and order. The Japanese, Germans, and Italians were acting aggressively toward other nations. The politicians of Britain and France put their own national interest in avoiding aggression by Mussolini before that of collective security and maintaining the integrity of the League.[56] To cite an example, they were willing to sacrifice part of Abyssinia if this meant they could avoid being targets of war. The League couldn't work once states began to act in the very way it had set out to avoid.

The League didn't succeed in restraining the aggressive powers that brought about the Second World War. It had however altered the way that statesmen and the public thought or spoke about war. There was no longer a belief in the unrestricted right to engage in war. War was understood to be a measure of last resort, to protect a state's interest, and starting a war was formally a crime. Punishing the crime remained a problem. With the Second World War, Britain, France, the USA, and USSR joined together to stop the aggression of Germany, Italy, and Japan. After the Second World War, there was once again a widespread feeling that this type of global war should not be repeated. The Second World War was begun by states that used force to violently alter the existing political and territorial status quo at a time when force was no longer seen as an acceptable means of pursuing changes or advancing policy.

The idea of prohibiting aggression surfaced again after the Second World War in the Charter of the United Nations. The United Nations was to replace the League. Like the League, the UN was based on the idea of collective security, that is, that each state shared a responsibility for every other state's security, and that there should be joint action against an aggressor. The UN was authorized to use force against any state that it saw to be a threat to world peace. In this respect, its main goal was to preserve international stability.

The Second World War was also followed by a review of the Geneva Conventions in 1949, and the release of four new conventions that summer. The task of the 1949 conference, attended by representatives of 64 states, was to revise and replace the Geneva Conventions of 1929 and the Hague Convention of 1907 related to the sick and wounded in maritime warfare and to prepare a completely new convention on the protection of soldiers.[57] The process began with a letter from the President of the ICRC in February 1945 to governments and national societies of the organization, which outlined a provisional program and invited them to help in compiling documentation.[58] The final product emerged out of a complex and political process of negotiation between these three actors. Every party sought to find some human limitations on the conduct of war. The main problem they faced was the extent to which war-making, at the time, was susceptible to limitations in the nature and use of weaponry.[59] The Second World War had given rise to such devastating developments in both areas that there was a shared concern about subjecting them to legal control. The sentiment was expressed by a Greek delegate, Professor Michel Pesmazoglu at the Preliminary Conference of the National Red Cross Societies in Geneva July 26–August 3, 1946:

> War has been transformed into butchery and belligerents strike army and civilian populations alike without any distinction between the two. However, all abuses lead to a reaction. … International conscience demands the condemnation of all these barbarous proceedings.

The world is amazed and stunned before these rivers of blood, these hillocks of bones, these mountains of ruins. ... A new crusade is being gathered together against these abuses. ... We have been convened here to accomplish this universal desire. ... We are conscious of the will of all those whose lives, either as hostages, deportees, or on the field of battle, were sacrificed to the madness of men who believed that the protection of human beings was merely a figment of the brains of intellectuals.

All these martyrs do not demand revenge but they cry out that their sacrifice shall not have been in vain. They ask to be the last victims of these theories according to which man exists only for the State and not the State for the happiness of its citizens.[60]

The delegates sought to achieve as many humanitarian goals as were conceivable given military and political realism. They did not manage to prohibit indiscriminate bombing from the air. Concern about this practice was widespread throughout all of the countries who had experienced the war, on both sides. The ICRC had always held the conviction that indiscriminate bombing was lawless and contradicted the fundamental principles of International Humanitarian Law to which treaty signatories were committed. But the issue arguably belonged more to the Hague legislation, which focused on the conduct of hostilities, than Geneva, which had traditionally emphasized the victims of war, and pressing it could have further complicated the task of the latter.[61] The emergence and use of the atomic bomb in Hiroshima and Nagasaki posed further considerations.

The result of the 1949 Geneva process of review was four conventions. The central concern of all four Geneva Conventions was the protection of victims of war, including (1) the wounded and sick in armed forces in the field, (2) the wounded, sick, and shipwrecked in armed forces at sea, (3) prisoners of war, and (4) civilians.[62] The distinction between combatant and noncombatant, which is the most crucial element of international humanitarian law, was maintained, although with a focus on civilians in the hands of the enemy. Armed resistance in an occupied territory was accorded greater legitimacy, provided certain military conditions were met.[63] The protection of soldiers and those who care for them was reaffirmed. A comprehensive code for humane treatment of POWs was developed.

Article 2, which was common to all four conventions, was one of the most important provisions, because it specified the conditions under which the Conventions were to apply and extended the conditions contained in the earlier convention.[64] Under this article, the conventions "apply to all cases of declared war or any other armed conflict which may arise between two or more of the High Contracting Parties, even if the state of war is not recognized by one of them." The earlier Geneva Conventions only applied in a case of war that was either validly declared or recognized by either belligerent as a state of war in international law. After the Second World War, and its grave humanitarian consequences, it became clear that the protection of war victims could not be left to the question of whether a legal state of war existed. The phrase "armed conflict" was devised as a solution to this difficulty.[65]

Protection in war

In addition to Just War theory, two further elements of moral thinking developed hand in hand. The first is the idea of humanitarian aid to those suffering from war. The second is the codification of legal conventions to guide the treatment of POWs and victims of war. The ICRC was and continues to be at the forefront of both. While early efforts focused on wounded and sick combatants and the rights of POWs, the field has since expanded to cover refugees and other civilian victims. Since the end of the Cold War, there has been an explosion of humanitarian efforts. New questions about the application of the laws of war have also emerged.

The final decade of the twentieth century saw the human displacement of the Gulf War, bloody interclan warfare in Somalia, ethnic cleansing in Bosnia, and genocide in Rwanda to name just a few of the more prominent examples of humanitarian disaster. Given the high-profile coverage of these events in the media, "humanitarian" has become a household word. Yet, despite its frequent use, the term remains ambiguous and it had no universally accepted definition.[66] While carrying a connotation of apolitical, it has often been used by political actors for political ends.[67] The ICRC is founded on the principle that humanitarian aid should be given to all in need of assistance, without discrimination, once belligerents have given their consent for the ICRC to do so. Consent can be problematic, however, in so far as warring parties may withdraw it when they no longer see a political or military benefit.

Post–Cold War humanitarian efforts have emphasized two types of war-related action: the provision of relief to civilian populations and the protection of their basic human rights. Thomas Weiss and Cindy Collins present these two forms of action as the core of an international humanitarian system, comprising governmental, institutional, and individual actors who respond to war-related disaster.[68] The specific tasks include gathering data about the severity of a crisis, negotiating with warring parties over the provision of aid, the mobilization of resources, and the organization of aid projects, including the delivery of goods, and assuring accountability.

These practices take place against a background where the traditional distinction between civilians and soldiers has all but lost its meaning. Humanitarian organizations deal not only with "right authorities," that is, recognized political leaders, but also insurgents, many of whom operate outside of international law.[69] There has been a dramatic increase in the number of emergency relief and human rights agencies, private and public, multilateral and bilateral, as well as a proliferation of nongovernmental organizations dealing with humanitarian aid. Far from the hopes that inspired the combatant–civilian distinction, 90 percent of the casualties of war, in some estimates, are civilian rather than military.[70] The apparent expansion of humanitarian activity may have more to do with an increase in attention than an increase in need, as well as better access to data from previously inaccessible areas with the end of the Cold War. The amount of funding for humanitarian assistance increased fivefold during the 1990s.[71]

New questions about justice

Many criteria of Just War have been codified in positive international law. In regards to *jus ad bellum*, just cause has been defined in terms of self-defense against armed attack or an international response to threats to international peace. While traditionally right authority was assigned to states, the UN Security Council has since the Second World War had the right to authorize action.[72] During the Cold War, the use of the veto by permanent members often stood in the way of action. The collapse of the Soviet Union opened up the prospect for greater cooperation but it often remains difficult for the Security Council to agree. Other actors, such as NATO or the USA, have on occasion stepped in to fill the gap. Even without the endorsement of the Security Council, some argued that NATO's bombing of Serbia was just since, in contrast to the invasion of Iraq in 2003, it had broad international support. The question of right authority has become much more complicated in a world of overlapping international institutions.

Conflicts since the end of the Cold War have raised important questions about Just War theory and its legal codification. Both Just War theory and international law presume that states are the primary and only legitimate actors, yet many of the conflicts emerging since 1990 have not centered on formal state actors. The phrase "War on Terrorism," coined after the attacks on the US World Trade Center and Pentagon on September 11, 2001, is a confusing category in this regard. The language of war has in the past referred to a contest between legitimate state actors and the language of terrorism to "criminals." The denial of POW status, and thus due process,[73] to "terrorists" detained by the USA in Guantanamo Bay gave rise to debates about the categories applied to these prisoners as well as the legality of denying any prisoner basic legal and human rights. International lawyers have been very vocal in making the case that the American administration is violating international law.

The US Administration of George W. Bush. has argued that these prisoners are "enemy" or "unlawful" combatants. Indeed, Al-Qaida detainees do not fit easily with the conditions of "prisoner-of-war protection" (1949 Geneva Conventions III, Article 5) or "combatant and prisoner-of-war status" (1977 Additional Protocol 1, Articles 43–4). The criteria for this classification include an organized group under responsible command, carrying arms openly[74] and conducting operations in accordance with the laws and customs of war. Prisoners who meet these conditions cannot be punished for participating directly in hostilities. However, Article 5 states that in cases of doubt, prisoners should be treated as POWs until their status is determined by a competent tribunal. Further, being denied POW status should not mean absence of legal rights. The Addition Protocol 1 (Article 45) maintains that those not entitled to POW status are still protected by fundamental guarantees.

Initially the United States was unwilling to classify either Al-Qaida or Taliban prisoners as POWs. On February 7, 2002, in the first major policy statement on the issue, the White House made a distinction between Taliban and Al-Qaida detainees. Since Afghanistan is a party to the Geneva Conventions and the Taliban represented something like a sovereign authority (although never recognized by the USA as the legitimate Afghan government), the Taliban would be covered under Geneva Convention III, although not with full POW status.[75] The larger problem of giving status to Al-Qaida prisoners raises two issues. The first is the more specific one of the American government's treatment of these prisoners and the hesitation to grant them basic legal rights. These concerns were exacerbated by the exposure of acts of humiliation and torture by American soldiers and private contractors of Iraqi prisoners in the Abu Ghraib prison. The second is the question of whether the Geneva Conventions need to be rethought and updated in light of the new wars.[76] Just War theory, and related legal conventions, focus primarily on the right of *states* to engage in war and the treatment of state combatants. These provide little guidance for wars involving non-state actors.

Conclusion

Moral reasoning at the international level is often understood to be more problematic than moral reasoning within a culture. It is shaped by questions about the efficacy or dangers of morality in a realm of power politics, the difference between individual and community morality and the potential conflict between the moral responsibilities of leaders to their own people and to the larger world. However, moral reasoning has long been a part of the practice of making decisions about war and normative "oughts" are built into the structure of the international system. Just War theory is the most long-standing framework for making ethical judgments about action in war. Part of this thinking has traditionally been incorporated in state military practice. As war has become increasingly destructive, blurring the distinction between civilian and combatant, efforts have made to further codify humanitarian laws of war, the foremost expression being the Geneva Conventions. Ethical arguments, often put forward by nongovernmental actors, such as peace movements, have played an important role in creating a political climate for normative change and institutional development.

Just War theory did not attempt to eliminate war, only to define the circumstances in which it could be considered just and to place restrictions on the way it was fought. The bloody experience of the First World War gave rise to widespread demands that war be outlawed and established institutional mechanisms to minimize its likelihood. These mechanisms proved to be ineffective as states began in the 1930s to place their national interests over the common interest and collective security. Attempts to eliminate war have not succeeded and arguably the practice of total war over the last century has become more destructive to civilian populations. Despite recent Western efforts to make war more "humane," the majority of casualties in modern wars have been civilian. Subsequently, there has been a dramatic expansion of efforts to protect and provide humanitarian aid to populations suffering from war. The proliferation of new wars since the end of the Cold War and, since September 11, 2001, the War on Terrorism, have raised questions about the need to rethink laws of war that have been defined in terms of states.

4
Legal Interventions

One fundamental criticism of international law, frequently heard from realists, is that states can ignore it with more or less impunity. In this line of argument, international law is made by states for their own purposes and advantage. If states wish to break the law there is no proper authority or judge to prevent them from doing so or to punish them afterwards. However, major breaches of international law are relatively rare. States observe the law most of the time and most of it all of the time because it is convenient, profitable, and helpful to do so.[1] States can break the rules with impunity but their reputation will suffer in the long term. In fact, those who do break or bend the law, make great effort to provide a legal justification for their questionable acts. The desire to justify acts on the basis of existing laws is a reaffirmation of their importance, even when these acts represent a violation. In this respect, much international law is normative in so far as it sets standards, building on what is already established practice to develop expectations of future behavior.

There is a habitual element of international relations, reflecting the practices and customs of state action, which has given rise to customary law.[2] For instance, proportionality or the attempt to establish criteria for limiting the use of force, is a fundamental customary principle.[3] Beneath these customs, or common shared practices of states, exists another level of fundamental principle, relating in particular to elementary humanitarian considerations. Some of these rest on pre-emptory norms (*jus cogens*), or that from which there can be no derogation. Many laws of war, and within this the subset of international humanitarian law,[4] can be placed in this category in so far as the fundamental aim has been to limit the cruelties and damage inflicted in armed conflict against specified opponents and to protect innocent victims. This is done, among others, by drawing lines between "forms of attack that are permitted and forms that are not, between weapons that may be used and weapons that may not."[5]

The laws of war, and more specifically international humanitarian law, can be distinguished from human rights law, although the two increasingly overlap. While international humanitarian law applies specifically to protection and rights in time of war and conflict, human rights law is a body of norms to be implemented in general, both inside and outside of war. Prior to the development of the latter, the relationship between a state and its citizens was not understood to be a problem of international law. As Hersch Lauterpacht stated, "The predominant theory is clear and emphatic: International law is a law of states only and exclusively. Individuals are only the objects of international law."[6] Summary execution, torture, arbitrary arrest, and detention beyond national borders had only been significant legal events in the past if the victims of these atrocities were citizens of another state, in which case they were treated by international law as bearers, not of personal rights, but of rights belonging to their government and ultimately to the state which it represented.[7] Since the end of the Second World War, human rights law has been universalized and applies regardless of regional, national, or other differences. It represents an ensemble of legal norms that focus principally on protecting the individual against crimes committed by the state.[8]

There is thus both a customary side to international law, on the one hand, and a normative or moral side, on the other.[9] The two together, while sometimes in conflict, have contributed to a deepening of international law. As discussed in the last chapter, legal codification has often been a response to problems arising from the increased destructiveness of war. Sovereignty and nonintervention were a response to the bloody Thirty Years' War. The Hague and early Geneva Conventions were a response to the increasing destructiveness of war in the nineteenth century and the First World War. The expansion of the Geneva Conventions and the development of human rights law were responses to the atrocities of the Second World War and the Holocaust.

These different bodies of international law, like Just War theory, are forms of intervention in so far as they seek to shape and limit the experience of war. Both stand outside any particular conflict and provide objective standards for judging behavior. The two differ, at least theoretically, in the relationship between judgment and enforcement. While Just War theory has provided a framework for judging the moral legitimacy of particular wars and the means by which they are fought, international law, like law more generally, is a formal mechanism for judging the legality of particular acts. However, as already stated, international law is distinguished from its domestic counterpart by the absence of an overarching authority at the international level to enforce the law in the event of a violation.[10]

International law emerges out of the customs and habits of states, while attempting to introduce moral limitations on their behavior.[11] During the Second World War, a new kind of problem arose which international law was not equipped to deal with, that is, the attempt by a government to destroy its own subjects. Sovereignty and nonintervention had during the Westphalian period been the defining principles of the state system. However, after the Second World War the horror of the Holocaust of European Jews forced the international community to address what had happened in Germany and throughout Europe.

The purpose of this chapter is to examine the tensions within international law that arise from the coexistence and codification of habitual practice and moral principle, particularly as these relate to the emergence of human rights law. The first section of the chapter will examine human rights law and, within this, the Genocide Convention, which is one of its most important expressions. The second section will examine the problem of international enforcement of human rights law, particularly as it relates to the concept of humanitarian intervention. The third section will examine the ad hoc War Crimes Tribunals and the potential of the new International Criminal Court. The fourth section will review some of the positive and negative potentials arising from the globalization of human rights law.

Defining human rights

The evolution of human rights law has been propelled by the ongoing effort to reconstruct an understanding of what it means to be fully human often in response to threats, such as the Holocaust, to this humanity.[12] A human right is one that everyone has by virtue of their humanity.[13] In this respect, human rights have been defined as natural, universal, and inalienable. Regardless of rights or duties as a citizen or as a member of a particular group, there are fundamental rights that cannot be renounced, lost, or forfeited. It is possible to give up citizenship of a particular country but not one's human rights. To say that human rights are inalienable means they cannot be transferred to another person. The first attempt to lobby for international human rights was the antislavery movement that emerged in the eighteenth century and later contributed to the abolition of the slave trade. If human rights are inalienable, if they cannot be transferred to another person, then it is an obvious violation of such a right if one person is owned by another.[14]

While the customary practice of states has rested on an assumption of sovereignty and nonintervention, some recognition of human rights concerns can be traced back to the beginnings of the state system. The Peace of Westphalia of 1648 provided certain guarantees for religious minorities, as did other later treaties.[15] The concept of "crimes against humanity" goes back to the nineteenth century. The French revolutionary Robespierre described King Louis XVI, as a "criminal against humanity."[16] An American observer, George Washington Williams, in a letter to the US Secretary of State, accused King Leopold's regime in the Congo of being responsible for "crimes against humanity."[17] The first appearance of the term in an international law context, during the First World War, was in a joint declaration from France, Great Britain, and Russia on May 24, 1915, regarding the atrocities committed against the Armenians:

> In the presence of these new crimes of Turkey against humanity and civilization, the allied Governments publicly inform the Sublime Porte that they will hold personally responsible for the said crimes all members of the Ottoman government as well as those of its agents who are found to be involved in such massacres.[18]

Reports of the number of Armenians killed range from 600,000 to two million. The rest were forcibly driven from their homeland. Yet, none of the perpetrators was ever punished.[19] The growing interest in international protection of human rights found further expression in the post-First World War peace treaties of 1919, which recognized the need for special protection of national minorities.[20]

However, it was only after the Second World War, during which Hitler rounded up and systematically annihilated the Jews of Europe, that human rights became a focus of international concern. Toward the close of the Second World War, Winston Churchill referred to the Nazi effort to exterminate a people as a "crime that has no name,"[21] which reflected the absence of appropriate words to describe the horror of Auschwitz.

The word "genocide" was coined by Raphael Lemkin, a Polish Jewish Legal Scholar, in his 1944 book, *Axis Rule over Occupied Europe*.[22] Genocide comes from the Greek "genos" meaning race or tribe and the Latin "cide" meaning to kill. The word quickly entered into international discourse and corresponded with efforts by Lemkin to develop a new concept of international law, within which genocide would be branded an international crime and one permanently outlawed by the world community. He was part of the staff of Associate Supreme Justice Robert K. Jackson, the Chief American Prosecutor at Nuremberg, although he failed to convince the prosecution to include his new word in the indictment of Nazi war criminals. Instead, Nazi war criminals were convicted of "crimes against humanity," among others.[23] The Nuremberg Charter seemed to indicate that crimes against humanity could only be committed in time of war, which set a troubling precedent for the future protection of human rights.[24]

Lemkin did finally succeed through his unceasing efforts, in introducing the word to the UN agenda. On December 11, 1946, the General Assembly of the United Nations passed Resolution 96(I), which formally declared "genocide" to be "a crime under international law which the civilized world condemns, and for the commission of which principals and accomplices ... are punishable." The law was further developed in the Convention on the Prevention and Punishment of the Crime of Genocide—commonly known as the Genocide Convention, which was adopted by the UN General Assembly on October 9, 1948 and came into force in January 1951 (UN Res. 260-IIIA).

The convention defined genocide as the deliberate and systematic destruction in whole or in part of a national, ethnic, racial, or religious group. Genocide includes two elements, which, at least in theory, have to be proven in trial.[25] The first element is the material facts, that is, that the destruction actually took place. The second is moral and regards the question of intent. The actions cannot have been accidental or committed without intent to do harm. Genocide requires a plan and an organized process committed by a group, rather than an individual. Because it implies a specific intent, and massive scale—the elimination of an entire group—genocide was named the ultimate crime against humanity.

The coining of genocide related to attempts to codify human rights law more generally.[26] The Covenant on Genocide was followed in December of the same year by the Universal Declaration of Human Rights (1948). The Declaration was adopted by the UN General Assembly without a dissenting vote. It was intended less as a legally binding document than "a common standard of achievement for peoples and nations." M.N. Shaw has raised a question about whether the Declaration has since become binding by way of custom, or the general principles of law, or by virtue of interpretation of the UN Charter itself as expressed in subsequent practice.[27] In the period since 1948 the United Nations has adopted treaties to address civil and political rights, economic and social rights, racial and ethnic discrimination, discrimination against women, torture, and the rights of the child.[28] The great majority of states—over 75 percent—have ratified the seven treaties.

After the Second World War, the Genocide Convention in particular and human rights more generally had widespread support at the international level. However, states had several incentives to water down the law or ignore it in practice. The foremost issue is the potential conflict between sovereignty and human rights. Sovereignty is the traditional concept of statehood, and is based on an objective territory, assuming a permanent population, an effective government, and a capacity for that government to engage in international diplomacy.[29] Human rights are part of a value system, growing particularly out of Western liberal democracy and Judeo-Christian moral standards. Ideally, the two work together, enhancing the human rights of citizens within states. The problem arises when the internal mechanisms of a government don't conform to liberal democratic principles. In this case, the conflict at the heart of international customary and normative law becomes evident.

The UN Charter made sovereignty and noninterference the hub of its legal apparatus. Article 1 of the Charter defines the primary purpose of the UN:

> To maintain international peace and security, and to that end, to take effective collective measures for the prevention and removal of threats to the peace, and for the suppression of acts of aggression or other breaches of the peace, and to bring about by peaceful means, and in conformity with the principles of justice and international law, adjustment or settlement of international disputes or situations which might lead to a breach of peace.[30]

That the emphasis is on sovereignty over justice is clarified in Articles 2(4), which states that:

> All members shall refrain in their international relations from the threat or use of force against the territorial or political independence of any state, or in any other manner inconsistent with the purposes of the United Nations.

Article 2(7) further elaborates that:

> Nothing contained in the present Charter shall authorize the United Nations to intervene in matters which are essentially within the

domestic jurisdiction of any state or shall require the members to submit such matters to settlement under the present Charter; but this principle shall not prejudice the application of enforcement measures under Chapter VII.

The United Nations did establish mechanisms to facilitate the pursuit of justice related to human rights and self-determination, but these were not to be sought at the expense of peace.[31] In the face of a massive violation of human rights by a government, the international community had to decide whether sovereignty, which includes the assumption of noninterference, should be overridden in order to address the problem.[32]

There have been several reasons for the weak observance of human rights law, relating in particular to the practicalities of implementation. First, in the post-war period states were rushed into a commitment to protect human rights. Human rights was tacked on to sovereignty, rather than integrated into it, without thinking about the consequences.[33] Those involved in the Nuremberg indictments did not want to set a precedent that could be used against them in the future. They were therefore careful to qualify the definition of crimes against humanity, in order to minimize its application, for instance, by specifying that it referred only to crimes during war. While the Genocide convention went further, Schabas argues that its definition is too narrow and restrictive.[34] It fails to cover many major human rights violations and mass killings perpetrated by dictators. The principal deficiency is that it applies only to "national, racial, ethnic, and religious groups." While in cases of state terror victims are chosen arbitrarily or because they have committed subversive acts, genocide relates only to victimization as members of a group.

Second, while there was agreement in principle, there were disagreements over interpretations of human rights law as the victors of the Second World War fell out among themselves. The superpowers in particular disagreed. The USA placed emphasis on civil and political rights, or the right to freedom from interference by the government.[35] Thus they were critical of the Soviet bloc countries for failing to allow free speech or for engaging in practices of arbitrary arrest or unjust treatment of prisoners. In the early 1980s, when American President Reagan accused the USSR of being an Evil Empire, he was in part pointing to the oppression of individuals and groups who had been imprisoned for speaking out about the human rights violations of countries that had signed on to the Helsinki Final Act.[36] By contrast, the East bloc defined human rights in terms of subsistence rights or the right to work, to education, and to health care.[37] A similar message could be heard from the Third World, based on arguments that the rights of the community and the need for order have to take precedence over those of the individual. Further, it has been questioned whether political and civil rights are that significant when one doesn't have enough to eat.[38] In the late 1980s, Soviet President Gorbachev was very critical of the fact that tens of thousands of people were homeless in the USA, the wealthiest country in the world, and that one quarter of the children were living below the poverty level.

Third, the central problem with human rights law is one of enforcement. There are few procedures for individuals to pursue claims against their own state. The International Court of Justice has not been open to individuals.[39] Further, responses to massive violations of human rights have in the past often been stymied by the conflicting interests of states. The UN Security Council has been authorized to approve the use of force.[40] However, the body was paralyzed during the Cold War by the ability of any of the permanent members to exercise the veto.[41] Other than Korea in the 1950s, there were no further collective security operations authorized by the UN until the Gulf War. The Korean vote was only possible because the USSR was absent. In any case, these acts were defined in terms of international security rather than humanitarian ends. Even in cases where there was a humanitarian outcome to an invasion by an individual government, such as Vietnam's invasion of Pol Pot's Cambodia, this was justified in terms of national interest.[42] States clung to their sovereignty and put human rights on the backburner, except as a weapon in the Cold War of words. During the Cold War the superpowers backed authoritarian regimes guilty of massive human rights violations in Hungary, Czechoslovakia, Chile, and El Salvador, to name only a few. There were no "humanitarian" interventions during the Cold War,[43] other than peacekeeping operations, which were primarily for the purpose of monitoring ceasefires. Nor were there any war crimes tribunals between Nuremberg and those in the 1990s for the former Yugoslavia and Rwanda.

While states attempted to ignore the commitments they agreed to in the human rights documents, nongovernmental organizations did use these principles to hold up a critical mirror to governments. This was not inconsistent with the intentions of Eleanore Roosevelt and Rene Cassen, who drafted the Universal Declaration of Human Rights. They saw NGOs as potentially more important than states in making the declaration into an effective instrument for preventing future horrors.[44] Human rights NGOs have played several roles. First, they have been involved in standard setting, or establishing the international norms by which the conduct of states can be judged, as well as fact-finding in relation to these norms. They have intervened on behalf of "prisoners of conscience" or on behalf of the oppressed. They have also been actively involved in the creation of various types of implementing agencies and institutions, or in politicizing human rights violations. In Eastern Europe in the 1970s, groups such as Charter 77 in Czechoslovakia and Solidarity in Poland used the Eastern bloc commitment to the Helsinki principles to expose the distinction between the promises made by states and their actual practice. In the West, an increasingly vocal chorus of voices protested the practices of Apartheid South Africa, as well as the abuses in Latin America by US-supported regimes. Amnesty International has played an active role in documenting human rights abuse.

Enforcing human rights law

The end of the Cold War brought an end to the superpower stalemate that stood in the way of common action by the UN Security Council. On August 2, 1990 Iraq invaded Kuwait after which the Security Council, led by the USA, authorized the first collective security operation since Korea. This was an action justified in terms of traditional concepts of sovereignty and noninterference. Because Iraq had violated the sovereignty of Kuwait, the international community in responding was upholding the central principle of the UN Charter relating to peace and security. Following the Gulf War, the international community was confronted with a new type of humanitarian challenge, beginning with the humanitarian emergency faced by the Iraqi Kurds. In Europe, after 50 years of saying "never again" the outbreak of ethnic conflict in the former Yugoslavia, accompanied by ethnic cleansing, gave rise to fears that genocide was happening once again and in Europe. In other hotspots, such as Rwanda, even more brutal massacres took place. The international community was forced to address the commitments it had made in the Genocide Convention. This raised several issues.

The first was a problem of definition. Genocide is a concept that has to be applied in practice. At what point can brutalities against a citizenry be placed in the category of genocide, thus requiring some action by the international community? The concept was applied with frequency in relation to the former Yugoslavia, fuelled by media representations that brought back the memory of Hitler's concentration camps. Despite the disturbing images, and the public outrage they engendered, the UN and NATO failed to act forcefully in Bosnia until late in the day. The UN

Security Council, among others, resisted use of the term genocide in Rwanda, precisely because it would accelerate demands for intervention.[45]

The second issue is whether humanitarian intervention, involving the use of force, without the consent of the authorities in the area, is legal. Strictly speaking, the majority of international lawyers say it is not.[46] At the heart of this claim is the conflict between sovereignty and human rights. The lawyers who argue against humanitarian intervention are referred to as restrictionists. They point specifically to the ban in Article 2(4) of the UN Charter on the use of force against the territorial and political independence of a state. The Security Council has legitimate authority under Chapter VII to authorize an enforcement action, but only if there is a threat to international peace and security (Article 39), not on humanitarian grounds alone. Although the jurisdiction of the Security Council under Chapter VII is only triggered by the existence of a threat to peace, a breach of peace, or an act of aggression, the Security Council has, since 1989, been increasingly willing to interpret the phrase "threats to peace" broadly.[47]

The opposing argument is that there are supreme humanitarian emergencies, such as genocide, or state-sponsored mass murder, or massive expulsion of a population by force, when ethical concerns should override the legal concern about sovereignty. In this view, international law should recognize a right of unilateral humanitarian intervention. One specific argument is that governments who massively violate human rights forfeit their right to sovereignty and nonintervention. Sovereignty thus comes with certain responsibilities toward one's citizens. If the state does not live up to these, other states are morally and legally entitled to intervene.[48] Consistent with this argument, the International Commission on Intervention and State Sovereignty (ICISS) has proposed shifting the terms of debate away from the "right to intervene" toward the "responsibility to protect." The latter rests on an interpretation of sovereignty that assumes the responsibility of a given state to protect its citizens. This perspective incorporates a principle of "human security" over more narrow definitions of national security. While the ICISS recognizes the potential difficulty of getting states to embrace the responsibility to protect, it sees the challenge as a necessary one:

> Nothing has done more harm to our shared ideal that we are all equal in worth and dignity and that the earth is our common home, than the inability of the community of states to prevent genocide, massacre and ethnic cleansing. If we believe that all human beings are equally

entitled to be protected from acts that shock the conscience of us all, then we must match rhetoric with reality, principle with practice. We cannot be content with reports and declarations. We must be prepared to act.[49]

The two distinct arguments regarding the legality of forceful intervention fit within two broader schools of thought, which Nicholas Wheeler describes as Pluralist and Solidarist.[50] The first, that is, the *pluralist*, overlaps with the realist position, although it is distinct from it. In this view, international society is made up of states and its rules are made by states on behalf of state interests. There is neither an international consensus on rules regarding humanitarian intervention nor an international organization that can make decisions about intervention independent of individual state interests. If the Security Council is often divided about the use of force, humanitarian intervention with international consent will be the exception and unilateral humanitarian intervention the rule. States acting on their own behalf will weaken an international order that has been built on shared rules of sovereignty, nonintervention and the nonuse of force. Unlike the realist position, which emphasizes the primacy of power considerations, pluralists are first and foremost concerned with the shared rules that constitute the society of states.

Like realists, pluralists are concerned that states won't intervene and risk the lives of their soldiers or invest economic resources unless vital national interests are at stake, although their primary concern is the danger of pursuing justice and morality in a world which, they argue, lacks agreement on these concepts. Humanitarian concerns may be a factor, but states are unlikely to act unless there is a coincidence of these with the national interest. This raises the issue of selectivity and the concern that actors will only undertake humanitarian action if other interests are at stake. Thus the ultimate criterion for intervention is interest rather than the gravity of the abuse. In this view, decisions to intervene on humanitarian grounds become dependent on shifting strategic considerations. Further, states may use humanitarian arguments to justify what are purely material interests. For instance, in Kosovo the action was presented as purely humanitarian but, one could argue, what was really at stake was re-establishing NATO as a legitimate post–Cold War actor after the repeated failures in Bosnia. A further objection from the pluralist perspective is that states have no business risking their soldiers' lives to save strangers. The first responsibility of state authorities is to protect their citizens.

The second school of thought is referred to as *solidarist*. Members of the world community, in this view, are not first and foremost states but individuals. Therefore the international community has an obligation to intervene if individual rights are being abused on a massive level. Justice should be the first priority. The measure of progress at this level is the degree to which sovereignty and the maintenance of order have given way to universalism and some notion of the common good. The solidarist perspective points to the need to construct a universal morality for individuals as members of a world community, to heighten the sensitivity of people in one place to wrongs committed in another in the interest of global justice. States, in this view, should be good international citizens and come to the aid of those who are in need.

While it is generally accepted today that individuals have a moral standing independent of states, or independent of their status as citizens of particular states, this acceptance raises a further question. At what point does a state's abuse of its citizen's human rights justify intervention in its sovereign affairs? It is generally accepted that this intervention is justified if genocide, or the deliberate effort to eliminate a people is taking place. But, as already suggested, it is not always easy to determine when genocide is occurring. The problems of definition and legality thus relate to the problem of who should decide when genocide is occurring, that is, the question of right authority, and subsequent enforcement. At what point is the problem sufficiently severe that the international community should override the sovereignty rule? Answering the question is often in part a problem of political will. While populations were horrified by the sight of human slaughter in, for instance, Bosnia, this was tempered by concerns about sending soldiers into harm's way in conflicts that did not intersect directly with the national interest.

It is not straightforward that soldiers in one state should risk their own lives in the course of saving strangers.[51] Particularly in the USA, the Vietnam syndrome continued throughout the post–Cold War period to provide a powerful restraint on sending soldiers to far-off wars. The experience of US peacekeepers in Somalia as part of UNOSOM II proved fatal to further US interventions. Images of soldiers being dragged before television cameras led to US withdrawal and tempered enthusiasm for intervention at a later time in places such as Rwanda. Humanitarian intervention was not only problematic because of the conflict with the sovereignty rule. In places such as Bosnia or Somalia a violation of sovereignty was less at issue than the conflict between the responsibility of intervening governments to protect their own citizens, including soldiers, and the humanitarian need for intervention in cases where the national interest was not at stake. Criteria for justifying humanitarian intervention will be examined in the next chapter. The central purpose of this brief examination has been to raise the complex legal questions posed by humanitarian intervention. How do we know genocide when we see it? Is humanitarian intervention ever legal? If it is, at what point is the scale of atrocities sufficient to override the sovereignty principle?

Punishing human rights violations

Law presupposes the possibility of following or breaking legal codes and, in the latter case, the prospect of punishment. The absence of a power to enforce and punish interstate violations of the law has been the defining feature of international experience. International law isn't worth the paper it is written on if it can't be enforced, or so realists argue. The other side of the coin is that states do follow the law most of the time. The presence of these formalized and agreed norms does shape state practice. The incidence of violation or the failures of enforcement are not so different than would be present in any domestic society.

The Nuremberg and Tokyo trials following the Second World War represented attempts to bring legal justice to the aftermath of war. They extended the traditional scope of international humanitarian law, by adding international criminal law and justice to the laws of The Hague and Geneva.[52] Both trials were highly politicized and, in the years following, were criticized for representing a form of victor's justice.[53] The losers were in the dock and acts by the victors, such as the bombings of Dresden, Hiroshima, and Nagasaki, never came to trial. The trials were US initiatives, which paved the way for the legal concept of crimes against humanity to be accepted as customary public international law. It further substituted legal process for the victims' urge for revenge.[54]

There were no new war crimes tribunals until the 1990s, when the Security Council created the International Tribunals for Rwanda (ICTR) and the former Yugoslavia (ICTY). These trials were based on the precedent of the post-Second World War tribunals and had the legal backing of the Universal Declaration of Human Rights and the Genocide Convention. The decision to create the ICTY in May 1993 represented the first time that the Security Council had created a judicial body to "maintain international peace and security under Chapter Seven of the Charter."[55] The ICTR, established in November 1994, shared the legal basis and jurisdictional power of the ICTY. However, as it was classified as an internal conflict, the Rwanda tribunal had no mandate to prosecute war crimes, and instead was tasked with prosecuting those indicted of genocide and crimes against humanity inflicted in a widespread and systematic manner on civilian populations.[56]

One development of the ICTY and ICTR was the redefinition of rape as an illegal instrument of war and an unacceptable military strategy. Rape had always been a violation of the laws of war, codified as a capital crime in Lieber's Code of Instructions as early as 1866. It could thus be prosecuted in domestic court or military court martial. In the post–Cold War tribunals, rape was placed in the category of crimes against humanity and individuals became criminally responsible for using it as an instrument of military strategy. The first conviction for sexual offense at the ICTY was on February 22, 2001, at which time Drogoljub Kunarac, Radomir Kovac, and Zoran Vakovic were sentenced to 28 years, 20 years, and 12 years respectively for crimes including rape as a crime against humanity.[57]

Another significant step in the direction of holding all individuals responsible for their criminal actions, regardless of rank and status, was the indictment of former President Pinochet of Chile, who was the leader of Chile after the 1973 coup that deposed democratically elected President Allende. Pinochet was arrested in London in 1998 based on a warrant issued by a Spanish court, which claimed he had murdered Spanish citizens during his term as President. A second Spanish warrant, after his arrest, accused him of systematic acts of illegal detention, murder, torture, and disappearance of people. Initially the British High Court decided that extradition to Spain was not warranted since neither the UK nor Spain had jurisdiction over crimes committed in Chile. Further, Pinochet, as a former head of state, was protected by sovereign immunity and could not be prosecuted by foreign courts. However, this decision was later overturned by the House of Lords, who decided that Pinochet should stand trial in the UK or be extradited to Spain for having violated international humanitarian law.

These ad hoc efforts represented attempts to apply the scrutiny of law at the international level and to determine appropriate punishment. They raise a number of crucial problems. In a world made up of multiple separate states, each with its own legal traditions, whose laws and procedures should provide the framework for judgment? For instance, one problem in the negotiating sessions leading up to the adoption of the Charter of the Nuremberg Tribunal was that each party brought their own legal concepts and experience to the table, that is, the common law adversarial system, which has evolved differently in the USA and England, and the civil law inquisitorial system, which took different forms in France and Russia.[58] It was no small challenge to create a new judicial entity that combined elements of the different systems and was acceptable to all parties. Despite the effort to combine legal traditions, the court still did not have the position of an impartial international authority. Because there is no impartial authority at the international level, there is a tendency for justice to be led by the victors and thus by their interests.

The International Criminal Court (ICC)

There was a significant effort to make the post–Cold War tribunals in the former Yugoslavia and Rwanda into *international* tribunals, to detract from accusations of victor's justice. But momentum was also building for a truly International Criminal Court. The concept of a permanent ICC goes back to 1919 and the Versailles Peace Treaty, although due to the unwillingness of the USA to implement the war crimes articles of the treaty (Articles 227–30) and concerns about regional stability, it never came into being. After the Second World War, the UN revisited the idea, but interest ebbed with the onset of the Cold War. The idea was renewed with the Velvet Revolutions that took place across Eastern Europe and the collapse of the USSR. On June 15, 1998, 160 states convened to negotiate a "statute and final act" for a proposed International Criminal Court. The UN Secretary General said that "[The ICC] promises at last, to supply what for so long has been the missing link in the international legal system, a permanent court to judge the crimes of gravest concern to the international community as a whole—genocide, crimes against humanity and war crimes."[59] The statute, which included 128 articles and 13 parts, established the court, its seat, and relationship to other international bodies, such as the United Nations, the jurisdiction of the court, the penalties it can impose, and the process of enforcement.[60]

The most contentious part of the negotiations regarding the ICC revolved around the jurisdiction of the court vis à vis domestic courts. The court was to deal with a range of traditional forbidden acts, including torture, extermination, and forced enslavement. Article 7 specified a range of further acts that had occurred since 1945, such as Apartheid, forcible transfer of populations, ethnic cleansing,[61] rape and forced pregnancy, enforced disappearance of persons, and gender persecution. In so far as specific states are potentially implicated on particular issues, it was bound to be inherently complicated to define and universalize the various crimes. For instance, the inclusion of "the transfer, directly or indirectly, by the occupying power of points of its own civilian population in the territory it occupies" (Article 8) as a war crime, gave rise to vociferous opposition from Israeli delegates, who saw it as a direct attack on Israel's policy of settling the West Bank.[62] A number of states, and the USA in particular, who have a large military presence abroad, primarily in the form of peacekeepers, were concerned that the court would be used to prosecute soldiers involved in duties beyond their borders for political reasons. To overcome some of the difficulties, the negotiators had to define levels of activity beyond which individuals or small groups would no longer fall under the jurisdiction of their domestic legal machinery, whether national or military, and would become accountable to the ICC.[63]

Although President Bill Clinton was on record as supporting the creation of the ICC, the USA has been the "main obstacle" to its creation.[64] As the world's most powerful state, the USA is less inclined than most to hand over a degree of its sovereignty to an international court.[65] It has the most to lose, given the prominent role of its forces abroad. The military's greatest fear is that commanders and ordinary soldiers will become the targets of politically motivated prosecutions. A further concern was the need for checks and balances on a single prosecutor, who it was feared might be influenced by personal and political considerations.[66] Despite these concerns, President Clinton signed the treaty in December 2000, although he did not send it up for ratification. President Bush has subsequently withdrawn the US signature, "unsigning" the treaty in May 2002.

International law has prioritized questions of peace over justice. The increasing momentum behind the ICC, and its focus on war crimes and crimes against humanity, call this hierarchy into question. Indeed, in one line of argument, some form of justice is a necessary condition for future peace, for the aggrieved to put the past firmly in the past rather than reproducing it in the future.[67] The relationship between injustice and the reproduction of violence will be examined in more depth in Chapter 8.

The globalization of human rights law

The last half of the twentieth century, and particularly the decade following the end of the Cold War brought an increasing recognition of universal laws and norms of human rights. While states were—unsurprisingly— reluctant to abide by these laws in practice, a global network of NGOs and INGOs, as well as an increasingly globalized media, have played an important role in mobilizing awareness regarding human rights violations, placing states under increased pressure to abide by the norms and laws they have agreed to. These are positive developments.

Nonetheless, any effort to produce global norms and laws is likely to have negative implications in a diverse world and to be an expression of power in and of itself. Globalization has involved complementary processes of integration and fragmentation. While Western countries, and particularly the states of the European Union, are increasingly integrated, many other areas of the world, some of which were objects of Western imperialism in the past, have suffered greater fragmentation. Recently decolonized states, which emerged along with globalization, have confronted global processes that erode sovereignty at the very moment they are attempting its consolidation. Traditionally, it has been assumed that the absence of a universal state meant that protection of individuals and their interests was primarily the responsibility of their governments. However, an erosion of sovereignty means an erosion of the ability of states to deliver these rights and responsibilities, especially as they relate to social and economic rights. In this respect, the lobbying of NGOs, and the mobilization of public opinion relating to human rights, has involved strengthening the link to other global policy domains, related to development, trade, and the environment.

The bifurcation cannot be separated from a longer history of exploitation. It is those states who in the past have been invaded or intervened upon by the wealthier Western states that are likely to be exploited through trade relations, as became clear during the 2003-G21 meeting in Cancun. They are also more likely to be receivers rather than senders of a culture of human rights. The legal apparatus of human rights law does not take into account the role of a history of violence and human rights violations by outside perpetrators into former colonies in shaping the contemporary politics of "failed states." Important questions need to be raised about the extent to which the politics of human rights law and enforcement reinforce the powerlessness of those who have historically been at the bottom of the political ladder.

Conclusion

Human rights law has emerged as a complement to the laws of war. In principle states can no longer act with impunity toward their own populations. This development nonetheless brings to the fore important problems regarding the tension between the primacy of sovereignty and nonintervention in international law, and the need to act in response to massive human rights violations, and particularly genocide. The central problem that distinguishes international law from domestic law is the absence of a centralized authority to enforce and punish violations.

While ad hoc efforts have emerged to internationalize enforcement and punishment of human rights violations these also have been dogged by the conflict between the sovereign immunity of leaders and the sovereign jurisdiction of states over their own citizens. The ICC provides a context for universalizing punishment of war crimes and crimes against humanity, but is no less impeded by the politics of sovereignty and the interests of the individual states who have created it than earlier more ad hoc efforts. However, consistent with the constructivist leanings of this argument, the problems arising from the conflict between sovereignty and human rights are less a reflection of the tension between an objective reality and the introduction of normative principle to it, than the emergence of two distinct sets of social rules at different times in response to a changing reality of war. Human rights was tacked on to sovereignty, rather than integrated into it, without thinking through the potential conflict between them.

5
Military Interventions

The last two chapters explored moral and legal interventions that have shaped the way that war or intervention are justified and constructed. Each provided a more or less formal framework for making judgments about the conduct of war. The next two chapters shift to the more specific policy choices involved in different forms of intervention. Realist theory emphasizes the influence of material interests on policy. The rational decision is one defined in terms of the national interest in power. Power is first and foremost expressed as military capability, but the latter also relates to economic power, including the strength of the economy and the capacity to produce or purchase weapons. From this perspective, power rather than moral or legal principle motivates state policy or, at best, principle is a vehicle for realizing more material interests. To say, by contrast, that policies are social constructs is to focus on how power and principle combine in historically specific circumstances to bring about a particular configuration of relationships. One objective of the following two chapters is to explore how the relationship between material power and questions of moral principle combine in the construction of economic and military policy and practice.

A second objective is to examine the choices involved in particular economic or military interventions. In addition to the power/principle nexus, policy-makers choose from a range of different types of intervention. In the military realm, intervention with force can take many different forms. It can be done purely in the service of national interest or for humanitarian ends. It may have the end of keeping peace or enforcing it. Force may be used as part of coercive diplomacy, in order to get an Other to stop or undertake some activity, or as part of a strategy of pre-emption, to disarm a regime before it has an opportunity to launch its weapons. There is no straightforward formula for making these decisions, which are inevitably shaped by a complex of factors.

The word intervention most often implies or refers to military intervention. Sovereignty and nonintervention have been the central rules of the international system. While states, such as the USSR during the Cold War, complained about the interference of other states in their sovereign affairs, for instance, relating to human rights, the main prohibition, enshrined in the UN Charter, regards the use of force for anything other than self-defense. This book looks more broadly at multiple practices of intervention and how these underpin or shape specific border-crossings. In this respect, the interventions explored thus far are closely related to the question of military intervention. Moral interventions, such as Just War theory, have provided a framework for thinking through the criteria for defining when a war is just and when the means for fighting war are just. Legal interventions from the UN Charter to the Genocide Convention have defined the conditions under which intervention is legal and illegal. These various legal interpretations raise questions about peace and stability or human rights as the rationale for intervention.

This chapter explores the complex criteria by which the use of military force is judged. There are military criteria for the evaluation of military strategy to bring about specific ends. However, the military means are often justified in terms of moral or legal ends. The purpose of this chapter is to look at different frameworks for judging military intervention in relation to several historical examples. The section on force and diplomacy will examine coercive diplomacy as a traditional tool of state power. The section on force and protection will analyze the relationship between the use of force and the end of protecting potential victims of war. The section on force and self-defense will explore the Bush Administration's new strategy of pre-emption, particularly as it relates to the end of self-defense. The range of options and criteria suggests the increasing complexity of the social and institutional background against which states and other actors must shape and construct specific policy choices. At the same time, these options are constrained by historical context. The dominant military logic for action has shifted over the last two decades from deterrence to compellence to pre-emption.

Force and diplomacy

Military intervention is often conceived as the intervention of one state in the affairs of another state on behalf of its national interest.

Intervention is sometimes a matter of brute force, that is, of one state imposing its will on another, as in Germany's invasion of Belgium in the First World War or its invasion of Poland, which sparked off the Second World War. However, more often than not an intervention involves some form of coercive diplomacy to realize a political end. As G.F. Hudson stated:

> As long as war was the *ultima ratio regum,* which could and did occur from time to time, the threat of resort to war if certain demands were not met or if vital interests were infringed was always present in peace-time in relations between states. In this sense, it can be said that in tra-ditional international politics the use of force has not been confined to actual war but has won its greatest successes when governments have been intimidated into compliance with the will of a stronger (or more determined) power without any clash of arms taking place.[1]

Diplomacy has been the handmaiden of war, providing a system of communication between states both outside and inside of actual conflict. Coercive diplomacy is a particular practice of diplomatic com-munication that involves the threat to use force. To coerce someone is to get them to do something they do not want to do. In this respect, it is a form of persuasion where the threat holds out the prospect of pain and presents a choice regarding the costs and benefits of complying with the threatener's demand. There are two broad reasons for making a coercive threat. The first is *compellence* which is an attempt to initiate action, that is, to get an opponent to do what they otherwise would not do or to get them to stop doing something they would prefer to continue doing.[2] The UN threatened Saddam Hussein with military action if he did not remove his troops from Kuwait. NATO threatened to begin a bombing campaign over Serbia if Milosevic did not sign the Rambouillet Accords. Both were attempts to compel actors to bring about a change in their activity. The message is that the actor can continue as he is, but there will be consequences for doing so.

A second reason for the coercive threat is *deterrence.* To deter is to stop an action before it takes place. Acquiring a mean sounding dog or installing a noisy burglar alarm in a house are both means to deter a bur-glar from breaking in. They communicate the likelihood of having a leg chewed off or being caught and thereby make the cost of this act higher than it would otherwise be. During the Cold War the USA and NATO had a policy of nuclear deterrence toward the USSR. This involved drawing a line across the middle of Europe and communicating that if the Warsaw Pact crossed that line the West would inflict tremendous pain, for instance, by launching a nuclear attack. The logic was that if the costs were sufficiently high, as was the case with nuclear weapons, the USSR would not even consider such a move.[3] Deterrence is a passive threat, while compellence is more active. The objective of deterrence is to discourage an opponent from taking certain actions in the first place for fear of the consequences. This contrasts with the objective of compellence which is to get an opponent to do something or stop doing something. The purpose of the threat in both cases is to communicate the cost of noncompliance and to make it sufficiently high that the opponent will comply.

Coercive diplomacy can thus be distinguished from the use of pure coercion or brute force. The latter involves imposing force on another and eliminating any choice. When the Serbs ethnically cleansed Muslim villages they used brute force. Cases of coercive diplomacy are different because the adversary is offered some space for choice. The purpose is to *persuade* them. For this reason, it represents a form of diplomacy. The threat to inflict pain becomes a bargaining tool. Bargaining involves at least two parties, each of whom have something to trade in exchange. One side brings the threat, the other side makes a choice of whether or not to comply.

The obvious advantage of coercive diplomacy over the imposition of brute force is that if it is successful, the use of force may be avoided altogether. Coercive diplomacy seeks to avoid escalation. The use of limited force may be used to signal the costs of noncompliance.[4] Ideally, the threat is manipulated in such a way that the opponent realizes it is in their self interest to comply before a single hair has been lost or a single bullet fired. Pure coercion requires only superior capability. The successful implementation of coercive diplomacy is more complicated. Peter Viggo Jakobsen, among others, has defined the factors that contribute to successful coercive diplomacy:[5]

- The threat has to convince the adversary that noncompliance is *too costly*. The threat has to eliminate any question of whether the opponent will suffer if they fail to comply.
- The threat has to be *credible*, which is in part a function of capability but not entirely. The threatener has to have a reputation for carrying out their threats. If they have made past threats and haven't followed through on them, future threats may seem hollow.
- Whether presented by a single state or a multilateral organization, involving several states, the threatener has to present a *cohesive*

identity. National threats from the USA are sometimes less than convincing if public opinion is not firmly behind the act. Likewise, threats by NATO or the United Nations have been less than credible given conflicting interests between member states.

- The threat must be perceived as *legitimate* by those watching, such as public or international opinion, although this factor will be more crucial for democracies than dictatorships.[6]
- The conflict cannot be perceived as *zero-sum*. In contrast to brute force, there has to be some common interest in avoiding a full-scale escalation, which means communicating that something is to be gained from bargaining. It is therefore as important to offer carrots for compliance as threatening the consequences of noncompliance. The chances of success are greater with a combination of carrots and sticks than sticks alone.
- The communication of both sticks and carrots *must be clear*. The adversary needs to know the potential rewards of compliance and how long they have to comply, which means setting a clear deadline for a decision. In addition, the adversary needs to be assured that compliance won't lead to further demands in the future.

In sum, to be successful, a strategy of coercive diplomacy has to be attentive to the specifics of a context. Success isn't just a matter of having military superiority but balancing this with a range of other issues, which may vary from context to context. A few examples highlight some of the issues.

The Cold War

The Cold War was an ongoing conflict between two relatively equal military powers, which differed from the classical period of diplomacy in Europe. While nineteenth-century balance of power politics required a willingness to change alliances as necessary, the Cold War was a stalemate that froze the map of Europe for close to 50 years. While war in the earlier period was fought with conventional weapons, nuclear weapons, increased the costs of war exponentially. By the time the Cold War came to an end the two sides together had tens of thousands of strategic nuclear weapons which could cross entire continents before exploding. A conventional war between the two sides could have escalated into a nuclear war. This made the cost of any war, at least in Europe, too great to consider. As a result, deterrence was the central strategy of the Cold War.[7] The USA made a threat that if the USSR initiated any kind of war in Europe, it would quickly escalate into nuclear war.

NATO members argue that this is the main reason why there was peace in Europe from the end of the Second World War until the end of the Cold War.

There was, however, one notable case of compellence, or of trying to get the Soviets to stop an action that was already underway: the Cuban Missile Crisis. In the early 1960s, the Soviets began to deploy missiles in Cuba. The United States perceived this as a threat in their backyard. The US President Kennedy threatened Soviet Premier Khruschev with a nuclear war if he did not withdraw the missiles. This lead to a series of interactions, often referred to as *brinksmanship*. Brinksmanship is an allusion to stepping to the brink or the edge of a precipice, where one could conceivably lose control and fall over the edge. The process has also been conceptualized as Chicken, which was a game played by teenage boys in 1950s-America, as depicted in the James Dean film, *Rebel without a Cause*. Chicken involves two cars racing directly at one another at high speeds and is a test of nerve to see who will swerve first to avoid a collision. The USA and the USSR were stepping to the brink of nuclear war and the question was who would change course first.

The threat was credible because nuclear weapons were involved and the cost of noncompliance was enormous. Reputation was less at stake in this case, since nuclear weapons had only been used once, when the USA dropped atomic bombs on Japan at the end of the Second World War. While this past did communicate a readiness to use them if necessary, the bigger issue was uncertainty whether the other side might in fact be crazy enough to step over the brink knowing the consequences. In this respect, nuclear deterrence involves a paradoxical relationship between the rational and the irrational. Any rational actor would pull back from the brink before a nuclear exchange, recognizing that the results would be devastating for both sides. Yet, for the threat to be credible there must be some measure of doubt. If there were complete certainty that the other side was rational, then the threat would lose some of its credibility since no rational actor would commit suicide. This tension between the rational and irrational was at the heart of the bargaining process. Khrushchev did back down and began to withdraw Soviet missiles. This was followed by major moves to improve communication between the two sides, so that future crises could be averted and to move toward some kind of control of weapons between the two sides. This is an example of successful coercive diplomacy in so far as the threat persuaded the USSR to back down without recourse to force. It should be noted that the relationship was not purely one way, in so far as the USA also made concessions, for instance, withdrawing its Jupiter missiles from Turkey.[8]

Post–Cold War

Post–Cold War cases of coercive diplomacy were less successful, at least in so far as avoidance of all but the most limited use of force is a criteria of success. This context can be distinguished from the Cold War period in a number of ways. First, the USSR dissolved in 1991 leaving the USA the sole remaining superpower. As distinct from the relative symmetry of the Cold War superpowers, post–Cold War cases of coercive diplomacy involved a clear asymmetry of power. For instance, both of the Gulf Wars, led by the USA, under UN auspices in the first case, involved an overwhelming superiority of forces against Iraq. Second, the end of the Cold War brought a great deal of optimism that it would be possible, now that the superpower stalemate was over, to make the UN into a viable institution for collective security. The "New World Order" would be characterized more by multilateral action based on common interest rather than narrow national interest. The emphasis thus shifted away from unilateral intervention within superpower spheres of influence to multilateral action to uphold international norms. Post–Cold War threats have thus been primarily intended to compel actors to stop bad behavior.

In the case of the first Gulf War, there was unanimous agreement by the UN Security Council about the need for a US-led collective security action in defense of the principle of sovereignty.[9] Iraq had invaded the sovereignty of its neighbor, Kuwait. The purpose of the UN collective security force was to compel it to withdraw its forces. The question is whether this act of coercive diplomacy fit the criteria of a successful strategy. Did it convince the Iraqis that the costs of noncompliance were great? Was it credible? Did it involve a combination of carrots and sticks? Did it communicate a clear deadline and assure that compliance wouldn't lead to future demands? (See Box 5.1.)

While the UN coalition was successful in ejecting Saddam from Kuwait, the strategy of coercive diplomacy was less than successful. There is a general view that the results of coercive diplomacy in the post–Cold War period have been poor. Coercive diplomacy failed in the Gulf in so far as it became necessary to launch a ground war to evict Iraq from Kuwait. Two other post–Cold War cases are worth mentioning. In Bosnia, coercive diplomacy did in the end play a major role in bringing the war to an end, when the USA realized its bombing campaign in the summer of 1995. But this was preceded by years of failure to follow through on successive threats, which severely damaged the credibility of both the UN and NATO as institutions.[10] Haiti was a somewhat successful case in that it led to the peaceful removal of the military regime

Box 5.1   Iraq: Criteria of successful coercive diplomacy

- **Convincing the adversary of the costs**

Given the asymmetry of power the two sides didn't play by the same rules. The threateners had an overwhelming superiority of firepower. The militarily weaker party had power to do damage on the ground. Thus, when UN forces threatened Saddam Hussein with the use of force to get him to withdraw from Kuwait, he took Westerners hostage and located them at vital military installations as human shields. He promised to release them if Western governments promised not to attack. The hostages were also used to divide the coalition, selectively rewarding countries that hadn't sent military forces by releasing their nationals. This did have the effect of making Western opinion even more hostile to Saddam. Despite the discrepancy of power, Saddam was amazingly defiant and, unlike the first President Bush, remained in power, until the invasion in 2003, which will be explored in the section on force and self-defense.

- **Credibility**

The threat against Iraq should have been credible. The UN delivered a clear cut ultimatum that Iraq had to get out of Kuwait by a specific date. There was a deadline for compliance and a massive deployment of 500,000 troops from an international coalition. The threat had the firm backing of the Security Council, including the USSR. The Arab countries were united in their support. This was the first post–Cold War security action and there was great optimism about the potential for success now that the USA and USSR were no longer working at odds.

In fact, the threat was not totally credible. When Saddam refused to comply to an ultimatum on February 23 giving him 24 hours to initiate an unconditional withdrawal, an international force, led by the USA, was sent in and he was ejected from Kuwait within one hundred hours. While the coalition was successful in liberating Kuwait, it was not a successful example of coercive diplomacy in so far as overwhelming force was actually used.

- **Carrots and sticks**

It has been argued that the threat didn't work in Iraq because no carrots were offered. At a certain point Saddam came to the conclusion that he was going to be attacked no matter what he did and there was no assurance that compliance wouldn't lead to further demands.

- **Clear communication**

The threat also may not have been taken seriously at the beginning because of mixed messages. Iraq had been a client of the USA during the war against Iran. Just before the invasion, Saddam had been assured by a US official that the consequences of an invasion would not be severe.

- **Attention to context**

In Iraq the Western powers didn't take into account how the past use of airpower would affect Saddam's calculations. In Vietnam, the superior power of the USA did not result in victory. Western experts had been raising doubts based on this precedent in advance of the campaign. Saddam may also have believed that he could draw the USA into a war of attrition and that the superpower would be unable to sustain public or coalition support.

and reinstatement of a democratically elected leader. However, in all three cases, ends were not realized until force was actually used.

Force and protection

The end of coercive diplomacy is to influence the behavior of an adversary. As a military strategy it may relate to diverse ends from humanitarian to peace enforcement. In this respect, coercive diplomacy may be a component of humanitarian intervention, but they are not the same. Coercive diplomacy refers to a style of communication and bargaining or the intent to persuade an adversary via the manipulation of threat. Humanitarian intervention refers to the humanitarian intent to alleviate suffering. In the Kosovo case, which will be explored below, NATO used coercive diplomacy as part of a humanitarian intervention, threatening both sides, but Milosevic in particular, to sign the Rambouillett agreement or suffer the consequences. This section takes the discussion begun in the last chapter a step further, to look at the relationship between the use of military force and humanitarian ends.

The meaning of humanitarian intervention is not straightforward and thus it is useful to start with a few distinctions.[11] The first is between the classical and the broad definition of humanitarian intervention. The classical definition of humanitarian intervention involves military intervention without the approval of authorities in the state where the intervention takes place, and for the purpose of bringing an end to widespread suffering or death among inhabitants. This contrasts with a broader, less precise meaning, in which humanitarian intervention refers to a major humanitarian action, not necessarily involving the use of armed force, and not necessarily against the will of the government.[12] In many cases the two combine in providing "peace support," as part of a multilateral military operation that serves the various ends of peacemaking. As Gow states, 'Whether the mission is straightforward imposition along agreed ceasefire lines or the activity of humanitarian aid or the defense of safety zones or enforcement—or a blending of these activities, it constitutes peace support. The main purpose of this support is to "buy time" for those engaged in the peacemaking process to pursue a diplomatic resolution of the conflict'.[13] One ongoing problem, particularly evident in Somalia and Bosnia, was that the distinct humanitarian aid and military options often were not clearly defined and their implementation became so intertwined that both ultimately suffered.[14]

The second distinction is between peacekeeping and peace enforcement. Peace enforcement refers to an attempt to impose a solution by means of force without first establishing the consent of the conflicting parties. While there is some overlap, peace enforcement is broader than humanitarian intervention. The Iraq case above can be considered as an example of peace enforcement that was not a humanitarian intervention, at least in any explicit sense. Peace enforcement is closely tied up with collective security and the idea that the international community should join together to stop an aggressor who threatens international peace and stability. During the Cold War, peace enforcement proved to be impossible because the USA and USSR could veto each other in the Security Council, resulting in a paralysis of action.

The end of the Cold War and the apparent success of the Gulf War gave rise to greater optimism about the potential for the UN to enforce peace. This was reflected in the 1992-pamphlet, *Agenda for Peace*, published by the UN General Secretary Bhutros-Bhutros Ghali.[15] The concept of humanitarian intervention extends the idea to potential action to enforce a solution in cases of gross injustice. Somalia was the first time the Security Council authorized the use of force on the grounds that humanitarian suffering constituted a threat to international peace and security.

Since peace enforcement has proven so difficult, the UN has historically put much more energy into peacekeeping. If collective security is joint action to impose a solution on an aggressor, peacekeeping was traditionally an attempt to stand in between two parties who had agreed to a ceasefire, in order to ensure that fighting would not resume. Peacekeepers aren't empowered to impose a solution on combatants, which represents a dramatic change from the past. The classical way to establish peace was to defeat an army. Peace was a side effect of winning a war, rather than an objective in and of itself. The peacekeeper, by contrast, isn't there to win, but to ensure that peace is maintained. The range of tasks undertaken by peacekeepers has broadened since the end of the Cold War, which means that soldiers are involved in activities that have not been a part of the soldier's traditional role. These include monitoring elections, helping lorries with humanitarian aid make their way through a war zone, or guaranteeing the safety of refugees trying to flee a conflict area. In post–Cold War conflicts peacekeepers have been sent into areas where there is no peace, such as Bosnia. They thus were often very vulnerable and stood in the way of peace enforcement. For instance, the Bosnian Serbs took peacekeepers hostage as a way to get NATO to withdraw its threat to bomb. It was impossible to consider a large-scale bombing campaign until the peacekeepers were out of harm's way.

Issues raised by humanitarian intervention

Humanitarian intervention raises a number of practical concerns in addition to the ones discussed in the last chapter. The foremost practical concern relates to whether the international community have the resources and support to carry out humanitarian intervention, whether narrowly or broadly defined. Since the end of the Cold War there has been a huge growth in demand for the peacekeeping and peace enforcement forces of the UN which has raised several problems. First, the excessive level of demand has overstretched the resources of the UN.[16] This has been exacerbated by the increasing globalization of the media. During the nineties, the televised suffering of people in conflicts from Somalia to Bosnia to Rwanda gave rise to demands to do something, yet the cost of sending UN forces into every trouble spot in the world would be excessive.

Second, the legitimacy and effectiveness of the UN have suffered because of its inability to decide or to act quickly.[17] Collective decision making can be very unwieldy. In addition, action depends on the willingness of individual countries to volunteer troops and resources. In several conflicts, decision-makers have been pulled apart by two competing public demands: the one explicit, to do something in response to the suffering, and the other implicit, that public support will quickly erode along with images of body bags coming back from a foreign conflict. The failure of the UN and NATO to act in Bosnia until very late in the day was a blow to their credibility. This failure provided an impetus to use force more quickly than may have been justified once attention shifted to the Kosovo case, as a way to restore credibility. In the latter case, NATO acted on its own, without approval by the UN Security Council.

The UN has taken steps to address some of these problems. On April 7, 2004, in commemoration of the tenth anniversary of the 1994-genocide in Rwanda, UN Secretary General Kofi Annan presented a five-point *Action Plan to Prevent Genocide*. The plan emphasizes prevention of armed conflict, through more cooperation at the regional level, better education, and the protection of minority rights; the protection of civilians in armed conflict; an end to impunity by bringing those responsible to justice; information gathering and early warning through a UN Special Advisor for Genocide Prevention; and, finally, swift and decisive action.[18]

Third, the nature of the conflicts and the actors involved have changed. The UN was set up to deal with conflicts between states where there was a clear center of authority. Many post–Cold War conflicts accompanied the breakdown of states, and were waged by the leadership of nongovernmental entities. As Brian Urquhart states, "… the problem of essentially internal violence raises a wider question of the UN's role in matters of peace and security; whether the organization's basic function is to deter aggression and stop conflict between states, or whether it now also includes dealing with massive episodes of violence and abuse of human rights *within* the borders of states—in other words a broad commitment to justice, law and order."[19] In this situation it can be difficult to identify precisely who should be involved in negotiations or who has the authority to assent to the presence of the peacekeepers.

The nature of warfare has also changed. Traditionally, a distinction has been maintained between soldiers and civilians; it was assumed that civilians should not be the target of war. Many of these post–Cold War conflicts involve the use of force against civilian populations. Ethnic cleansing is the premier example. This raises issues of how to protect dispersed and vulnerable citizens.

The preceding section raised questions about criteria for judging the success of coercive diplomacy. In cases where coercive diplomacy or peace enforcement are used for humanitarian ends, further criteria for success relate to humanitarian ends and means. Nicholas Wheeler has formulated several key questions to guide these criteria.[20]

- Was there a humanitarian cause? A humanitarian cause has been equated with a supreme humanitarian emergency, where the only hope of saving lives depends on outsiders coming to the rescue. This would be a point when human rights violations have reached such a magnitude that they shock the conscience of humanity. As already suggested, identifying this point is not a straightforward matter and waiting until the situation has reached emergency proportions precludes preventative action. In the Bosnian case, many people asked whether military action at a much earlier stage of the conflict—when the political will didn't exist—would have been more successful, before the conflict spiraled out of control. On the one hand, this criterion raises a question about who decides what is clear evidence of genocide and how to reconcile the moral imperative for speedy action, before millions have died, with the Just War requirement that force should always be a last resort.
- Was there a declared humanitarian end in view?
- Was there an appropriate humanitarian approach? Was action carried out impartially and were the interests of the intervenors compatible with a humanitarian purpose?

- Were humanitarian means employed?
- Was there a humanitarian outcome?

These criteria largely mirror Just War thinking. Some of the issues raised by their application in concrete circumstances are evident in a few post–Cold War examples.

Somalia

In Somalia the humanitarian tragedy grew out of civil war and the disintegration of the state following the fall of the Siad Barre government in January 1991.[21] Somalia was divided along clan lines, and as full-scale war erupted, the country disintegrated into violence between these clans. The war devastated agricultural and livestock production, which was compounded by a draught. The result was a famine that killed 300,000–350,000 people in 1992. The Security Council didn't respond to the disintegration of the state in 1991. Its first act was to impose an arms embargo. The country was already flooded with arms from the two Cold War superpowers. After negotiations with the UN Envoy, a ceasefire, which included provisions to allow a UN monitoring mission into Somalia to oversee arrangements for humanitarian assistance, was agreed in March 1992. In April, the UN Security Council approved a UN operation, pursuant to the ceasefire agreement and in July 50 unarmed UN military observers were deployed to Mogadishu to monitor the ceasefire. The ceasefire didn't hold and the country collapsed into general lawlessness. In August the UN humanitarian relief effort, Operation Provide Relief (UNOSOM I) began, with 500 peace-keepers to assist with delivery of aid, with the consent of the main clan leaders. They were angered, however, after an announcement by the Secretary General of the UN that 3000 troops would be sent, with or without the consent of clan leaders, to protect the humanitarian relief supplies. Deteriorating security prevented the UN mission from delivering food and supplies to the starving Somalies, as relief flights were looted, food convoys hijacked, and aid workers assaulted. After the UN appealed to its members to provide military forces to assist the humanitarian operation, US President H.W. Bush responded, proposing that US combat troops lead an international UN force to secure the environment for relief operations. On December 5, the UN accepted his offer and Bush ordered 25,000 US troops into Somalia. The US-led United Task Force (UNITAF) was dubbed Operation Restore Hope.

After the election of Clinton in 1993, the UN authorized UNOSOM II, a UN operation with expanded enforcement power, whose mandate stressed "the crucial importance of disarmament" of the Somali people, which was to take over from the US-led UNITAF. The expanded operation's mission went beyond providing humanitarian relief, calling for the UN to facilitate "nation building."[22] By the end of March, 28 nations had sent contingents to Somalia in support of the new operation and the US official handed over command to the UN in May. After 24 Pakistani soldiers were ambushed and massacred, during an inspection of a Somali arms storage site, the UN Security Council issued an emergency resolution calling for the apprehension of "those responsible" for the massacre. Aidid was not mentioned specifically but it was in effect a call to apprehend him. US and UN troops then began attacking targets in Mogadishu associated with Aidid, which turned into a war between the peacekeepers and the clan leader. As the crisis escalated, American military were wounded and killed in attacks which attracted the attention of the American media and led to the deployment of US Army Task Force Rangers. What began as an operation focused on the delivery of humanitarian assistance, turned into a manhunt. For an examination of this intervention in terms of the criteria above see Box 5.2.

Kosovo

Kosovo is a powerful symbol of Serb nationalism, and has been claimed as the sacred birthplace of the nation.[23] In 1974, Tito gave autonomy to the Kosovo Albanians, who comprised 90 percent of the population. This act alienated the Kosovo Serbs and fanned the flames of the nationalist movement. In 1989 the Kosovars were stripped of their autonomy, which was followed by a series of measures that forced thousands of people from their jobs, closed their institutions of higher learning, and prohibited publications in their language, as well as introducing family planning for Albanians. Out of this crackdown, a nonviolent resistance movement emerged, headed by Ibrhim Rugova, the president of the Association of Writers in Kosovo. The organization, called the Democratic League of Kosovo, was both a political party and a mass movement. Like Solidarity in Poland, the League adopted a political strategy of acting as if.[24] Kosovo Albanians would act as if they lived in an independent and sovereign republic even though they were brutally repressed. They sought to prevent any type of violent revolt and to internationalize the problem by seeking to get others outside involved.

The end of the war in Bosnia and the Dayton Accords should have addressed the situation in Kosovo. Instead Kosovo was largely ignored and Dayton strengthened Milosevic's rule.[25] The lack of attention to Kosovo was a tremendous blow to the prestige of the nonviolent

Box 5.2 Somalia: Criteria for humanitarian intervention

- **Was outside rescue the only hope of saving lives?**
Probably. Clan warfare was making it impossible to get food to people who were starving.

- **Was there a declared humanitarian end in view?**
The humanitarian end was to get goods to a starving population. Given the clan warfare, and the problems with distribution, it was unlikely that the food would get through without military assistance.

- **Was there an appropriate humanitarian approach? Was action carried out impartially and were the interests of the intervenors compatible with a humanitarian purpose?**
While the initial goals were on track, problems emerged after the UNOSOM II mission shifted to a focus on hunting down one of the clan leaders, Aidid, after he killed Pakistani peacekeepers. The mission then turned into a manhunt which deflected from the aid mission and was contrary to the humanitarian rationale. In so far as there were civilian casualties of this effort, the result was to alienate the Somali people, strengthen political support for Aidid and to come under fire from international public opinion. Other countries participating in the UNOSOM II mission were also critical of the increased risk to UN peacekeepers that resulted from this shift of course.

- **Were humanitarian means employed?**
One element of the manhunt was raids, without warning, against Aidid, during which civilians were killed. This gave rise to a tit for tat response and a decision by Aidid to target US soldiers, given an awareness that seeing their soldiers injured and dead would touch an American weakspot.

- **Was there a humanitarian outcome?**
There was no long-term humanitarian outcome. The USA pulled out in 1994 because of the harm done to its soldiers. The mission was left to the UN, which failed to disarm the factions. It withdrew in 1995 leaving Somalia to its own devices.

movement and to Rugova, who had for years been telling people to be patient and assuring them that their interests would be taken into account in a final settlement on the former Yugoslavia. A turning point came in February 1996 when the KLA came onto the political scene with a campaign of bombing against Serb targets. For two years the KLA used clandestine tactics, but by early 1998 was well equipped enough to launch an offensive against the Serbs in the Drenica Valley.[26] The Serb security forces responded with attacks against the KLA. In the process, Serb forces burnt villages and drove hundreds of thousands of Kosovars from their homes. In 1998 the Western powers brought the warring parties to peace talks in Rambouillet, France. The negotiations were backed up by the threat to use force if the two sides couldn't reach an agreement. No agreement was reached and in March 1999, NATO's bombing campaign began.

The Serbs in Kosovo were engaged in ethnic cleansing before the bombing campaign began, but the numbers were fairly small. It was estimated that some 500 Kosovars were killed and 400,000 displaced in

---

Box 5.3   Kosovo: Criteria of humanitarian intervention

• **Was outside rescue the only hope of saving lives?**

The purpose of the bombing campaign was to stop the ethnic cleansing of Kosovo Albanians. Instead the onset of the bombing campaign accelerated the ethnic cleansing, generating a huge humanitarian catastrophe. Within weeks of the bombing, thousands of Kosovar Albanians were killed, 600,000 were driven from their homes to refugee camps in surrounding countries and hundreds of thousands more were internally displaced within Kosovo. This may or may not have happened on this scale in the absence of the bombing campaign. The bombing campaign also did not compel Milosevic to concede within a few days—as originally expected—to a NATO-led force to protect the Kosovars. Given his claim since 1987 that the Serbs would never be defeated again, it is surprising that NATO leaders assumed that Milosevic would give in so easily. Contrary to expectations, the bombing campaign lasted 78 days. A larger more counterfactual question can also be raised about the failure to support the non-violent campaign and whether a different and more peaceful outcome could have been secured by acting earlier with other forms of intervention.

• **Was there an appropriate humanitarian approach? Was action carried out impartially and were the interests of the intervenors compatible with a humanitarian purpose?**

Initially, NATO was seen by many to be acting as the airforce of the KLA, a concern that was only reinforced by the terms offered to the Serbs at Rambouillet. The Serbs were willing to accept an international force that didn't include NATO countries, but NATO insisted it had to be a NATO force, which Serbia saw as a violation of its sovereignty. The Serb rejection of the plan legitimated NATO's campaign. Arguably, the choice structure presented to the participants made the bombing campaign, rather than an agreement, inevitable.

• **Were humanitarian means employed?**

NATO lost some of its moral high ground in part because of the refugee crisis generated by the onset of the campaign and in part because of the number of civilians, particularly Serb civilians, killed during the course of the bombing.

• **Was there a humanitarian outcome?**

Kosovo was liberated, which brought the Kosovo Albanians more political autonomy than they would have had without the bombing campaign, but it set the stage for a new round of ethnic cleansing as thousands of Serbs fled in fear of Albanians seeking revenge. Far from creating the conditions for a new multiethnic politics, the Serbs found themselves on the receiving end of a new order of ethnic apartheid.

the year prior to NATO's action.[27] As the campaign began, the Serbs escalated their efforts with the massive evacuation of refugees and the massacre of thousands of Albanian Muslims. NATO originally thought that Milosevic would back down after just a few days when faced with massive bombardment. The campaign lasted 78 days and there were ongoing questions about the likelihood of succeeding without a ground campaign. Nonetheless, when NATO tanks rolled into Kosovo they were treated like liberators (see Box 5.3).

Neither of these two prominent cases of specifically humanitarian intervention met the criteria. In the first case, the failure can be attributed to the diversion from the original humanitarian goals. In the second case, although the liberation of Kosovo now tends to be seen in a positive light, many have argued that it exacerbated the crisis rather than solving it. The question is whether force can ultimately be successful in resolving an ethnically based conflict or whether it will inevitably exacerbate the wounds.

Force and self-defense

The end of the Cold War brought a shift away from an emphasis on nuclear deterrence toward questions of peace enforcement and humanitarian intervention. The attack on the twin towers of the US World Trade Center and the Pentagon on September 11, 2001, brought about another strategic shift. If the post–Cold War period was dominated by optimism about the possibility of multilateral action, the post-9/11 world saw America retreating into unilateralism. If the strategic focus of the Cold War was deterrence, and of the post–Cold War compellence, it shifted to pre-emption in the name of self-defense after 9/11.

The USA, the world's hyperpower, became on September 11, 2001 the victim of an ubiquitous network of terrorists who used conventional airplanes to destructive ends. It is not that the terrorist threat was new, only that it was, after this date, elevated to the center of US foreign policy. Indeed, over the previous sixteen-year period there had been 2,400 terrorist actions directed at US interests.[28] But the USA had applied a military response only in three of these cases: the 1986-Libyan bombing of a West German discotheque; the 1993-Iraqi attempt to assassinate US President G.H.W. Bush in Kuwait, and the 1998-bombing of two US embassies in East Africa by bin Laden operatives. However, the USA did have a counterterrorism policy, which included, among others, refusing to make concessions or strike deals with terrorists, bringing terrorists to justice for their acts, isolating and applying pressure to state sponsors of international terrorism, and strengthening the ability of other countries to combat terrorism through cooperative efforts.

Despite this pre-existing strategy, September 11 came as no less of a surprise than the end of the Cold War. The academic field of security studies was still focused primarily on great powers and interstate conflict and the literature on terrorism was scarce.[29] In the 1990s the US intelligence community believed that state support for terrorist groups, including Al-Qaida, was declining.[30] The new terrorist organizations, in contrast to the hierarchical and skilled practitioners of the 1980s, were diffuse, amorphous, and populated by amateurs. An international terrorist network thus seemed unlikely, given the numerous ethnic, national, and socio-economic differences standing in the way of unity between different factions.[31] But, as in the case of the ending Cold War, predictions were wrong.

The international network of terrorists were an expression of the new wars of the twentieth century. They were characterized by a highly unconventional and decentralized approach and asymmetrical operations to the end of bypassing the superior military power of nation states. The terrorists wore no uniforms and could infiltrate and blend into the population they set out to attack. They could make use of information age technologies, such as cell phones, fax machines, email, web sites and the internet.[32] The distinction between civilian and military targets became irrelevant. The laws and conventions of war would not constrain terrorists and their state sponsors who sought to use weapons of mass destruction on civilian and nonmilitary targets.[33] In a 1997 interview, Osama bin Laden described Al-Qaida as "a product of globalization and a response to it."[34] Information age technologies and cyber networks made it possible for Al-Qaida to recruit, communicate, establish cells and operatives, and to attack targets globally.[35]

While the terrorist attacks of the 1990s were placed in the category of crime, US President George W. Bush labeled the attacks on the World Trade Center and Pentagon "an act of war" and claimed, in his remarks to the graduating class at West Point in 2002, that September 11 represented a "new kind of war fought by a new kind of enemy."[36] In his National Security Strategy, announced in September 2002, a comprehensive strategy for combating weapons of mass destruction (WMD) was presented. The strategy included the following:[37]

- Proactive counterproliferation efforts to deter and defend against the threat of terrorism, ensuring that detection, active and passive defense counterforce capabilities are integrated into the transformation of defense and security systems, and the doctrine training and equipping of US force and those of allies.

- Strengthened nonproliferation efforts to prevent rogue states and terrorists from acquiring materials, technologies, and expertise necessary for weapons of mass destruction. This included strengthening diplomacy, arms control, multilateral export controls, and threat reduction to stand in the way of states and terrorist who seek WMD and, when necessary, to interdict materials.
- Effective consequence management to respond to the effects of WMD use. Acts to minimize the effects of the use of WMD against populations would deter those who possess such weapons and dissuade those who seek to acquire them by persuading them they cannot attain their desired ends.

At the heart of the new strategy was a belief that the reactive posture of the past, that is, deterrence, would not work against leaders of rogue states willing to take risks with the lives of their people. Deterrence also wouldn't work against suicidal terrorists. Therefore, the USA had to act against emerging threats "before they are fully formed."[38] The National Security Strategy further states that "While the U.S. will constantly strive to enlist the support of the international community, we will not hesitate to act alone, if necessary, to exercise our right of self-defense by acting pre-emptively."[39]

The UN Charter (Article 51) states an inherent right of individual or collective defense in the case of an armed attack. This right to self-defense includes defensive action in anticipation of imminent attack to frustrate a pending attack. Criminal law also includes use of violence to prevent an attack on oneself. In this respect, pre-emption and self-defense are not in conflict. Neil Livingston points to three responses to terrorism: reprisals, pre-emption and retribution.[40] All of these represent coercive measures short of war but ones that are also applicable to war more generally. All of them have a legal justification under Article 51 of the UN. He argues: "If terrorism is accepted as a form of aggression, especially if sponsored and supported by foreign governments, then the United States may adopt and employ proactive measures as a traditional form of self-help while attempting to find peaceful long-term solutions to the problem."[41]

Livingstone made this argument prior to September 11, 2001 and at a time when terrorism was in the category of crime. He thus relies on an analogy to domestic crime, arguing that just as conspiracy to commit a crime is illegal in domestic law, conspiracies by foreign terrorists to harm the interests or property of the USA should be illegal in advance of an actual attack and provide an appropriate justification for pre-emptive action.[42] Does this logic change when terrorism is placed in a framework of war? The legal argument favoring pre-emption in cases of self-defense would seem to apply equally to crimes as to war. However, as Crawford argues, a "war on terrorism" blurs the spatial and temporal limits implied by the term war and thus any potential application of Just War theory.[43] Given terrorism is ubiquitous and ongoing, any counterterror effort defined in terms of war is equally unlimited in its length and reach.

Because it is impossible to protect all assets from terrorism in all places, a premium is placed on prevention. As Donald Rumsfeld, the US Secretary of Defense under Bush stated, "The only defense against terrorism is offence. You have to simply take the battle to them because everything—every advantage accrues to the attacker in the case of terrorism. The choice of when to do it, the choice of what instruments to use and the choice of where to do it, all of those things are advantages of the attacker."[44] The counterterrorism campaign of pre-emptive annihilation thus potentially crosses the boundary into a preventive military mission, including counterproliferation and regime change in "rogue states." As Crawford states:

> By emphasizing total security on a long-time horizon, the administration has elevated potential threats to a status that goes beyond the limited notion of justified pre-emption in the face of the threat of imminent attack. Indeed, the administration's pre-emption strategy is actually, in large degree, a preventive (early offensive) war strategy which seeks to maintain US pre-eminence by reducing or eliminating the military capability of potential adversaries even before potential rivals have acquired those capabilities—and in the absence of a clear intention and plan to use weapons against the USA. Preventative war strategies are generally considered unjust.[45]

The argument for legitimate pre-emption based on self-defense relies on a requirement of "imminent threat," yet US President George W. Bush has said it would be dangerous to wait until threats become imminent. The congressional resolution that authorized the use of force in Iraq talked only of the country's continuing weapons capacity.

Many scholars have argued that the cause of self-defense after September 11 is just.[46] Most conclude that there is a clear *jus ad bellum* or just cause for the War on Terrorism as a response to September 11.

However, the US emphasis on the use of overwhelming force raises important questions about the *jus in bello* or just means and in particular whether the response is proportionate. In the context of Afghanistan, the US administration was deliberate in defining its mission in Just War terms. In so far as the attacks on the World Trade Center and Pentagon deliberately targeted and killed thousands of noncombatants in peace time, a response was justified. In Afghanistan, they claimed the response was a last resort, pointing to the demand that the Taliban regime hand over Al-Qaida before the bombing began on October 8, and giving them a second chance to produce bin Laden and others after the bombing began. In the face of their refusal, war came to be seen as inevitable.

The campaign was designed to follow *jus in bello* principles. There was an emphasis on noncombatant immunity, although the high number of US noncombatant deaths on September 11 were used as an excuse for Afghan noncombatant deaths or, they were justified by the doctrine of "double effect." According to the double effect, deaths may be permissible, however regrettable, if the military goal of action was just, the noncombatant injuries weren't intended, or the military benefits outweighed the unintended consequences for civilians. Further, the US provision of humanitarian assistance via air drops was a central element of the moral argument made by the Pentagon.

The invasion of Afghanistan, whatever its faults, did involve a link between the terrorists who attacked the USA and the counterterror action that followed. The invasion of Iraq in 2003 rested on much more questionable grounds and reveals the critical role of accurate intelligence in determining a threat that has not yet been realized. While the *jus ad bellum* for the Iraq invasion was the threat posed by Saddam Hussein's WMD, in the aftermath no evidence of these weapons was found. Given questions about just cause, the means of fighting the war, the *jus in bello*, with overwhelming force were disproportionate, unless placed in a framework of humanitarian intervention, which was emphasized after the fact by leaders in the USA and UK. The concept of punishing a crime prior to its occurrence is inherently problematic. It requires a high degree of accurate intelligence. In the Iraq case, the intelligence communities in both the USA and UK operated on the basis of widespread assumptions that were not borne out once troops went into Iraq.[47] In a strategic sense, a pre-emptive doctrine is extremely destabilizing, in so far as American acts provide a precedent and legitimation for others states, such as Israel or Russia, to adopt a similar strategy in their respective regions.

Conclusions

The three strategies discussed here have had resonance for policy makers in distinct historical circumstances. The emphasis on superpower deterrence in the Cold War period was replaced by an emphasis on multilateral compellence and humanitarian intervention in the post–Cold War period. Since September 11, 2001 this has given way to a unilateral strategy of pre-emption in the name of self-defense. However, within any one period, policy makers have had to be selective in determining the appropriate response to specific situations. Compellence was an important element of the Cuban Missile Crisis during the Cold War. Deterrence was implicitly in operation in the post–Cold War world given the extant nuclear arsenal of the USA. After September 11, deterrence does still play a role in US relations with "axis of evil" states and the invasion of Iraq in 2003 had a humanitarian element, although WMD were the main rationale for the invasion.

The criteria for the three approaches differ. The criteria for determining the success of coercive diplomacy are primarily strategic. In the case of humanitarian intervention, which may involve coercive diplomacy, these strategic concerns may intermingle with specifically humanitarian criteria. In this respect, a case like the bombing of Serbia can be judged in terms of multiple criteria, focusing on the success of efforts to compel Milosevic or the success in achieving the humanitarian end of stopping ethnic cleansing. Humanitarian criteria are closely related to the criteria of Just War theory. The pre-emptive strategy of the USA after September 11, 2001 represents a departure from coercive diplomacy, either in the form of deterrence or compellence, in so far as its end is not persuasion but the elimination of weapons before they can be used. While international law allows for pre-emption, reprisal, or retribution in self-defense, the USA has reserved itself the right to act without evidence of imminent threat, and thus easily crosses the boundary into preventative war, which is not justified in international law. While the *jus ad bellum* for Iraq was not humanitarian, the invasion did arguably produce a humanitarian end in removing Saddam Hussein from power. However, the failure to find weapons and the lack of evidence of a link between Saddam Hussein and Al-Qaida—and thus to the War on Terrorism—raise serious question about whether this Iraq invasion can be categorized as a Just War.

6
Economic Interventions

Policies regarding post–Cold War military interventions often posed difficult questions about who should intervene and whether action, to be legitimate, required support by the international community. They further revealed a conflict between national interest and support for international norms. Similarly, the history of economic intervention since the end of the Second World War has been shaped by the tension between profit and the interest of various states in exporting arms, on the one hand, and questions of principle related to limiting the proliferation of arms. In addition to various international agreements to stop the spread of nuclear, chemical, and biological weapons, economic sanctions have, particularly since the end of the Cold War, been an important tool for limiting the access of dangerous regimes to WMD. Decisions to sell arms to another country, that is, engagement in the arms trade, are no less interventions that shape the potential or likelihood of war than decisions to withhold arms or military equipment, as a form of economic sanction.

The expansion of the arms trade, particularly since the Second World War, has been met with global pressures to sanction states that use weapons for ends that contravene international norms. While there were glimpses of this relationship during the Cold War period, particularly in relation to South Africa, the tension between a global arms trade and the need to limit and sanction these weapons has defined the post–Cold War period. It is unusual to combine an analysis of the arms trade and economic sanctions. The two are most often dealt with as separate and largely unrelated topics. Yet, there are numerous examples of former client states in the arms trade that later became targets of economic sanctions, with Iraq being the most visible example. A client of the USA during the war with Iran, it became, after its invasion of Kuwait, a target of economic sanctions lasting over a decade. Osama bin Laden, a "freedom fighter" trained and funded by the USA in the 1980s, became in the 1990s a "terrorist." Since 1995 the US government has taken steps to impose sanctions on terrorist groups by freezing assets and criminalizing transactions with them.[1] Much of the concern about proliferation of WMD, particularly since September 11, 2001, relates to the likelihood that they will end up in terrorist hands. "Rogue states," which are thought to harbor or support terrorists, have thus been the target of economic sanctions, from Libya to Iran. The relationship between the arms trade and economic sanctions becomes more evident if their recent historical evolutions are juxtaposed.

During the Cold War the superpowers flooded the globe with arms. In its aftermath, states have been forced to negotiate the complex tension between economic dependence on the arms trade, on the one hand, and, on the other, the need to re-establish control over "rogue states" and "terrorists" through economic sanctions against the backdrop of widespread proliferation. The first section on the arms trade will examine the evolution of the global arms trade since the Second World War. The next section will explore the evolution of economic sanctions as a weapon of statecraft and its relationship to the arms trade. The section on profit and principle will explore some of the complex tensions that emerge out of the relationship between these two forms of economic intervention.

The arms trade

A central question raised by the literature on the arms trade is whether the availability of weapons increases or decreases the likelihood and severity of war. Two contrasting answers have framed this debate. On the one hand, most analysts would argue that there is a positive correlation between an increase in global arms sales and the likelihood of war. One major work has argued that the weapons trade is associated with an increased probability of participation in war and an increased severity and magnitude of the resulting war.[2] On the other hand, deterrence has provided a counterargument. As the old saying goes, if you want peace, prepare for war. States arm so that others will fear the cost of attacking them and thereby lead a peaceful, if insecure, existence.[3]

These arguments are often drawn on to shape policy toward arms sales. Governments like to present the appearance of laissez faire, and a disinterest in the arms business, and historically have done so. However, in the context of the global arms trade this is not the case. When an American president claims that one party in a central or South American revolution is villain and one friend, they prohibit arms shipments to the one while transferring them to the other.[4] Who gets arms and who does not shapes the politics of a conflict. But policies regarding the weapons trade also have economic consequences for the exporter, including an influence on employment, the performance of important sectors of the economy and living standards. As Hartung and others have argued, leaders in the major arms supplying states, many of them peaceful democracies (which, according to Democratic Peace Theory, do not fight each other), actively promote weapons sales, but their exports go to war zones. This is done to maintain domestic political support and to meet the interests of economic and security policy.[5]

The Second World War significantly increased the number of arms available at the global level. Two processes worked together in the expansion of a global arms market. First, the major powers continued the production of arms at the Second World War levels and generated large surpluses of weapons beyond their needs. The pace of production of new weapons exceeded the rate at which arms were destroyed in war or rendered obsolete.[6] Britain sought exports in order to produce at a higher rate and reduce the unit costs of weapons, given the expense of re-equipping its forces. It wanted to maintain its prominent global role through the arms trade. Exports from the USA had primarily a political motivation in the context of the emerging Cold War, but also provided economic benefits. Second, the process of decolonization created a large number of new states who wanted to acquire arms, both for purposes of security and national machismo. Britain, the former imperial power, and the USA, the new superpower, dominated the arms trade until the 1950s, when France and the USSR became exporters.[7]

The period after 1966 saw a number of changes. The recovery of Western Europe from the Second World War was almost complete. As the economies of various European countries became stronger, West Germany, Italy, the Netherlands, and Spain, as well as France, expanded their arms market, creating an increasingly competitive environment. With the easing of tensions in the European theater, as a result of the détente process, the developing world became a focus of attention. The interest in arms by developing countries was spurred by decolonization. Weapons were a symbol of prestige and jet fighters became the defining symbol of statehood for the newly independent states.[8]

With the emergence of the second Cold War in the early 1980s, there was a growing number of arms suppliers in a contracting market. The result was a larger number of suppliers chasing fewer markets and the structural overproduction of arms, as well as an increase in illegal and semilegal arms sales. Both superpowers were arming proxy forces in the developing world. US President Reagan armed "freedom fighters" in

Afghanistan following the Soviet invasion there, as well as in Cambodia, Angola, and Nicaragua. The Iran–Iraq War created a huge demand for weapons, but also resulted in the imposition of national restraints on their export. However, there was an economic incentive for governments and manufacturers to covertly approve exports, or to covertly back one side or the other. The Iraqi government became a patron of the USA, France, Britain, and Western Germany, while Iran was supported by Israel. In response to the overflow of surplus arms, attempts were made to control the flow of advanced technology to the developing world through nonproliferation agreements. In response, a semiclandestine market emerged through which some states sought to develop their own technology.

After a decline in its international status in the 1970s, Britain, during this period, surpassed France and the USSR in the arms trade, cementing its place as the world's second arms exporter after the USA.[9] In the 1980s and into the 1990s, the manufacture of arms spread beyond the Cold War alliance system, as many developing countries began to produce small arms, guns, and munitions.[10] Both the increased export to and production within developing countries represented a change in the use of weapons. The armies of the two Cold War alliances primarily acquired weapons for the purpose of stockpiling, in an attempt to spend the other side into surrender. By contrast, purchasing officials in developing countries wanted weapons to increase their status, to control the public, and to siphon off corruption money.

The end of the Cold War saw a further proliferation of arms with the flow of weaponry from the former USSR and Warsaw Pact to the open market at competitive prices. Eastern Europe emerged as a potential market, a trend that was strengthened by plans for NATO expansion. The flow of semilegal and illegal arms was spurred on by gunrunning in the context of emerging ethnic and regional conflicts and by the redirection of export control concerns away from the former Warsaw Pact states to a small number of "rogue states," including Libya, North Korea, Iraq, and Iran. During this time there was a surge in the demand and supply of arms available on the black market. Concerns about proliferation also shifted away from conventional weapons to WMD, and particularly chemical and biological weapons.

Economic sanctions

Decisions regarding the export of arms are one form of policy intervention. But governments and other actors also often withhold arms or other forms of trade for diplomatic ends. Throughout the Cold War period the search for profit was balanced by a growing global consciousness and a desire to hold states to widely accepted international norms. An *Economic sanction* is a general term for a penalty that is imposed for the purpose of coercing compliance with international law or to compel a nation to alter its policies. In this respect, an economic sanction is a form of coercive diplomacy by economic means, that is, it is a tool of power to get states to do what they otherwise would not do.

Two other related concepts are often subsumed by this term. The first is the *boycott*, which has become a way for normal citizens to express disapproval and to hopefully bring about change by refusing to buy goods or undertake acts that will benefit an oppressor. The word originated in County Mayo, Ireland in the late nineteenth century. Captain Charles Boycott was an English estate manager whose collection policies so outraged the impoverished Irish tenants that they refused to harvest crops for him.[11] Although prior to the coining of the word, the American refusal to buy British goods after the enactment of the Stamp Act of 1765 is another example of a boycott. More recently, in the 1980s, a widespread international boycott of Nestle's products was mobilized in protest of practices related to the marketing of baby formula in the Third World. A boycott is a way of retaliating against unjust practices and relies on the assumption that economic power rests on the willingness of large numbers of people to purchase a product or assist in its production.

While a boycott cuts off the production of certain products, as a form of economic retaliation, an *embargo* is a concept of international law that refers to a ban on the movement of goods to a foreign country. An embargo is typically imposed in time of war or threatened hostilities. It may be used to aid or limit a war effort, to either coerce another state or to support domestic commercial activity by preventing scarce resources from leaving the country. The UN imposed an arms embargo on the former Yugoslavia in the early 1990s in order to keep the conflict from escalating. Another example of an embargo was the refusal to sell grain to the USSR in 1980–81 in reprisal for the Soviet invasion of Afghanistan.

Boycotts or embargoes can be used as economic sanctions, but an economic sanction is not equal to either of these. Drury and Chan define sanctions as the actual or threatened withdrawal of economic resources to affect a policy change by the target.[12] Thus, while punishment may be an element of sanctions, the word is fundamentally tied to an expectation or demand for a change in behavior. Sanctions have historically been a complement to military warfare. The siege is the oldest form of total war, which in its simplest form involved surrounding an enemy camp or fortress and waiting for the defenders to run out of food and drinking water. The principal aim was thus to starve a protected population into submission. The blockade, its sea-based equivalent, is a way to interrupt foreign commerce, to prevent goods from getting to enemy ports, and thereby to deny the enemy access to foreign goods. For instance, during the American Civil War, President Lincoln ordered an economic blockade against the Confederate States as a way of denying them access to foreign goods, and succeeded in sealing off 3500 miles of coastline. Both sieges and blockades were traditionally used as complements to military strategy in a context of warfare. In the twentieth century, with the development of international institutions, the policy objective of economic sanctions has broadened. Particularly since the First World War, economic sanctions have become part of an effort to resolve international disputes without recourse to war or to coerce targets into conformity with international norms.

The incorporation of economic sanctions into the covenant of the League of Nations represented the first attempt by states to make an ethical commitment to isolate other states that weren't complying with the norms of international society. The American President Woodrow Wilson, who was one of the main architects of the League, referred to economic sanctions as "shutting the doors and locking an aggressor in."[13] The strategy proved controversial, however. Some states resented the obligation to impose sanctions in relation to issues that did not bear directly on their interests. Some also saw the sanction weapon as poorly defined and in need of strengthening. In practice, the League was reluctant to implement economic measures in times of crisis, as evident in relation to Manchuria and Abyssinia. During the Second World War, following the breakdown of the League, both the Axis and the Allies did effectively use economic sanctions against the other as part of warfare. This, more than the experience of the League, convinced the architects of the UN after the Second World War to include sanctions as an option of international policy. While economic sanctions have historically been a complement to military force in war, the League and the UN made them into a coercive tool for the community of states to enforce norms of good international behavior or to prevent recourse to war.

It is only recently, however, since the end of the Cold War, that economic sanctions have become a tool of multilateral diplomacy. Between 1945 and 1990, two-thirds of the sixty cases of economic sanctions were initiated and maintained by the USA. During this period, the UN only imposed economic sanctions twice, against Southern Rhodesia in 1966 and against South Africa in 1977.[14] Given the Cold War conflict, agreement to impose multilateral sanctions was difficult to reach, since the Security Council was hamstrung by the veto power of the permanent members, and not the least the USA and the USSR. The ethical demand for sanctions thus tended to become caught up in the ideological conflict between East and West. Sanctions were most often used as a means for the USA to demonstrate its resolve against communism. US sanctions on Cuba served this purpose, although they were unsuccessful in dislodging Fidel Castro.[15] The other, and somewhat more successful, focus of sanctions was the continuing oppression of black majorities by white minorities in the former colonies.

When sanctions were imposed on Rhodesia in 1966 it was still a UK dependent territory.[16] An earlier General Assembly Resolution had called for steps to restore all rights to the non-European population, but, following the election of Ian Smith's Rhodesian Front Party, the Security Council declared that the UK should not transfer sovereignty to South Rhodesia until "fully representative government had been established."[17] Smith wanted a constitution that would enshrine white minority rule indefinitely. When in 1965 he announced a Proclamation of Independence, the Wilson government in the UK condemned the act as illegal, a rebellion against the crown, and instructed the Governor of Rhodesia to inform Ian Smith and his colleagues that they no longer held office. This was followed by the progressive imposition of economic sanctions by Britain and other states, which in 1966 was reinforced by a UN Security Council Resolution (232) calling on member states to implement selective mandatory sanctions against the Smith government, including the prohibition of exports to Rhodesia of petroleum, armaments, vehicles, and aircraft and on imports of Rhodesian agricultural products and minerals. These failed, however, to bring an end to the Rhodesia "rebellion" or to persuade the Smith regime to terminate its racist policies. In 1968, under Chapter VII, the Security Council acted to define and enforce a mandatory program of economic sanctions (Resolution 253) which imposed a ban on all exports to and imports from Rhodesia, prohibited the transfer of funds to Rhodesia for investment, denounced the Rhodesian passport and severed links with the Smith regime.[18]

While the sanctions were widely circumvented by companies and states friendly to Rhodesia, radical movements in the region were increasingly successful and the USA and UK were eager to limit any potential damage to future Western interests. The sanctions were lifted in 1979 after an agreement was signed between black leaders and representatives of the white minority, who acceded to black majority rule in

Rhodesia. On April 18, 1980 Robert Mugabe became the first black Prime Minister of an independent Zimbabwe. The role of the sanctions was somewhat ambiguous. On the one hand, they contributed to the process of undermining white rule, although they were less significant than the guerrilla war, the independence of Angola and Mozambique and pressure from South Africa for a settlement.[19] On the other hand, the economic and moral weight of sanctions were said to have contributed to a negotiated settlement.[20]

While the UK and the USA took a lead role in Rhodesia, in the case of South Africa, the imposition of sanctions was preceded by and coincided with a global campaign to influence public opinion.[21] As early as the 1950s, prior to large-scale decolonization in Africa, some member states of the United Nations asked that apartheid be put on the international agenda because it represented a violation of the Universal Declaration of Human Rights. Sanctions were first imposed in the early sixties in response to the Sharpeville massacre in South Africa, in which 69 blacks were killed by police. The incident provoked worldwide condemnation of the South African regime and a call for sanctions. In response, the UN Security Council passed Resolution S/4300, with the UK and France abstaining, which condemned the violence and called for an end to apartheid. In 1962, the United Nations General Assembly passed a non-binding resolution (1761) which called on the members "separately or collectively, in conformity with the Charter" to break diplomatic relations with South Africa, to close ports to South African vessels, to forbid vessels flying their flags to enter South African ports, to boycott South African trade, and to suspend landing rights for South African aircraft.

In the following decades, further resolutions were passed, with fluctuating or conditional support from the members of the Security Council and particularly the USA and the UK. In 1976, hundreds of blacks, many of them children were killed in riots in Soweto, which had been triggered by inequities in the educational system. These events intensified international condemnation of the apartheid regime, and raised concerns among foreign investors about the stability of South Africa. In 1977, 11 US multinationals announced that they would adopt six principles, defined by Reverend Leon Sullivan, the first black board member of General Motors. The Sullivan Principles related to equal opportunity in the workplace. By 1985, 170 American businesses had signed on to the Sullivan Principles, which set conditions for American businesses to stay in South Africa, including their desegregation and the equal treatment of black and white employees.

By 1987, the USA, the UK, and the Federal Republic of Germany were still voting against mandatory sanctions in the UN, but a de facto worldwide embargo had already gained strength over the years.[22] Nongovernmental organizations played a large role in the mobilization of opinion that led to the ostracism of South Africa and its increasing isolation. A widespread campaign of disengagement was organized to encourage companies, banks, churches, and states to pull their investments out of South Africa as a way of isolating the regime and pressuring it to change.[23] There was also a sports boycott that focused on keeping South Africa out of the Olympics.

The United States only took the lead at a late stage, after world opinion had been organized against apartheid. In 1981, the US administration of President Ronald Reagan announced a policy of "constructive engagement" with South Africa, which was a recognition of the "limits on the US capacity to use negative pressure to achieve policy results in South Africa." The new policy, formulated by Assistant Secretary of State for African Affairs Chester A. Crocker, included relaxation of diplomatic and economic sanctions imposed under previous administrations, including allowing more South African honorary consuls in the USA, granting visas to the South African rugby team, relaxing controls on nonlethal exports to South African military and police and on restrictions on exports of dual-use military equipment and technology.[24] Against the background of growing international pressure, by the autumn of 1986, Congress was prepared to enact the Comprehensive Anti-Apartheid Act, despite President Reagan's vigorous opposition. Reagan vetoed the legislation but the House of Representatives and Senate overrode the veto. Nelson Mandela has since said that there was no doubt that economic pressure played a central role in the collapse of apartheid.[25] The driving force of the USA behind the campaign was crucial. However, in contrast to the post–Cold War cases, the US government was pushed into action by campaigners on the ground.

Post–Cold War sanctions

The end of the Cold War brought a number of global changes that have increased the use of sanctions. One important factor was the elimination of the USA–USSR rivalry. Because the USA was no longer bound by the need to counter Soviet influence it could be more selective and demanding in its engagement with various countries. For instance, while the nuclear pursuits of Pakistan were largely ignored in the 1980s, due to the need for cooperation in the battle against Soviet influence in Afghanistan, the USA held the country to a higher standard of conduct in the 1990s, imposing sanctions following Pakistan's nuclear test.[26] Sanctions were lifted after September 11, 2001 in exchange for Pakistan's support in the War on Terrorism.

The absence of superpower rivalry also enhanced the role of the UN. While the US use of sanctions during the Cold War was primarily unilateral and directed at other sovereign states, since the end of the Cold War it has become more common for the UN to impose multilateral sanctions. While mandatory sanctions were only imposed by the UN twice between its founding and 1990, they were imposed on 11 countries and four political movements in the decade following the end of the Cold War.[27] In the post–Cold War period there has also been a dramatic increase in the number of non-state entities sanctioned by the United Nations and the development of mechanisms for this purpose.[28]

During the Cold War virtually all major initiatives, conflicts and crises centered around the actions of states. Since 1990, both supranational and sub-state actors have played an increasing role. In addition to the UN, this includes the mobilization of actors who put pressure on states to take international norms seriously, particularly relating to human rights. But it has also included actors, such as terrorist organizations who seek to exploit processes of globalization for violent ends. Terrorist groups such as Al-Qaida and the liberation Tigers of Tamil Eelam have used global networks to advance their agendas. Companies and businesses are another form of non-state actor that have become more able to operate outside the purview of the nation-state.

As already suggested, the reason for imposing sanctions has also changed. From 1914–90, the USA was likely to use sanctions against states to constrain or influence their external behavior or to destabilize a regime. With the exception of the Carter Administration in the 1970s, which put human rights at the core of its foreign policy agenda, the internal behavior of a regime was rarely the focus of sanctions. Since 1990, sanctions have been used both by the USA unilaterally and multilaterally within the UN to promote democracy and human rights or to limit the proliferation of weapons. The goal, originally formulated by the League of Nations of using economic sanctions to reinforce international norms has since 1990 become more of a reality. However, the practice has also exposed some of the moral dilemmas raised by this form of intervention. Three examples from the 1990s reveal some of the issues.

In an effort to avoid fanning the emerging conflict in Yugoslavia, the UN passed resolution 713 in September 1991 calling on all states to implement a general and complete embargo on all delivery of weapons.

A second resolution in 1992 implemented more comprehensive sanctions, including trade, against Serbia and Montenegro.[29] While the embargo restricted arms to all participants in the conflict equally, the existing supply was distributed unequally. The Serbs had acquired the bulk of the military arsenal of the former Yugoslav army, which gave them a military advantage over other ethnic groups. Croatia was able to circumvent the effects of the ban and build up its forces because of its long coastline. This set the stage for the Bosnian Muslims to become the main victim of both the embargo by the international community and of the Serbs, given their inability to compete militarily. As the Serbs and Croats tried to carve up Bosnia, the Muslims became the target of ethnic cleansing as they were squeezed into a handful of besieged towns. The international community was reluctant to intervene with force and, at the same time, refused the Bosnians the means to defend themselves. By 1993, the Bosnian government announced that it intended to sue the UK in the International Court of Justice for conspiring to genocide in their opposition to lifting the UN embargo.[30] Increasingly the Bosnians were supplied covertly with arms from the USA, Turkey, and other NATO powers, as an alternative to forceful intervention. Finally in August 1995 the US House voted to end participation in the UN arms embargo. While the intention of the embargo was to limit the scale of fighting, given the existing imbalance in the region, it worked to the disadvantage of the weakest party.

In Haiti and Iraq economic sanctions were more directly imposed in support of ethical norms and as a way of punishing a recalcitrant state. However, in both cases the result was widespread suffering and starvation of the populations in those states. Sanctions were imposed on Haiti for the purpose of restoring democracy and human rights.[31] Democratic elections, which international monitors including the UN and Organization of American States (OAS) judged to be fair, brought Bertrand Aristide to power in Haiti in October 1990. He was deposed a year later in a military coup led by Raoul Cedras, which plunged the country into chaos.

Both the UN General Assembly and the OAS condemned the coup, but the OAS was the first to take action. Within ten days, the OAS had passed two resolutions recommending diplomatic, economic, and financial sanctions against the Haitian government. In mid-1992, the OAS (resolution 3/92) called on member states to reinforce the embargo, to freeze the private assets of the Haitian military, and to deny port access to ships trading with Haiti. In 1993, the UN Security Council (resolution 840) imposed an oil and arms embargo on Haiti, one of the world's most desperately poor countries, as well as freezing its foreign assets.[32] The new Clinton Administration also began to talk about restoring Aristide to power.

In October Clinton announced that he was sending 700 American troops under the UN flag to ensure the peaceful transition to democracy. The UN passed a further resolution (875) urging all UN member states to ensure the strict implementation of the embargo by halting and inspecting all ships traveling to Haiti. Clinton sent six naval destroyers to enforce the new sanctions. While the Cedras regime was increasingly isolated, the sanctions were also exacting a grim toll. A mission from the Harvard Center for Population and Development Studies, which visited Haiti in July 1993, revealed that shortages of drugs, supplies, and electrical power had lead to breakdowns in primary health care. Bottlenecks in public transportation had reduced access to health facilities, leading, among other things, to a decline in immunization coverage and a rise in deaths from measles and other infections. Between 1991 and 1992, the proportion of total deaths attributed to measles increased from 1 to 14 percent.[33] The team estimated that one thousand children were dying each month as a result of the sanctions.[34] Food shortages were causing malnutrition, encouraging disease, and dramatically increasing mortality rates. The UN oil blockade made it impossible for starving people to travel to feeding centers or for aid workers to deliver food to the villagers. As the situation worsened in 1994, the Security Council authorized a multinational force to go in and remove the Haitian military leadership. As UN authorization for a US initiative, the action was hailed as a great success for US foreign policy.

While it is often claimed that economic sanctions are directed at regimes, rather than civilian populations, it is invariably the latter who suffer. Haiti raises a question about whether a policy implemented for ethical reasons can justify morally objectionable outcomes such as mass starvation. There are further questions about the ethical framing in light of long-standing US interests in the region. The involvement of CIA in the original military coup that toppled Aristide, and the link between the Haitian leader's dependence on the US military and accession to IMF/World Bank plans for Haiti, highlight these concerns.

The sanctions against Iraq present the ethical problem in more dramatic terms.[35] Iraq has been compared to a medieval city under siege, cut off from outside assistance and deprived of adequate food, water, medical care, and the means of subsistence. The strangulation of an entire society was made possible by the emergence of a global capitalist economy, with the collapse of communism in the East.

Sanctions were initially imposed in response to the Iraqi invasion of Kuwait. However, after the Gulf War ended, sanctions were used to pressure Iraq to destroy its WMD. As a result, a degree of sovereignty was taken from Iraq and an intrusive foreign presence in the form of weapon's inspectors was imposed for years. The weapons inspectors, who in the beginning were primarily American, were given access to buildings and institutions at the heart of the Iraqi security apparatus. Also, a complex system for blocking the flow of goods to Iraq was constructed. The reduction of the civilian population to poverty, disease, and starvation has been attributed by some to the economic sanctions themselves, and by others, to Saddam's deliberate attempts to deprive the population.[36]

Whatever the case, 88,000 tons of bombs had been dropped on Iraq during the first Gulf War over a period of six weeks,[37] arguably a disproportionate level of destruction in view of the declared UN aim of expelling Iraqi forces from Kuwait. The population, already devastated by the bombing, then had fresh sanctions imposed on it, which made it close to impossible to rebuild their shattered society. They were denied sewage treatment, free drinking water, medical facilities, and food in adequate supply.[38] By 1993 the UN Food and Agricultural organization reported that sanctions had paralyzed the whole Iraqi economy and generated persistent deprivation, leading to chronic hunger, undernutrition, and massive unemployment.[39] A 1999 UNICEF study claimed that malnutrition hadn't been a problem prior to the embargo, but estimated that by 1997 one million children under five were chronically malnourished.[40] In 1997 a conservative estimate suggested that 5600 children under five were dying every month as a result of the sanctions regime.[41] When former US Ambassador to the UN, Madeleine Albright was in 1996 confronted with the fact that half a million Iraqi children had died as a result of sanctions, she replied that, from the US perspective, this was a price worth paying.[42] Others have since argued that the long-term sanctions against Iraq, lasting over a decade, represent a violation of the 1977 Geneva Additional Protocols I (Article 54) which prohibit the starvation of civilians as a method of warfare. Many other international covenants and declarations include similar themes. This raises important questions about whether policies intended to punish recalcitrant leaders justify widespread suffering on the part of vulnerable groups in society.

Profit and principle

The Iraq example raises a further question about the relationship between policies related to arms sales and economic sanctions. Iraq was armed by the USA, UK, France, and West Germany during the Iran–Iraq war. Later the United States became the main force behind sanctions to limit and destroy Iraqi weapons. A similar, if less direct, relationship is evident in Afghanistan. In the 1980s, President Reagan imposed a grain embargo on the USSR for its invasion of Afghanistan. The USA then armed the Mujahideen, with congressional approval. The act not only fueled the conflict, but increased the quantity of sophisticated weapons in the hands of "freedom fighters" such as Osama bin Laden, and strengthened the global network of fundamentalists, who would later, in the twenty-first century, necessitate the War on Terrorism, and a further invasion of Afghanistan. Even before September 11, 2001, the Security Council (Res. 1333) had imposed an arms embargo and other measures on the Taliban in Afghanistan.[43]

The conflict between the arms trade and economic sanctions was perhaps most glaring in the British relationship to Indonesia following the proclamation by the British Foreign Secretary, Robin Cooke, in 1997, that Britain would formulate and implement an "ethical foreign policy."[44] The intention was to make the promotion of human rights a central concern of British foreign policy and to review arms sales to ensure that they were not used by foreign governments who repressed human rights. In a speech on July 17, Mr. Cook stated the commitment:

> Britain will refuse to supply the equipment and weapons with which regimes deny the demands of their peoples for human rights. Last month, I announced a review of government criteria for the licensing of weapons for export. That review will give effect to Labor's policy commitment that we will not supply equipment or weapons that might be used for internal repression.[45]

Attention to the ethical component of arms sales was not entirely new. Following the Sharpeville massacre the UK was forced to restrict the sale of Saracens and other arms to South Africa, given their potential role in internal repression.[46] During the Vietnam conflict, in the context of the "special relationship" to the USA, the UK was faced with the tension between its commitments to the USA and the desire of the British government to avoid providing equipment that would be used in that conflict. However, by virtue of the explicit commitment to put human rights before arms sales, the ethical foreign policy of the 1990s represented a departure from the past.

The potential hypocrisy of an ethical foreign policy by the world's second largest arms manufacturer became evident against the background of conflict between Indonesia, which has one of the worst human rights records in the world, and East Timor, which sought independence. In the days following the August 30, 1999 elections in East Timor, the brutality of the Indonesian government was made visible to the world. The military had supplied the anti-independence militias with weapons and, in many cases, participated in destroying the country.[47] While there had been a deliberate policy of mass executions on ethnic grounds since 1975, the UN presence in 1999, accompanied by journalists and television crews, assured that the horrors would be recorded. When it became obvious that the Indonesian military had an active role in preventing a transition to democracy in East Timor, the British government began to take a tougher line, pressuring President Habibe to accept the deployment of a UN peace force. Cook issued a strong statement condemning "the appalling brutality" and demanded "an urgent response from the international community."[48] Cook and the Foreign Office played an important role in supporting an international coalition and in drafting a Chapter VII Security Council Resolution mandating an Australian-led force to restore peace and security in East Timor, which represented a departure from the lukewarm response by British governments in the past.

However, consistent with that past, New Labor continued to supply weapons to the Indonesian government, claiming that Indonesia had a right under the UN Charter to buy weapons for self-defense. This was particularly problematic given evidence that "defense" forces were used to violently police a territory that was never recognized as a *de jure* part of Indonesian sovereignty.[49] After 19 days of anarchy in East Timor, Cook was still making the claim that "[t]his Government had refused to license any arms exports that might be used against the people of East Timor."[50] Many have since come to the opposite conclusion, that is, that British-made hardware was used for the systematic internal repression of East Timor.[51] The British government then did give a partial acknowledgment of the contradiction between the human rights goals of the ethical foreign policy and its continuing export of arms. On September 11, 1999 the government suspended the delivery of six Hawk "trainer" jets equipped with sophisticated air-to-ground weapons. A bit late in day, the government took steps to support the EU arms embargo and to take action to suspend further arms exports.

Conclusion

The relationship between the arms trade and economic sanctions since the end of the Cold War exposes several tensions. The first, on the part of the major exporters, is between the desire for profit, on the one hand,

and the desire to manage the proliferation of weapons, on the other. The proliferation of weapons, particularly in the 1980s, is not unrelated to the proliferation of economic sanctions in the 1990s. A second tension regards the politics of arms. Decisions to export weapons may be used as an expression of approval of the practices of recipients, just as the Reagan administration exported arms to "freedom fighters" engaged in struggles with Soviet forces. However, as former friends later became armed enemies, they often became the focus of sanctions. The third is a tension in international law between the right of nations to the responsible transfer of arms for self-defense (Article 51) and the Universal Declaration of Human Rights. Exports justified in terms of external defense are often used for internal repression. A fourth tension regards a question about whether the export of arms or the imposition of sanctions serves to fan conflict or facilitate resolution. Greater availability of arms can make conflict more deadly and may fuel fighting, as it did in Afghanistan in the 1980s. However, according to conventional wisdom, a peaceful resolution of conflict and a negotiated settlement are more likely if there is a symmetry of power. While sanctions may be intended to reduce the ability of a rogue state to engage in conflict, as in Iraq, they may also contribute to a regime's power, as a nation closes ranks around its leadership, as in the case of Serbia. While an arms embargo directed at multiple parties may be intended to limit a conflict, it may, in a situation of asymmetry, place the weaker party in a vulnerable position, as in Bosnia. Finally, economic sanctions have since the First World War been viewed as an alternative to the use of force. However, they also raise important moral questions in so far as populations, rather than their errant leaders, may suffer most as a result. The post–Cold War experience has raised questions about the potential to develop "smart" sanctions that will more directly target the military capacity of repressive regimes.

7
Cultural Interventions

Chapter 5 explored the distinction between a pluralist and a solidarist approach to questions of military intervention. That discussion posed the problem of who should intervene and to what end. The distinction also relates to contrasting assumptions about the possibility of community. In the communitarian view, the world is made up of many distinct cultures, each with its own language, moral system, and social structure. The inherent diversity of the international system, or communities within it, means it is impossible to define the "right" or "good" life in universal terms. A cultural and moral life are only possible within the state. Another more cosmopolitan perspective emphasizes the possibility of universal laws. In addition to being members of national and local communities, we also belong to a human community, which is the basis for defining a common global life.[1]

At the heart of this contrast is a question about the extent to which the radical differences between societies preclude a more global culture. Increasingly, scholars have tried to reconcile the two opposing frameworks, arguing that attention to difference can be compatible with the cosmopolitan project, in so far as communication, dialogue, and inclusion provide the basis for moving toward a more universal notion of justice. It is less a case of either a universal culture or a world carved up into mutually exclusive cultures than the possibility of communication, conversation, and understanding between them.[2]

The cosmopolitan/communitarian debate revolves around the relationship between sovereignty and global society. But it implicitly relates to questions of war, conflict, and intervention at all levels of society. Cultural difference can be a source of conflict. Many ethnic conflicts revolve around disputes over which culture will be dominant in a particular territory, including which language or which cultural practices will be officially recognized. The various ethnic groups in the Balkans were first and foremost concerned about the consequences of being second class citizens in a state dominated by another group. At the international level, questions about forceful intervention may be framed in terms of a universal moral code or legal order. However, existing universal codes are largely derived from Western culture and may be in conflict with the moral codes of more localized cultures. At the same time, international actors have played a vital role in encouraging or facilitating dialogue between conflicting actors as a number of civil conflicts were internationalized during the 1990s.

This chapter will explore the different ways in which cultural interventions contribute to the constitution of war or its transformation. As Valerie Hudson points out, culture is both one of the most elusive and most easily understood concepts in the social sciences. Everyone has had the experience of interacting with others of different background whose actions or words seemed surprising or unpredictable. Its elusiveness relates to the difficulty of pinning the concept down in a theoretical sense, given the vagueness of its boundaries.[3] I use the word culture to refer to several levels of experience. First, culture can be thought of as a layer of identity and practice, which overlaps with other layers of culture, beginning with the thicker localized practices at a group or national level, to the international culture of states, to the thinnest level of a cosmopolitan culture defining a common humanity.[4] These cultural lines can also delineate lines of conflict as, for instance, in the West vs. Islam or Protestant vs. Catholic. Culture in this use is very closely tied to the politics of identity. Second, culture can refer more generally to the communication of meaning in language or visual image as interventions that shape the potential for war or peace. Propaganda has traditionally been an important form of intervention that has attributed—albeit distorted—cultural meaning to conflict, thereby contributing to the construction of war. By contrast, dialogue has increasingly provided a context for actors engaged in long-standing conflicts to begin to break down established assumptions and fixed categories of us and them, in order to re-describe the potential for new forms of identity, interaction and thus conflict transformation. This has often been facilitated by the intervention of outside mediators. The last chapter explored the dramatic proliferation of arms with the end of the Cold War and its role in fanning conflict. This same period saw an increasing effort by actors in South Africa, Northern Ireland, and the Middle East to move beyond a logic of force toward one of dialogue.

Culture, language, and rules

Language is often thought to be irrelevant at the international level, for several reasons. First, the world is made up of multiple languages, which by definition makes communication across boundaries difficult. Wars are often fought over the question of which language and which set of associated practices will dominate in a given space. However, from its beginning, international society has depended on a diplomatic system, indebted to a common language (French traditionally), a set of common rules and a common etiquette, as well as an emphasis on negotiation to the end of avoiding war.

Second, the international system is an anarchy characterized by the constant threat of war. Truth is often one of the first casualties of war and lying one of its central speech acts. The diplomat, as representative of the state, has often been referred to as "an honest man sent to lie abroad for the good of his country."[5] Yet, diplomats exercise extreme care in formulating the language of documents or public statements. As John Vincent noted, why would states bother with language or moral proclamations if the words, even if less than truthful, are of no significance?[6]

Third, policy-makers and academics often claim that rogue states or terrorists understand no language but that of force. The international system is a place of war where talk with real words is cheap. But even the language of force is a language. It is a language of threat, communicated in part with the implements of force and in part with language itself. As NATO's credibility problem in Bosnia in the mid-nineties illustrated, over-whelming physical capability may be a sufficient condition for commu-nicating threat. However, the necessary condition of successful coercive diplomacy is the ability to persuade others that a threat is real. As explored in Chapter 5, the ability to persuade depends in part on reputa-tion, often derived from a past correspondence between word and deed.

Finally, in a situation defined first and foremost by conflict, dialogue is by definition problematic and thus of minimal importance, again because the words of the other cannot be trusted. As Presidents Reagan and Gorbachev noted near the end of the Cold War, they had become accustomed to talking about the other, rather than to them. Nonetheless, diplomacy has been conceived as the "dialogue of states."[7]

The objections can be restated in positive form, thereby revealing the central role of language in diplomacy. In fact, diplomacy is an excellent example of the many different layers at which language operates at the international level. The concept of sovereignty is constitutive of the international system, and thus of the identity of the diplomat. Sovereignty is the precondition for practices related to the balance of power. The balance of power is said to preserve the international system because it preserves sovereignty. Sovereignty exists only by virtue of social recognition by the community of states. If sovereignty is constitutive of the rules of the game, lying is an act within these rules, and the good diplomat learns how to do this effectively as a player. The shared customs and rules of diplomacy are an expression of international society, based on a recognition that this culture should be preserved. Dialogue between states is at the core of diplomacy, as is the idea of minimizing the resort to force. The language of threat and force (coercive diplomacy) is at its most effective when it avoids the actual use of force. It is often assumed, particularly by realists, that states may not keep their promises if it is not in their interest to do so. Yet there are many layers of "promises" that states do maintain on a daily basis. Even the language of threat can be seen as a promise of sorts, in so far as its meaning and credibility depend on a reputation for consistency between past words and actions.[8]

While the "secret" diplomacy of the European system was replaced after the First World War by an "open diplomacy" through which public opinion played a much larger role, this change only reinforced the importance of public language in diplomatic maneuvers. As Herbert Butterfield once stated:

> Since 1919 it is possible that there has been a further change or development in technique. A certain move may be made in foreign policy not so much for the sake of its immediate diplomatic effect, but rather with an eye to the impression that it will make on public opinion either at home or abroad. In a converse manner, one suspects that certain lines of propaganda, adopted at home, really envisage some negotiation with a foreign power—that is to say, even an article in a newspaper or a question in the House of Commons may itself be a move in the diplomatic game.[9]

Butterfield further noted that the rules of this game were those of a recognizable cultural group, involving members of a Western "club," ready to compete for position within the club, but also anxious not to destroy the club itself. The "club" defined itself in opposition to others outside, barbarians or potential future players (such as Hitler) who threatened the game itself.[10]

At the macro-level of international society the language of diplomacy is constitutive of an international culture, or, more specifically, what diplomats think and say. Standing above this international culture is a thinner cosmopolitan culture, which defines the principles of a common humanity. Standing below is the thicker culture of any national group, or other more localized practices that define identity.

Constructing communication

The communitarian/cosmopolitan debate revolves around a question about the relationship between different levels of culture and how the conflict between them is to be resolved. The purpose of this section is to explore how the possibilities have been articulated within theoretical debates. This provides a stepping stone for examining more specific forms of communication, such as propaganda or dialogue, in a context of war. Each argument, to a different degree and with different emphasis, recognizes the potential for overcoming the communitarian/cosmopolitan divide. Each shares an implicit, if in some cases under-theorized, agreement about the importance of dialogue and conversation as a means to bridge cultural difference. However, they do not sufficiently address the distortions which constitute communication in a context of war and how these would be overcome to make dialogue possible.

Andrew Linklater has adapted the Discourse Ethics of Jurgen Habermas to an argument about the potential for global dialogue and conversation as a path to more universal agreement and thus a more universal culture.[11] Habermas reworks Kant's "categorical imperative," in which norms can only be considered valid if they have been universalized.[12] However, unlike Kant, the universal does not emerge out of a process of private reasoning. Instead universal norms emerge out of a process of discourse and argument between concrete and situated actors. Universal consent emerges out of a cosmopolitan community in which no one is excluded and there is a "unconstrained dialogue of equals." All actors should be motivated by a willingness to be persuaded by the "unforced force of the better argument."[13] The process of reaching agreement requires that agents be able to reflect on their own starting position and to change, recognizing how their own views reflect personal bias or local and cultural influences that others do not share.

Linklater argues that recognition of the individual and emancipation of humanity requires a form of community that transcends the state. This approach to cosmopolitanism attempts to strike a balance between universalism and particularism.[14] A cosmopolitan community requires that all individuals have an opportunity for equal participation in a conversation that will determine their own lives. As such, the goal is to expand the values of the *polis* to the international realm. In this conception, the sovereign state is inherently problematic in so far as the search for consent among a domestic population sets the stage for practices of exclusion of those outside. Universal consent requires openness and reflexivity between agents who are willing to engage in conversation involving reciprocal critique and in which there is no certainty of who will learn from whom.

Linklater argues that Discourse Ethics seeks to critique all forms of systematic inequality that prevent active participation in dialogue.[15] However, the model assumes an "ideal speech situation" within which participants will rationally move toward some kind of consent. It does not sufficiently address three problems. First, communication requires a common language. Historically the only bridge between different language cultures has been the diplomatic culture of sovereign states, which is a Western construct and has depended on the language of dominant powers. Second, the language of communities in conflict is often distorted by propaganda or, as will be explored in the next chapter, widespread trauma, which raises questions about the assumption of rationality underlying the Habermasian framework. Third, the language of conflict is often primarily strategic. Rather than seeking consent, propaganda seeks the advantage of the user. While presenting an ideal of universal consent, the question remains how communities, particularly those engaged in long-standing conflict, would be able to even begin such a dialogue much less sustain it. While war is not the focus of these scholars, war is a central feature of international life and its dynamics are thus crucial to understanding the potential for dialogue.

Post-structuralists have identified a further problem with the cosmopolitan perspective of discourse ethics. They argue that the search for consent can become an expression of totalizing power.[16] If Critical Theorists such as Habermas or Linklater seek universal agreement, post-structuralists highlight questions of otherness and the need to destabilize realms of discourse where difference has been excluded, assimilated, or denied. Like Linklater, they criticize the state as an exclusionary source of community. Like the Critical Theorists, post-structuralists agree that freedom or responsibility is linked to the possibility of communication between concrete others. Like them, the goal is a dialogue that crosses lines of difference. However, the end of universal agreement would, from this perspective, be part of the problem rather than a solution. Freedom lies in the ability to transgress boundaries.[17] It is freedom from totalization in any form, including a totalized universal agreement. It is difference itself that is to be celebrated. Freedom is about speaking, listening and being heard, and not being excluded from communication and conversation.[18] No single voice can come to dominate or "stand heroically upon some exclusionary ground, offering this ground as a source of a necessary truth."[19] An ethical relationship between self and other requires contestation and negotiation. All ethics arise from a relationship to otherness.[20] The universal responsibility to otherness entails a permanent critique of totalization and a struggle on behalf of difference rather than attempting to eliminate it. While recognizing that actors are situated in a social matrix, which shapes their subjectivity, post-structuralists are concerned with "disturbing and unsettling," pushing at the boundaries of understanding in which the subject is enmeshed.[21]

Both theoretical positions attempt to bridge the communitarian/ cosmopolitan divide. The first strives to reach a truly cosmopolitan end where all actors are included in a global dialogue based on shared consent. The second strives to maintain an uncertainty, where a dialogue of difference both pushes at the boundaries of more communitarian assumptions and resists any totalizing and universalizing discourse. Both assume dialogue is possible without problematizing the process by which barriers to dialogue would be overcome or how it would be conducted in the absence of a common language. Both streams are critical of universalized notions of sovereignty, which often assume culture and dialogue to be possibilities *within* the state, but not outside. Yet, conflict is not by definition between states and dialogue may be as problematic for actors at war over the definition of state, as in Northern Ireland or the former Yugoslavia. Dialogue is clearly desirable in a situation of war or conflict. The key question is how actors would find it possible to begin a conversation with others who, they have long assumed, only understand the universal language of force.[22]

War and propaganda

Propaganda is one of the most obvious sources of distortion in the communication of war. The word propaganda has developed a very negative connotation and is associated with the deliberate manipulation of meaning by unscrupulous sorts. Propaganda, it is assumed, is propagated by "evil" regimes, such as Nazi Germany or the USSR, which did in fact use the word in the naming of ministries. By contrast, liberal democracies, who refer to comparable offices as Departments or Ministries of Information, tend to avoid the word. However, propaganda, as a process for sowing, germinating, and cultivating ideas, is as old as human communication. The Ancient Greeks regarded "rhetoric" as a form of persuasion. Aristotle believed that the purpose of persuasion was to communicate a point of view. As Philip Taylor argues, the most effective propaganda is not based on pure lie, but builds upon "facts and credible arguments, approaching to the extent possible the whole truth, and relying more on reason than emotion."[23] The word was first used by the Vatican in the seventeenth century in regard to its defense of "the true faith" against the Protestant Reformation. Its more recent negative connotation dates primarily from the excess use of atrocity propaganda during the First World War.[24] It was the British who, during that war, set the standard for the modern "scientific" use of propaganda. Much admired by Hitler in *Mein Kampf*, the British, in contrast to the Germans, were skillful in the selective and rational deployment of facts, avoiding falsehoods in the belief that, if exposed, they would jeopardize the credibility of the facts that had been used.[25]

The aim of propaganda is to persuade and, in a context of war, to persuade people that violence is an acceptable course of action. It is a weapon in the arsenal of power and a psychological instrument for mobilizing power. To be convincing, it must rest on some substance and myth must be rooted in some reality.[26] As distinguished from education, which teaches people how to think, propaganda teaches people what to think. In this respect, propaganda is in part dependent on culture but may also play an important role in highlighting and thus mobilizing elements of a culture. In this context, the mass media has been an important form of third party intervention. The emergence and institutionalization of propaganda represents a shift from face-to-face communication toward mediated forms of communication in which a third party intervenes in the process between sender and recipient.[27]

The word propaganda emerged against the background of the Reformation and coincided with the invention of the printing press, which made it possible to manufacture newspapers, political pamphlets, or books in mass circulation. The print medium was a necessary condition for nation- and state-building in so far as it made it possible to imagine community across a larger geographical space.[28] In a village, a sense of community depends on one's direct relationship to people. With the invention of the print medium it became possible to transmit an understanding of community identity, for instance, as French or English, over a greater distance, to include people who would never meet face-to-face. The process of nation-building involved the consolidation of common rules of language and grammar, common symbols, and rituals, such as flags or national anthems, and the writing of national histories.[29] Historically, the print medium played a role in the construction of the nation and the state from what would otherwise be vast territories that separated people with different dialects who had little in common. From this perspective, education or teaching people how to think has been less distinct from propaganda, that is, teaching them what to think. The development of national education systems was part and parcel of extending the imagined community over large territorial expanses.

Arguably, the development of electronic media has enhanced the potential for a more universal identity, which transcends the nation state, and thus the potential for a universal culture. The development of the nation-state relied on the construction of a common language within a given territory. This obviously does not exist at the international level, although English is increasingly the common language of international discourse. Television relies on language, but it also relies heavily on image. On television one can witness the suffering of people half way across the world without being able to know them directly or speak their language. This may increase the potential for identification with others on the basis of a common humanity.[30] The images of the planes crashing into the World Trade Center Towers in New York on September 11, 2001 were repeatedly flashed across the media and did not require words to engender a source of horror in the observer. The observation of violence does not require language. However, its propaganda value rests on some interpretation of the violence, that is, its meaning and what it implies for action.[31]

The globalization of the media, both print and electronic, has enhanced the potential for its use to persuade.[32] But this can also involve a complex process and interweaving of image and culture at several levels. In the post–Cold War period, this was evident in cases of ethnic conflict, such as the former Yugoslavia. Within the former Yugoslavia, in the late 1980s, the Serb media made a deliberate effort to construct a Serbian identity.[33] It did so by evoking certain officially sanctioned rituals, such as the mass baptism of Serbs and Montenegrins in Kosovo Polje, and a procession of the alleged remnants of the fourteenth century Prince Lazar through Serb populated villages and monasteries.[34] The televising of these rituals made it possible to transcend their local character and reaffirm the bonds between Serbs scattered over the former Yugoslavia. The purpose of this campaign was to restore the Serb nation. The central claim was that the Serbs had been the victim of successive conquerers throughout history. After 1987, in particular, the Serb state- and church-controlled media published and broadcasted material that stressed the victimization of Serbs in Yugoslavia and the danger faced by the Serb nation if the Federation continued to ignore its plight. The power of the message was built on historical symbols. The persecution by the Croatian Ustasa, who were puppets of Hitler during the Second World War, was an experience of genocide that was transposed into the present—all Croats became Ustasa and thus capable of Genocide.[35] Milosevic also evoked the defeat of the Serb nation in 1389 in Kosovo as a symbol, arguing the Serbs would never be beaten again.[36] In this respect, historical events, beyond the experience of any living person, were drawn on to mobilize and politicize ethnic identity, and to construct the Serbs as victims in search of justice.

Rumors of the rape of Serbian women by Albanians in Kosovo were also taken up and exploited by the media. Even though Kosovo had the lowest rate of rape in former Yugoslavia, the media created a reality in which Serb women had been systematically raped by Albanian men.[37] This became a symbol of Serb martyrdom and the rape of the Serbian nation. This was the background against which rape became a weapon of war used by Serbs against Muslims in Bosnia. The construction of Serbia as an imagined community, threatened by genocide from its neighbors, became a call to war.

The media in Serbia, and later the other nations of the former Yugoslavia, deconstructed Yugoslavia as a multicultural entity, high-lighting and emphasizing the separate national identities. At the international level, the press played a much different role, in giving meaning to the slaughter and thus shaping how the international community should respond. On the one hand, images of mayhem were cast as the re-emergence of ancient tribal hatreds that were destined to resurface after the demise of Tito, who had kept the lid on nationalist tensions. A similar story was told in Rwanda. The conclusion of this type of story was that the perpetrators were mad (and the observers by contrast were sane), so there is really nothing much that could be done.[38] In the case of Rwanda, which had been part of the Belgian colonial empire, this message also reinforced the idea that the inhabitants couldn't govern themselves, the implication being that decolonization had been a mistake. On the other hand, the press also perpetuated images that evoked a common humanity. The televised image of a starving Bosnian man, standing behind barbed wire, probably did more than anything to change the meaning of the conflict.[39] Suddenly images and memories of concentration camps and genocide were brought into Western living rooms. The promise of "never again" and the Universal Declaration of Human Rights became important arguments for doing something in response.

In Rwanda, contrary to the image of complete anarchy, genocide was perpetuated by tight control over the media.[40] The hatred was deliberately stirred up by leaders. Yet, there was a clear reluctance on the part of outside actors to use the word genocide, precisely because it would then require some form of action. During the mass slaughter in Rwanda in 1994, the Clinton State department and the National Security Council drafted guidelines instructing their spokesmen not to use the word genocide.[41] The word genocide, as discussed in Chapter 4, carries an obligation to take action. The Holocaust had become a benchmark of atrocity. To apply the term to a situation is to create an imperative to act. To compare a crisis to the Holocaust is to claim that they are morally equivalent in intent and scale.[42] In Bosnia, the images of concentration camps in Europe once again and public demand that something must be done, finally led to military intervention. In Rwanda, governments dragged their feet even more and were successful in distancing themselves from the language of genocide, even though the degree of violence was much greater.

Propaganda cannot easily be separated from larger processes of socialization, whereby identity, difference, and culture are defined within an "imagined community." It has historically played an important role in persuading populations about the need to go to war. In so far as propaganda suggests deliberate manipulation to some end, media can play an important role in this process. During times of war, governments impose restraints on the media and have unusual powers of censorship. However, ideally, in democratic societies, the media is detached from any particular political agenda. Since the end of the Cold War it has also played a role in mobilizing public opinion on behalf of human rights and thus moving governments to act.

Constructing conflict

National media may be an important tool in mobilizing conflict. This may involve dramatizing some aspect of a culture or assumptions prevalent in a culture to a particular end, blocking out more tolerant meanings. When conflict is sustained over a long period of time, these meanings can become a part of the culture and particularly resistant to change. When conflicts are referred to as intractable this often means they are irresolvable. But intractable can also mean stubbornness or resistance to resolution. If conflict is irresolvable, the only option is management to reduce the adverse affects. However, as stubbornness or resistance to change, intractable can mean there is some space for making a situation more tractable such that a transformation is thinkable. This requires seeing conflict not as a natural feature of the world but as a social artifact that develops out of a particular kind of interaction. If conflict is constructed it doesn't just spring from the ground like a mushroom. It develops and escalates in stages. The following is one way to think about the sequence.[43]

The first stage is the perception of a threat. The threat may be objective, for instance, a neighbor is building up their stockpile of arms. But the key issue is one of meaning and attribution. If the arms are being stockpiled for fox hunting in the spring this doesn't impinge on the observer's identity—unless of course one is an animal rights activist. On the other hand, if the meaning of this act is somehow related to who you are—perhaps you belong to different religious communities—then the threat becomes closely bound up with your identity.

A second stage is a distortion of the threat. Once the threat is perceived as a threat to a group's identity, there is a tendency to view any further act within that framework. Goebbels, Hitler's propaganda minister, created subtle association in film between Jews and rats in an attempt to highlight and give meaning to the Jewish threat.[44] Acts of aggression since the Second World War have been repeatedly placed in the framework of another "Hitler."[45] George W. Bush was masterful in making an association between Saddam Hussein and Al-Qaida, which had no basis in fact, but came to believed by a majority of Americans, and provided justification for the invasion of Iraq. Even when a connection between image and ground is missing in fact, once the association has been made and reinforced it becomes difficult to detach any observation from the framework of meaning.

A third stage involves rigidification. As two parties interact, they increasingly develop a rigid and impermeable construct that blocks out any information about the Other that would appear conciliatory. Definitions of self and the Other begin to harden and crystallize into a common framework, like the rules of a game. Thus the Other comes to possess all bad qualities, and the self all good. This places a distance between the self and the threat, which leads to dehumanization. The Other is not like the self, but evil, and therefore less than human. This is a necessary step for the use of violence. It has been a core aspect of military training to teach soldiers to dehumanize the Other.[46]

A fourth stage is collusion. As the rules of the game solidify, the two parties begin to collude in maintaining the conflict. This is paradoxical. As the identity of the self becomes increasingly wrapped up in a conflict, there is an interest in maintaining it. To destroy the conflict would be to destroy one's identity. At this point it would appear that the parties are trapped. They may not want to get out, since this would mean a loss of identity. Even if they do, they may not know how. They have developed common rules of interaction, which seem to be part of the world as it is. Both act as if the other can only be an enemy.

A play written by Edward Albee in the 1960s, called *Who is Afraid of Virginia Woolf?*, illustrates the dynamics of an intractable conflict.[47] The main characters, George and Martha, were a married couple who over the course of their marriage had developed a pattern of acting and reacting to the other, in a tit for tat game. One would strike and the other would strike back. Each of them understood the rules of the game, including what would set the other one off and how to retaliate. In this respect, they each were doing the same thing and this kept the conflict going. Occasionally, one would get tired and try to change the situation, for instance, by saying something conciliatory, but the other only looked at this suspiciously, placing it within the framework of their common game, and responding in a way that would draw the other back in. Both of them may have wanted the conflict to end, but they were caught up in the logic of their interaction, which was larger than either individual. Kenneth Waltz, in his classic *Theory of International Politics*,[48] used George and Martha as a metaphor for socialization into anarchy. The metaphor is also apt for intractable conflicts more generally.

A similar kind of pattern is evident in situations of intractable conflict. Both sides feel themselves to be victims of past injustice, which they believe justifies their retaliation. The result is an unbreakable spiral that each is unable to step out of. They may want to get out, but don't know how. By the collusion stage, the conflict is a system or a culture in itself and parties to the conflict cannot find their way out.

Conflict, negotiations, and dialogue

The two definitions of intractable presented above relate to two alternatives: the management of conflict through negotiations, and the transformation of conflict through dialogue. Negotiation and dialogue are often used synonymously but they can be distinguished. Taylor and Pitkin have argued that negotiation and dialogue are distinct forms of life.[49] Taylor points out that "negotiation" is inseparable from "the distinct identity and autonomy of the parties, with the willed nature of their relations; it is a very contractual notion." Pitkin argues that dialogue belongs to the realm of "moral discourse," which also relies on a vocabulary with rules. The latter is more appropriate to a context in which one party has been injured and seeks redress as well as the healing of a relationship. She quotes Stanley Cavell who says of dialogue and moral discourse:

> It provides one possibility of settling conflict, a way of encompassing conflict which allows the continuance of personal relationships against the hard and apparently inevitable fact of misunderstanding, mutually incompatible wishes, commitments, loyalties, interests, and needs, a way of healing tears in the fabric of relationships and maintaining the self in opposition to itself and others.[50]

Negotiation and dialogue often go together. However, as ideal types they relate to conflicts at distinct levels of culture, as introduced at the beginning. Despite Watson's claim that international relations is a "dialogue of states," this dialogue has taken the form of hard-headed negotiations rather than open-ended dialogue to the end of healing. Negotiations rely on an adversarial model,[51] where the actors are sovereign entities with clearly defined national interests which they are fully justified in promoting and protecting. Because there is no over-arching world government, it is a legitimate concern of sovereign states to act to preserve their own independence and survival. This gives rise to a competitive and adversarial framework of communication. Each state has a clear legal identity and authority to act and they are juridically equal, if not equal in fact. Further, they are often competing over scarce resources, such as land or military and economic might. The end of negotiations is dividing up this pie, such that each side tries to get more for themselves at the expense of the other. This happens through a process of bargaining, during which each side tries to maximize their own self-interest.

While negotiations have been a part of post–Cold War peace processes, from Northern Ireland to the Middle East to Sri Lanka, and these have involved territorial, military, or economic concerns, dialogue was arguably a necessary precondition to any kind of negotiated solution. These conflicts were noticeably different from those between states. First, as already suggested, negotiations are more likely to be effective if they take place between relative equals. However, in many civil wars or ethnic conflicts, there is a clear asymmetry between a government in power, which has more military strength and legitimacy and an opposition, which has less of these.[52] While the government has a clear legal identity, the identity of the opposition may be less clear. As a result, it may be difficult to establish who has the authority to negotiate on behalf of the opposition or the identity of their legitimate representative. Often governments refuse to recognize anyone in opposition as a legitimate negotiating party. The ANC in South Africa, the PLO in Israel-Palestine and the IRA in the North of Ireland were all referred to as terrorists. Almost by definition, terrorists are denied the right to speak, as symbolized in the banning of Gerry Adam's voice from British television until the mid-1990s. The stigma of terrorism must in some way be overcome before negotiations will even be thinkable since they necessarily involve direct communication.

A further expression of asymmetry is the greater role of the government in determining the rules of the game. It is both participant and umpire, at least in the absence of an outside intervenor. The problem was glaringly obvious when violence erupted in East Timor in 1999. The government was inflicting violence on the East Timorese who were declaring their independence. Prior to the arrival of UN peacekeepers, it was also assumed that the government should restore order. The government had military might and legitimacy on their side, even as the international community recognized the long history of government repression as the problem. If the government writes the rules of the game, the opposition, from a position of inferiority, petitions or contests a grievance. Yet, the failure of negotiations and the eruption of violence are most often due to a failure by the government to address a deeply felt grievance. Once violent conflict is underway, a government may prefer to turn the asymmetry into an escalation, in order to destroy the rebellion. Insurgents may try to break out of the asymmetry by linking up with an external host state and neighbor, at which point the conflict becomes in effect international. The proxy wars during the Cold War are examples of civil conflicts that became wrapped up in the USA–USSR rivalry.

Second, negotiations in divided societies often involve complex issues of identity, which can't be resolved by dividing up the pie, and where those involved, unlike sovereign states, have to continue living together in some way. Parties may prefer a complete divorce, and this is often a part of their demands, as in Kosovo or Palestine, but the international community is usually reluctant to grant sovereignty in cases of civil conflict and, unlike a married couple, the parties involved can't simply pack their bags and move to a new place. Conflict in divided societies is often over goods that can't be divided, such as fundamental human questions of culture and identity as part of a community. While some goods, like land or trade are divisible and therefore negotiable, many communal conflicts revolve around nonnegotiable needs for cultural, religious, ethnic, and national self-determination. The Orange Order in Northern Ireland often claims that it is their culture and the right to express it, for instance by marching, that is at stake. Culture is not negotiable in the same way that a trade agreement is.

A particular school of thought, referred to as the Human Needs School, argues that intractable conflicts between nationalist groups revolve around fundamental needs of identity, culture, and legitimacy and shifts attention to the processes by which people gain the ability to fulfill their own needs.[53] This rests on a different concept of power than the adversarial model of negotiations. The adversarial model relies on a coercive notion of power, where the side with the most bargaining chips gets the largest piece of pie. By contrast, the human needs model emphasizes power as the ability to act together to realize needs relating to identity and culture. Conflict in divided societies is not purely about material interests. It is first and foremost about the need to be recognized as legitimate. Conflicting and competing mythologies, cultures, and histories may be at stake.

Conflicts in divided societies may be particularly resistant to change because, out of the spiral of conflict discussed above, two mutually exclusive stories of past suffering have come to compete in the same space. The Jews brought a story of the Nazi Holocaust with them to the construction of Israel; the Palestinian story revolves around their displacement and repression since the creation of the Israeli state. Further, conflict is maintained by a process of mutual demonization. Each side sees the devil in their opponent and any potentially conciliatory action is likely to be viewed as a ploy. As discussed above, in a situation of heightened tension, observation and judgment are not based on individual character and action, but assumptions of what the "Other" is like and what can be expected of them, which then clouds judgment and reproduces the conflict. As the conflict is locked in place it becomes a psychological wall. It may even take the form of a physical wall, such as the Berlin Wall, which separated East and West Germany during the Cold War, but the physical wall is merely a symbol of the psychological barrier of suspicion, fear, and deception. Negotiations are likely to give way to no more than a continuing cycle of recrimination in these circumstances.

The Humans Needs School thus proposes an alternative to the adversarial model, referred to as *integrative bargaining*. Integrative bargaining is a point of departure for an outcome that recognizes and integrates the needs of the two sides and is thus more likely to lead to a positive sum outcome rather than victory for one side over the other. The goal of integrative bargaining is to re-describe the conflict and redefine the relationship. A first step is to contextualize the aggression, to look at the historical conditions that gave rise to the rivalry, attempting to step out of the pattern of mutual recrimination. This involves a shift away from assumptions about the natural aggressiveness of the other, to the negative experiences of both sides and an understanding of how previous wars and violence have conditioned each to feel threatened. Integrative bargaining is an attempt to unfreeze the adversarial framework. The end is a positive sum notion of security, in which each side's security is dependent on that of the other. It is no easy matter to reframe a relationship that has been defined, in some cases, by centuries of animosity, and where conflict has become a part of the respective cultures. The point, however, is that the negotiating process, not to mention any kind of equitable agreement, will not even get off the ground in the absence of some form of mutual recognition. The Palestinian recognition of Israel's right to exist, in accepting UN Resolution 242, for instance, was crucial to getting the peace process there underway.

Negotiations at the international level belong to a diplomatic culture, which grew up in Europe. Diplomats have been socialized into a common diplomatic language, even if they come from a multitude of different national cultures. This type of common knowledge and shared background assumptions can be quite important for effective communication, although it is by definition more problematic than within a national culture. Given the common origins in Western culture, problems are more likely to emerge in negotiations between Western and non-Western negotiators. Raymond Cohen makes a distinction between the low context culture of negotiations in America and Europe and the high context culture of some other parts of the world.[54] In the former case rationality and results are key and it is assumed that anything can be bargained away. By contrast, in a high context culture there is more emphasis on building up an ongoing relationship with one's counterpart and maintaining face may be a crucial factor. In addition, cultural signals may be more distinct and embedded in all kinds of meanings which, if not understood, may lead to frequent misunderstanding.

Thus participants in negotiations, even when speaking a common diplomatic language, may be operating on the basis of two different sets of cultural rules. In this case, the process of communicating may itself exacerbate the problem rather than eliminate it. In the north of Ireland the differing language of the two parties is a marker of the conflict itself. The designation of this space as the north of Ireland, by those with nationalist or Republican identity, points to the political goal of removing partition so that the entire island becomes a part of the Republic. By contrast, Northern Ireland or Ulster designate a territory within the UK. This example has less to do with a failure to understand the language of the other, than different rules for speaking about the conflict which are in themselves constitutive of a politics. It is hard in this situation to imagine how the language might be reframed to allow for a more integrative solution.

In some cases, the north of Ireland included, opponents may understand each other all too well. Richard Holbrooke, the negotiator in Bosnia, referred to a common assumption that was shared by all the participants from Bosnia.[55] It is standard negotiating procedure in the Balkans to refuse to accept anything that comes from the other side without trying to change it. The tendency was so pronounced during the Dayton negotiations that it became a joke: the best way to confuse someone in the Balkans was to accept his initial proposal without change, at which point he would change his own position!

It may also be the case that cultural and linguistic differences are a part of what perpetuates misunderstanding, as one would suspect in negotiations between Palestinians and Israelis. Thus, either dialogue or negotiations need to recognize the potential role of semantic differences in meaning or cultural differences in communication and hopefully limit the misunderstandings that flow from them.

Dialogue and third party intervention

Successful negotiations require that the asymmetry between players be addressed, a shift from an adversarial model toward the potential for integrative solutions, and recognition of the role of linguistic and cultural differences in communication. If parties have been in conflict over a long period, it is hardly surprising that successful dialogue or negotiations will require some kind of outside mediation. *Mediation* is the involvement of a third party who is not directly involved in the conflict.[56] This may be an individual, such as George Mitchell, who was invited by the Irish and British governments to mediate in Northern Ireland. While initially suspect because of his Catholic grandfather, he managed to win the respect of both sides and played an important role in bringing about the Belfast agreement. Mitchell's involvement will be discussed in more depth in the next chapter.

States may also take on the role of mediator. When a major power like the USA is in this position, their power may be either a benefit or liability, depending on how successful they are in using positive and negative incentives to pressure the parties. In the Middle East, the USA has historically favored Israel, which has given the superpower important leverage while contributing to a perception of bias in the negotiations. These considerations were absent for a country like Norway which, as a middle power, off the beaten track, was unable to dictate anything. Instead, the facilitators in Oslo were able to create a relaxed atmosphere and get down to the business of thinking through a range of potential solutions.

International organizations, such as the Organization for Security and Cooperation in Europe (OSCE), the United Nations or nongovernmental organizations (NGOs) can also play a mediating role, but often more in facilitating dialogue rather than formal negotiations. The Europeans were less than successful negotiators in the former Yugoslavia given the difficulty of presenting a united front. In the late 1980s, some 45 NGOs in the Middle East were actively trying to break down barriers of mistrust and misunderstandings between the Israeli's and Palestinians.[57] The OSCE has established a High Commissioner for National Minorities for the purpose of preventative intervention in ethnic conflicts.[58]

Mediation can take many forms. The key is that the mediator is outside the conflict and perceived to be neutral. They are usually invited by disputants to play a role at a time when they have recognized that it is in their interest to seek an agreement, and that they need outside help to rise above their ongoing conflict. Ripeness is a key concept that refers to the timing of dialogue or negotiations at a point when adversaries are ready to begin direct communication.[59] Any kind of agreement is highly unlikely if disputants are unwilling to consider an alternative to conflict.

Conclusion

Cultural interventions play an important role in shaping the meaning of conflict or war. Political leaders or the media may mobilize cultural difference in constructing or perpetuating war. Dialogue, facilitated by third-party intervenors, may provide a venue for re-describing conflict, thereby opening the way for an integrative solution. While dialogue has recently become a theoretical focus in International Relations scholarship there has been insufficient attention to the different issues raised by dialogue at the international level between states and within divided societies. While the theorists of dialogue identify the state as the problem, diplomacy has historically provided a common language for dialogue between states. The adversarial model that has been characteristic of negotiations between states is less appropriate for conflicts characterized by asymmetry, a lack of recognition of at least one party, and where issues of culture and identity are at stake. Conflicts of this kind require more of a dialogical model, not unlike that envisioned by the theorists, but also must go further to problematize the conditions under which dialogue would become possible in a situation distorted by conflict, where both sides understand the other to be capable of no language other than that of force. Models of negotiation, like the theoretical models of dialogue, tend to assume the rationality of actors. The next chapter takes this discussion a step further. Past societal trauma is examined as a barrier to rational engagement and various "therapeutic" forms of intervention are explored.

8
Therapeutic Interventions

The last chapter explored the role of cultural interventions in shaping the meaning of conflict, including the role of propaganda and dialogue. While propaganda tends to exaggerate or distort the threat posed by others, and sanitize the violence of the "self," dialogue is about breaking down the misperceptions that arise from an ongoing absence of direct communication in a context of war. The media was discussed as the primary source of intervention, shaping the perceptions of a larger public, and generating support for action of one kind or another by governments. Dialogue was presented as a process by which estranged collective selves begin to engage across the lines of conflict. While the potential role of a third-party intervenor was raised, a further dimension of dialogue, and other processes of moving out of conflict, requires separate exploration.

One theme of this book is the correspondence between the increasing destructiveness of war and attempts to address and minimize its excesses. The twentieth century saw two World Wars, the Holocaust, Hiroshima and Nagasaki, as well as ethnic cleansing in the Balkans and Rwanda, to mention only the worst atrocities. While numerous efforts have been made to address the moral or the legal or the economic dimensions of total war, there has been far less attention, until recently, to the social, psychological, and political consequences of widespread social suffering, trauma, and loss. In the literature of international relations, losses in war are often studied quantitatively and specific thresholds are used to delineate different categories of violence. As Stanley Cavell argues, the failure on the part of social scientists to acknowledge the individual and social suffering in war is an act of violence in itself.[1] It pushes the humanity of victims out of sight and transforms questions of meaning and loss into a matter of quantification.

Past trauma in war often provides justification for contemporary action toward new enemies. As discussed in the last chapter, 1389 in the vocabulary of the Serbs or the Holocaust in the vocabulary of Israel and others have provided a framework for mobilizing public emotion and action. Interestingly, a "therapy" metaphor has often been used in relation to practices such as dialogue, Truth and Reconciliation Commissions or reparations. Each of these represent interventions that seek in different ways to break the pattern of war by coming to terms with the past. The purpose of this chapter is, on the one hand, to explore the relationship between past trauma experienced by a community and the reproduction of violence and, on the other hand, different modes of therapeutic intervention to the end of moving out of a cycle of violence. Neither trauma nor therapy have a place in the literature of international relations, given their origin in a psychological grammar focusing on individuals. Nonetheless, both have a political expression in the world that deserves attention.

The first section examines the concept of trauma as a basis for thinking about political trauma. The section on political trauma explores the potential role of trauma in the construction of conflict. The section on therapy examines several forms of therapeutic intervention which have had a political manifestation. In the final section the tension between therapy as individual experience and therapy in a political context is explored in relation to several post–Cold War conflicts.

What is trauma?

The meaning of trauma is not straightforward, at least across time. Prior to the nineteenth century it referred to a physical lesion or wound, primarily from battle. In the nineteenth century it was psychologized with the development of a science of mind and memory, which, as Ian Hacking argues, wrested the human soul from religion and drew boundaries around the human memory that had not previously existed.[2] He points to a much longer history of collective memory that precedes the individual assumptions of psychology. The dominant trend at the moment is back to the body and neurological shock.[3] What began, for psychoanalysts, as a gender-specific female experience originating with child abuse, became, with the emergence of the railway accident and "railway spine," and later, shell shock in the First World War, a condition including men, which was closely tied to the legal pursuit of compensation or pension. In the 1980s, Post-Traumatic Stress Disorder (PTSD) was accepted as an official diagnostic category by the American

Psychiatric Association.[4] This followed a political struggle waged by psychiatric workers and activists on behalf of the large number of Vietnam war veterans who suffered from the undiagnosed psychological effects of war-related trauma.[5]

Trauma has been associated with a number of symptoms,[6] some of which are more conducive to a social and political manifestation than others. The first is a state of hyperarousal or permanent alert, which includes an expectation that the danger may recur at any moment. In this respect, definitions of trauma overlap with more conventional definitions of the security dilemma, derived from Hobbes "state of nature." Hobbes emphasized that positive emotion cannot find expression in war, precisely because of the continuous fear of attack by others.[7] The second is a continuing intrusion of the past in the present such that the traumatized may relive the traumatic event long after the actual danger has passed. As the Israeli psychiatrist Moses Hrushovski notes:

> Traumatized people cannot resume the normal course of their lives, because the trauma repeatedly emerges long after the dangers of the trauma have passed. They relive the event as though it were continually recurring in the present, not only in their dreams and thoughts, but also in their actions. Often they reenact the traumatic moment ... wishing thereby to change the traumatic encounter retroactively, so that they can, as it were, overcome it differently this time.[8]

Trauma may give rise to a tendency to replay the traumatic event in the present, in order to do it differently. In this respect, traumatized individuals may bring a pattern of past interaction with a perpetrator into present interactions with others. One possible consequence of "doing it differently" is that the former victim places himself in the position of perpetrator in order to avoid the experience of humiliation.

A third symptom is constriction, which means emotional numbing or dissociation from the painful experience. Traumatized individuals may insulate themselves from stimuli they associate with the trauma, which contributes to their isolation from potential sources of support. Trauma has also been associated with silence and the inability to speak of the traumatic event, which may be a function of a neurological shutdown, fear of speaking in the context of continuing danger, or the impossibility of capturing horrific events in words.[9] It constitutes the individual as fundamentally isolated, and corresponds with a collapse of community,[10] of those roles and meanings that had structured every day life,[11] and a loss of feelings of being protected.[12] Given the centrality of isolation and the inability to speak, any notion of political trauma would seem to be a contradiction in terms. If trauma results in a collapse of community and individual isolation, how can it be constitutive of social identity? If trauma involves an inability to speak of the traumatic event, how can it possibly play a role in politics, which necessarily relies on language? Given the emphasis on the individual and the "unspeakable" why use the concept of trauma to talk about collective politics?

Political trauma

Trauma is a useful category because it adds a new dimension to the analysis. It introduces an element of emotion and emotional numbing into international politics, which is largely unexplored territory.[13] But it is much more than emotion. Trauma is the human equivalent of nuclear radiation in so far as the effects may last well beyond the violent and traumatic experience, continuing to contaminate social relationships long into the future. The powerful pull to replay the past and to avenge humiliation provides a focus for analyzing the reproduction of violence. Trauma is an existential position in which "trauma time,"[14] a ritual reliving of the past, intersects with historical linear time, such that the traumatized may live in the present as if it were the past, thereby contributing to the construction of the present and future.

Most literature on trauma in war focuses on the impact of the environment on the individual. Trauma may thus arise from experiences of torture, terror, or rape, which may isolate the individual and which may be so terrifying that it is "unspeakable." There are, however, a few psychologists or psychiatrists who have theorized about the experience of group trauma. Vamik Volkan has developed a psychoanalytic theory of unresolved group mourning based on the concept of a "chosen trauma."[15] He distinguishes normal group mourning from unresolved mourning. For instance, in disasters, such as the crash of the US space shuttle *Challenger*, group mourning was fairly uncomplicated. After the initial shock, society became involved in a variety of religious and cultural rituals and, over time, the collective mourning faded away. However, some collective tragedies are more complicated and involve long-lasting damage. These include more monumental calamities, often related to war, where the group is left dazed, helpless, and too afraid, humiliated, or angry to even initiate the mourning process.[16] In cases marked by humiliation and helplessness, a version of the trauma may remain in the minds of the victims long after the overwhelming physical danger disappears.[17]

In Volkan's theory, those aspects of the self that are unacceptable, for example, humiliation, are enveloped and externalized to others who fit the perception of the traumatized self.[18] This does not necessarily take a malign form. He provides the example of a boy who grows up with deformities who, once the deformities are removed, goes on to work for the handicapped. Another enveloping strategy may involve a group distancing themselves from a traumatic memory, as many Israelis in the first 20 years after the Holocaust, distanced themselves from survivors.[19] Projection of one's own humiliation on to an "other" is another distancing strategy. The Israeli psychoanalyst, Rena Moses-Hrushovski uses the concept of deployment to describe a process, at either the individual or the collective level, of dissociation from painful emotions of shame.[20] Deployment involves the creation of a rigid structure of roles and organization for the purpose of protection, which closes down the possibility of direct communication with the other, and results in a life-long battle against "enemies," which have been a source of repression, harm, or humiliation. Deployment, like Volkan's "enveloping," is a response to trauma and the inability to mourn loss.

While pathbreaking, the psychoanalytic theories don't sufficiently problematize the relationship between individual trauma and social experience. Volkan refers to "mental representations" of the humiliation that become consolidated in shared feelings, perceptions, fantasies, and interpretations. The transgenerational transmission of trauma relies on a concept of "psychological DNA" which only reemerges under certain conditions.[21] Volkan suggests that a large group "unconsciously" defines its identity through the traumatic memory and passes it from one generation to another. But arguably a collective experience of humiliation is more than the sum of "psychological DNA" or the mental representations of traumatized individuals and, far from existing in the unconscious, is embedded in narratives of social memory.[22] When the target of humiliation or fear is a group, these emotions necessarily find expression in language. If meaning, already a social phenomena—as distinct from unconscious images or psychological DNA—is placed at the center, the individual experience and the collective experience naturally intermingle. Individual identity is constituted in a cultural context where a shared past resonates back in individual values and meaning. As Kerr states: "There is nothing inside one's head that does not owe its existence to one's collaboration in a historical community."[23] Individual emotion may find more direct expression in political emotions, thereby minimizing the experience of isolation and re-establishing a sense of community, grounded in negative emotions toward an "Other."

A "common enemy" can act as a source of social cohesion that in turn acts to lessen the isolation of individuals and diminish feelings of loneliness and depression.

An example demonstrates the relationship between individual and political trauma. Rachid, an Algerian terrorist, provided a personal testament to the British newspaper, *The Observer*.[24] He argued that Osama bin Laden's skill was to transform a history of grievance into a universal struggle, but emphasizes that he is merely a symbol of a pan-Islamic movement that pre-existed him by hundreds of years and will outlive him. He states:

> It takes more than the speeches of bin Laden to turn an Islamist into a terrorist. It takes years of feeling abused. To make me kill, my torture needs to be personal. To send me into a fury, I need flashbacks of suffering, not empty ideological concepts. The Algerian government's tyranny has made the struggle feel real enough. Terrorist volunteers came running because of the blood that they tasted on their punched lips. ... Maybe if he didn't have the paranoia about being deported or extradited to his death, he might have cared about his life. He might have believed in freedom if he hadn't seen the West back bloody regimes and oil wars. He may not have felt so desperate if poverty hadn't forced him into exile; illegal, paralyzed, scratching a living for the smallest slice of pie. Maybe if he didn't feel abused and that all Muslims are abused, now and throughout history, he might not have been so hasty to redirect the world stage.

The terrorist, in this testimony, is motivated by a history of abuse, going back to imperialism but most directly finding expression in authoritarian regimes backed by the West. In this non-Western context the "average Algerian is a stranger to the individual 'I' identity." Joy and pain are collective experiences, such that the suffering of each other is one's own. The political attempt to reverse the humiliation, by joining in the terrorist cause is mixed up with an idealized and romantized image, in this case, concentrated on Allah and the psychological, spiritual, and emotional support from others. The common experience of abuse binds together a traumatized culture in a common cause.

In conditions of collective humiliation, political leaders, such as Osama bin Laden, Hitler, or Milosevic, may consolidate their power base by rallying these emotions. In *Mein Kampf*, Adolph Hitler argued that the key to successful war-time propaganda is simplifying an emotional message,[25] appealing to the masses, rather than the intelligentsia, and pounding this home again and again. For him, propaganda was a means to an end, which was the struggle for the unity of the German nation. The First World War provided a simple emotional message of this kind. The unity of Germany at the time the war broke out was contrasted with betrayal by the Weimar government and the Jews. Hitler portrayed himself as ready to revert Germany's humiliation and to reunite the German people. The message was reinforced by Hitler's visit to the former battlefields of the First World War, after which he was greeted by millions of adoring Germans as he returned to Berlin. The readiness of public opinion for further sacrifice in the German context was the seedbed within which Hitler and the Nazis constructed a cohesive national identity. The Nazis strategically manipulated existing sentiments to their own ends.[26]

Political narratives may be mobilized by political leaders to consolidate their power. From this perspective, a people who have undergone widespread suffering may be vulnerable to leaders who are able to give expression to their unresolved feelings about a past trauma. Hitler gave voice to emotional states that were unexpressed among the public. As Bromberg and Small state:

> The abundant, almost unheard of expression of hate and rageful anger ... fired [Hitler's] successful orations ... [He spoke] the unspeakable for them. His practice of touching off hostile emotions rather than conveying mere critical ideas was wildly successful.[27]

Rather than a community attuned to its suffering in war, the emotions were turned inward to betrayal and outward to humiliation by others. In Mein Kampf, Hitler refers to the Versailles treaty as "this instrument of boundless extortion and abject humiliation." He goes on to speak of the "common sense of shame and a common hatred" among sixty million people that would "become a single fiery sea of flame."[28]

Therapy

From the perspective of the security dilemma, a change in the balance of power, as represented by the rise of Hitler or Milosevic, requires that the balance be redressed. However, once situated in a framework of trauma, this response is somewhat troubling since a further experience of defeat or humiliation may reproduce the conditions for future violence. Arguably, the allies took this on board in dealing with Germany after the Second World War. Rather than being isolated and humiliated, as happened after the First World War, Germany, after a trial of individual leaders, was integrated into the European Community of states. Once placed in a framework of trauma, the logic of response changes. At the point that Germany had mobilized its power and become a threat, a military response may have been the only option. The question is whether there are other opportunities to address the trauma of a community, either to prevent it from developing, to break an existing spiral of conflict, or to firmly situate the experience in the past. This is largely unexplored territory, although the "therapeutic" experiments of the post–Cold War period provide an empirical basis for beginning to think through the possibilities.

These are all examples of conflicts that were ongoing and seemingly intractable. The last chapter broached some of the possibilities for re-describing and rethinking a conflict of this kind. The objective here is to explore these possibilities more explicitly as "therapeutic" options. While therapy, no less than trauma, has been associated with the individual mind, both have an implicitly social or political element. In a situation where two parties bring an experience of past trauma to their interactions, such that they always interact with the other "as if" the past is about to recur, the context itself comes to be characterized by hypervigilance, intrusion, and constriction. Once two parties are wrapped up in the logic of acting and reacting to one another, the pattern may seem impossible to change, even if they would like to. They can't get out of the situation themselves. When an element of trauma is involved, dialogue will not take place in an ideal speech situation of rational individuals, as suggested by some of the theories explored in the last chapter.

In Albee's *Who's Afraid of Virginia Woolff?*, George and Martha were caught up in a situation of this kind. They lived in a world of distortion, revolving around an imaginary son, and where emotions were numbed by alcohol. The play ends on a pregnant note, with both of them wanting to find a way out of their shared past. As individuals they might visit a marriage therapist. The question is what the equivalent of marriage therapy would be in a situation of protracted conflict? Arguably in this situation unguided dialogue would easily degenerate into further conflict and a repetition of the pattern in the absence of a third party. Several concepts at the heart of the therapeutic process are evident in the examples explored below.

First, therapy usually involves someone from outside a conflict, that is, a therapist, who can help the parties to stand back from their relationship and look at it from a new angle. This involves helping the parties to become more reflexive about their own actions toward the other. As mentioned in Chapter 1, to be reflexive means to be capable of stepping outside one's context and to become conscious of how one's own actions contribute to a pattern. Reflexive sounds a bit like reflection—as in seeing one's reflection in a mirror. But it goes a step further. In an intractable conflict, parties often mirror the behavior of one another. One side drops a bomb, the other retaliates. They are doing the same thing. If I look in a mirror and raise my hand to strike the image, the image strikes back at me. Reflexivity is a further step beyond mirroring a reflection. In the mirror you see only the Other. Reflexivity means stepping outside, to see your self interacting with the other. Looking at them through the mirror, the Other is the source of the problem. They are evil. They have committed all kinds of injustices. Thus, the harmed party is justified in retaliating. Once one is able to step outside the conflict, and survey its dynamics, each side is better able to take responsibility for their own actions. Once they recognize that they are involved in a common game, that they have constructed together, they are more able to act consciously rather than simply reacting to what the other is doing. Tit for tat requires two players. If one refuses to hit back, it becomes increasingly difficult for the other to justify their own aggressive actions.

Second, therapy involves listening and acknowledgment. Conflict is conditioned by an experience of individual and social suffering. An experience of injustice, humiliation, and of not being heard may propel conflict by both sides. A cycle of mutual recrimination and blame by definition involves a denial by each side of their own responsibility in causing the other's pain. In the absence of acknowledgment, violence may be reproduced in the search for vengeance and retribution. Repressed pain and trauma create blocks with psychologically adverse effects. It is a cornerstone of modern psychology that expressing emotions, and talking through traumatic experience is necessary for recovery.[29] Victims need to re-experience trauma in a safe environment. Listening and acknowledgment require a safe place, where victims can speak without fear. This is inherently problematic in a situation of war.

Third, the search for acknowledgment relates to a desire for reparation and apology. Acknowledgment is the prior or constitutive condition of the latter. In individual therapy, the therapist plays an important role in acknowledging the client's pain; he or she may or may not then assist the client in seeking some form of legal compensation. In the political world, this is inevitably more complex. Demands for apology are inherently political since they represent an acceptance of responsibility for injustice, which then entails some form of compensation. This will be discussed in more detail below.

Therapy is a word that, like trauma, is associated with a Western individual model comprised of a person with a psychological disorder who consults with an authority, who helps them to return to a normal state. The abnormality resides in the individual, the problem is medicalized and depoliticized, although psychotherapists do, in various ways, take account of the larger familial or societal context in which a problem originated. This is the most visible model for therapy and one that has found a significant place in American culture in particular, and Western culture more generally. To talk about therapy as a political response to trauma in war necessarily requires looking to other formulations of the therapeutic.

Remembering and expressing terrible events are pre-requisites to restoring social order and healing individual victims. Since therapeutic models tend to focus on the latter, it is unclear what therapy would mean in a social and political context of war. While the metaphor is frequently employed, and there are therapeutic elements of different approaches to conflict transformation, there has been no theorization of how therapy at the societal level would necessarily differ from individual therapy. A first step in this process is to look at some of the "therapeutic" assumptions employed in situations of conflict transformation and problems arising from their application in a societal context.

While the therapy metaphor has found a place in the literature on conflict resolution its implications have not been fully explored. In what follows, I examine the therapeutic elements of four different scenarios: dialogue, Truth and Reconciliation Commissions, one-on-one therapy with individual victims of war, and demands for reparation. These represent less a menu of choice than processes that address different elements of a conflict at different stages and in quite different ways. Each also raises a particular type of problem that reveals the difficulty of applying a psychological framework to a social and political context of war. The problem is different in each case, but each revolves around this tension.

Dialogue

Dialogue is a potential and process that is prior to the end of a war. The key question is how actors, caught up in an intractable and violent conflict, which may have been underway for decades or even centuries, would find it desirable to talk with an Other who, it is presumed, understands no language but that of force. This may be combined with a perception that one party to the conflict is a "terrorist," and therefore not a legitimate partner in dialogue, as was the case with Sinn Fein (IRA) in Northern Ireland and the PLO in the Middle East. As in a destructive marriage, therapy is not going to be an option unless the parties are willing to begin the process. There may be any number of incentives to do so, from war weariness to a change in the larger context. The end of the Cold War, for instance, changed the strategic calculations for the different actors in the conflicts mentioned above.[30]

But, for two reasons, moving out of conflict is not a purely rational calculation. First, as already discussed, parties entrapped in the logic of conflict may try to change but may be continually drawn back in.[31] For this reason, therapy is a useful metaphor for the involvement of an independent third party in the transition from one framework for understanding a relationship to another. In this respect, George Mitchell, invited by the British and Irish Governments to chair the independent commission for the peace talks in Northern Ireland, was a therapist of sorts. As the chair, he established a set of principles to govern the talks. These represented a contract by which the participants committed themselves to these principles and to one another. The core was a willingness to renounce the use of violence. In so far as the end of the process was a society governed by democratic and nonviolent practice, the peace process provided a training ground. Participants whose relationship had been characterized by mistrust, suspicion, and an inability to compromise, could begin to learn a new game.

In his book, *Making Peace*, Mitchell presented the challenge of his role in Northern Ireland:

> At the heart of all of the problems in Northern Ireland is mistrust. Centuries of conflict have generated hatreds that make it virtually impossible for the two communities to trust each other. Each disbelieves the other. Each assumes the worst about the other. If there is ever to be durable peace and reconciliation, what is needed is the decommissioning of mind-sets in Northern Ireland. That means that trust and confidence must be built over time by action in all parts of society.[32]

Mitchell identifies the problem as a lack of trust. The lack of trust was the motor behind the tit for tat violence. Thus, the tit for tat was not only military, but political, and psychological. The two demons in Northern Ireland, he states elsewhere, were violence and intransigence.[33]

Walking out of meetings, withdrawing from the talks or violent retaliation were the standard forms of reaction to any perceived injustice. The lack of trust generated a climate of suspicion where the boundaries between truth and falsehood became blurred. Confidentiality was not respected; in the context of the negotiations, news was leaked before meetings had even ended. Stories were fabricated, and blown up in the press, until the lie became more real than life itself.

The weapons were not the cause of the problem but rather the implements of a political logic driven by fear, suspicion, and fantasy. Thus, one key move by Mitchell was to shift the emphasis away from the decommissioning of weapons to a decommissioning of mind-sets. It was not that the weapons were unimportant; rather the mind-set that gave rise to the violence was prior. The political intransigence had to be dealt with for any agreement to be possible. Since more weapons can always be procured, decommissioning would not make a difference if the rules of the game had not changed.[34] Even in the presence of rational incentives to move toward an agreement, the participants needed assistance in stepping outside the patterns of violence and intransigence that had become so central in their dealings with one another.

The distortion, deception, and manipulation that constitute a pattern of war are a second reason why the shift towards dialogue involves more than rational calculation. Therapy involves a process of disentangling actors from a set of deeply engrained and distorted assumptions that drive destructive practice. If the parties are trapped, they have to be guided out of the logic of tit for tat into a commitment to respect and acknowledge the other. In a situation of conflict, this is akin to a paradigm shift where the relationship between the two parties is placed in a new framework of meaning. The conflict resolution literature has elaborated the dynamics of this process.[35] The conflict analyst, as therapist, creates a space for parties to step back from the conflict and to articulate their separate stories of suffering and persecution. In so doing, an effort is made to disentangle various assumptions about the other, for example, that they are demons who always act with malign intent, to help each to acknowledge how the acts of the Other have been conditioned by their own experience of suffering. The hope is that through a process of structured dialogue parties will begin to put themselves in the shoes of the other and to reframe both the conflict and the potential solution. This "analytic empathy" represents an acknowledgment that the other has also suffered and provides a basis for beginning to re-describe the conflict such that an integrative solution, rather than a mutually exclusive bargain, might be possible.[36]

Structured dialogue is a process involving small groups and—in so far as there is a desire to influence policy—elite groups. The process is akin to a form of marriage therapy that is, by definition, larger than individual minds, since it involves both parties to a destructive conflict, and the goal is some type of reconciliation. When two individuals enter marriage therapy they are not only dealing with their individual psychology but with the logic that has come to structure the relationship between them. In a social conflict, involving distinct groups, it is even more obvious that it is a *social* relationship, attitudes and behaviors, shared by members of a group that drives the violence. Nonetheless, the social process does not easily extend beyond the interactions between individuals to a larger political context. Most of the meetings with Mitchell took place in private behind the scenes. Unlike the couple in marriage therapy, Gerry Adams and David Trimble, for instance, had to re-enter a very public, political arena. The literature has not elaborated on the more public element of drawing the larger populations of both sides of a conflict into the process of changing games.

The process of getting to the Belfast agreement was a very public one of transforming incentive structures such that various actors involved could begin to engage in a serious dialogue.[37] The public dimension was essential: without public support, elites would be unable to realize the outcome of a dialogue. While face-to-face negotiations began in the months after the Belfast agreement, by 1999, when George Mitchell was called back to Review the agreement, the peace process was about to derail. The people of Northern Ireland had endorsed the process but the leaders were having a hard time disentangling themselves from old habits. Mitchell then took the political leaders out of the public limelight, to a secluded retreat, where, over dinner, the various parties spoke face-to-face, about food and families as well as politics. A process that was nearly off the tracks set off once again.[38]

The face-to-face meeting was crucial. As in the meetings between Reagan and Gorbachev as the Cold War was ending, recognition of the Other as "human being" and not purely scheming politician, moved the process forward onto a new level.[39] However, in both cases, this stance was difficult to maintain after returning to the more public political maneuvering. In fact, in the period since the Review politicians have been pulled from the center by the extremes. For instance, in the elections of 2000 and 2003, the more extreme parties, that is, the Democratic Unionist Party (DUP) of Iain Paisley and Sinn Fein, were successful at the expense of the more moderate Ulster Unionist Party (UUP) of Trimble and the nationalist party (SDLP) of John Hume, the two main architects of the Belfast Agreement. Further, there has been a hardening of sectarian divisions in society since 1999. The institutions created by the agreement have, for the time being collapsed. The question of how elite-level dialogue relates to a more public process of re-description requires further exploration.

Truth and reconciliation commissions

Dialogue as a form of "therapy" in Northern Ireland or in Oslo, between the Israelis and Palestinians, focused less on the trauma of war than the boundaries defining the political conflict and the possibility of resolution. The role of intervenors, such as George Mitchell or the Norwegians, respectively, was crucial. The focus was on beginning to talk against the backdrop of war. By contrast, the Truth and Reconciliation Commission (TRC) in South Africa was part of the reconstruction following a change of government. The relationship between individual and social context is different. In dialogue, a group engages in a process of rethinking the boundaries of the conflict and the relationship to the Other. In a Truth and Reconciliation Commission, individual victims are the focus but the end is both individual and societal healing. In the South African context, for instance, individuals were encouraged to break the silence and speak of their suffering under apartheid. In this act the individual experience was situated in a larger social and political context, as a part of a process of collective healing and reconciliation.

After Nelson Mandela was released from prison he helped to negotiate an end to apartheid. One of the crucial questions was how the new government would deal with the events and consequences of the apartheid period. The answer to this question made explicit reference to the African concept of *ubuntu*, which means humanness or an inclusive sense of community that values everyone. With *ubuntu*, unlike Western conceptions of therapy, the healing of the individual and society are inseparable.[40]

In 1994 the South African Parliament created a TRC. The task of the commission was to uncover the facts of the apartheid regime and to work to overcome ignorance and denial on the part of the general community and government officials. It was based on a hypothesis that the testimony of victims and perpetrators, offered publicly to the commission, would create an opportunity for individuals and for the nation as a whole to heal. As religious leaders and churches became increasingly involved, the language of forgiveness became more prominent.[41]

The therapy metaphor is perhaps even more relevant to the TRCs than to dialogue, since the process of the commission echoed many assumptions of psychotherapy as well as religious confession.[42] The process was based on an assumption that telling and hearing the truth is in and of itself healing. Individuals who have suffered need to tell their story to someone who will listen seriously and validate them with official acknowledgment. This provides a point of departure for individuals to begin to reintegrate these narratives of atrocity in their whole life story. Public truth-telling takes the atrocity out of the individual experience of suffering and of silence, and transforms it into an indictment of the social context. The focus is less on collective guilt for the past, than creating collective responsibility for the future.

This functioned on three levels: (1) a personal catharsis through talking about terrible personal traumas; (2) moral reconstruction, by producing a social judgment and moral account for the historical record; and (3) political consequences, which included an assessment of whether or not to prosecute given the risk of further violence and instability.[43] The hope was that by facing the truth about what happened the dignity of the victimized and the humanity of the victimizer might be restored.

One observer said that the purpose of the public hearings was to help ALL South Africans to recognize their complicity in apartheid. It was thus group therapy for 41 million people![44] Therapy required identification and recognition of the various forms of abuse that constituted apartheid, the hope of moving from denial of the brutality to an open articulation of it, and thus the potential for apology and healing. Unlike the War Crimes Tribunal, which focuses on meting out justice to the perpetrator, the emphasis of the TRC is on breaking the silence that has surrounded the experience of suffering by individual victims. This rested on a recognition that unacknowledged wounds would continue to fester long after the cessation of fighting and may in the future explode into new conflicts. While repressed emotional pain and trauma create a blockage with psychologically adverse affects, giving victims a chance to tell their stories can help them to regain their dignity.

While generally positive, this form of social therapy raises another issue related to the individual/social relationship. Speaking of painful personal traumas can open up wounds. TRCs do not offer long-term therapy, but a one-shot chance to tell one's story. Psychologists have raised questions about whether a one-time catharsis can result in real psychological healing. In one-on-one therapy few therapists would push their clients to address the worst of their suffering too quickly, particularly when it is rooted in an extreme trauma.[45] Given the large number of victims in South Africa and the time constraints, adequate follow-up support services were also not available. While the catharsis was effective for some, others were devastated afterward. Some people were re-traumatized by giving testimony, resulting in a number of debilitating physical symptoms, such as confusion, nightmares, exhaustion, loss of appetite, and sleeplessness,[46] symptoms which fit in the category of PTSD. While dialogue does not sufficiently address the public/political context, TRCs raise questions about the consequences of public truth-telling for individual victims of trauma.

War therapy

Truth and Reconciliation Commissions are "therapy-like" in their attempt to create a space for individual victims to speak of their pain and receive official recognition of their suffering; however, the potential after-effects and the need for long-term therapy have not been adequately taken into account. In other conflicts, such as the former Yugoslavia, a variety of international efforts have been mobilized to provide more individual therapy to victims of rape and other forms of trauma. Because this is therapy in a literal sense, I will elaborate less on the practice than in the other sections, focusing more on the problem. The problem, in this case, relates to the application of an individual psychological model in a context of war.

Models of PTSD often assume trauma to be an individual experience.[47] The PTSD concept was developed by US psychiatrists dealing with victims of the Vietnam War. This context, in itself, was unique. In contrast to past wars, where entire platoons or regiments from a particular area served time together, in Vietnam soldiers began and ended their term of duty alone rather than as a member of a regiment or platoon. The further isolation of individual Vietnam vets, who returned to a hostile political environment, with few support services, has been identified as one source of the high incidence of ongoing trauma associated with Vietnam, relative to past wars.[48] This example suggests that trauma may in large part be a function of social isolation and an inability to give positive meaning to the experience of war, unlike, for instance, the veterans of the Second World War.

War therapists have increasingly questioned the assumption underlying Western models of therapy that meaning is generated within individual minds.[49] Instead, meaning is grounded in social and cultural practice and language. Psychological theory often rests on a distinction between "inner minds" and an outside world, and thus a separation between the two. The end result of therapy is thus self-reflexivity, where the self is made more self-aware and detached, and can find a more rational way to interact with the outside world.[50] This raises three questions. First, is this an accurate depiction of the relationship between self and world, if language and meaning are understood to be fundamentally social and cultural phenomena? Second, is this a particularly Western conception, which is less applicable to other cultures? Finally, what are the limits of focusing on individual rehabilitation in a context of war?

War is a social and political phenomenon. The trauma of war is not like physical trauma, where one passively receives a blow from an external source.[51] Trauma relates to the destruction of a social world, which may include a change of identity (e.g., to combatant or rape victim), the loss of loved ones and meaning within a community, as well as the physical destruction of one's living space. To identify trauma as a purely individual phenomenon in these circumstances may reinforce the social isolation that is one source of the trauma itself. The strength of the South African TRC was that it attempted to clearly situate the suffering of individual victims in a larger social and political context. The question is whether individuals who are treated alone, in the absence of a larger societal process, are able to adequately make this link and thus, whether the therapy helps them to situate their suffering within a larger social and political whole. This is further exacerbated if these individualist assumptions are contrary to the indigenous culture, either invalidating more localized forms of healing and healers or providing no basis for social reconstruction.[52]

The imposition of an outside model not only invalidates more indigenous practice; it also disempowers, by constructing the local people as "victims" who require outside help. Pupavac has argued that models of trauma management, imposed on entire societies after war, assume war to be a form of psychological disfunctionalism.[53] This disfunctionalism is constituted on a discourse of the "pre-political frail, vulnerable victim who must be protected and enabled through therapeutic intervention," a discourse that is not qualitatively different than earlier colonial discourses. She questions the assumption that individuals in a society that has experienced war necessarily experience trauma. Her primary concern is the relationship between the medical rationalization for intervention and the power-political process of attributing war to "traumatized nationalism." There is another fundamental problem raised by her depiction. If one expression of trauma is helplessness and a loss of control over one's life, then interventions that disempower rather than empower are likely to exacerbate or even construct trauma from what would otherwise be a normal process of social reconstruction and grieving loss.

Reparations

Acknowledgment is a central concept of therapy. In that context it is the individual therapist who acknowledges the past suffering of the client, as well as the client him or herself. In a larger political context, not only acknowledgment of the perpetrator, but that of society at large, is important. But acknowledgment is a complex process. Individual perpetrators may be unwilling to acknowledge their wrong doing, either because they have not admitted it even to themselves, but also because of the potential for punishment. Similarly, entire societies may be reluctant to acknowledge past wrongdoing, particularly until the injustice has been politicized.

Whether an act of aggression is condemned or supported is highly dependent on social practices and assumptions. Sharon Lamb argues that cultures often condition individuals to be victims or perpetrators. For instance, anger and aggression is more acceptable in boys and is often not allowed in girls. The more entitled a person feels, the less empathic and socially responsible they will be.[54] Gender is one basis by which certain individuals within a culture are assumed to be entitled at the expense of others. But entitlement can also be a function of other social categories such as race or ethnicity or religion. White Americans grow up with a sense of entitlement to wealth, safety, or opportunity, which has historically been denied to African Americans, in particular, but other minorities, as well. The long history of imperialism was based on assumptions of entitlement on the part of Europeans vis à vis the subject peoples they colonized. These assumptions of entitlement are often embedded in categories of language that construct hierarchies, associated with who is strong or weak, who is violent or civilized, and who is allowed to feel anger or injustice. They constitute a part of the emotional scaffolding of a culture, which can stand in the way of acknowledging the injustice done to entire sectors of a society. They may further provide the justification for acts of discrimination, pillage, or ethnic cleansing.

The end of the Second World War, and the acknowledgment of Nazi genocide, has given rise to another potentially therapeutic practice at the international level in the form of reparations, which imply an act of acknowledgment of past injustice.[55] Since that time, Germany has made payments of some 13.7 million US dollars to assist Israel alongside payments to individuals.[56] Reparations can take many different forms, from monetary payment, to the return of stolen homes, art, or the bones of loved ones. They may involve an explicit apology, the creation of memorials or other gestures of restorative justice. Reparations are a symbolic gesture and an effort to give victims a chance to reclaim their dignity and history. At the same time, they are paradoxical in so far as they represent a search to repair the irreparable.

Acts of reparation contain positive potentials particularly when combined with apology. Together they provide a response to mass atrocity that demands a recognition of wrongs done without any obligation of the survivors to forgive. They potentially meet the need for vindication without vengeance. They send to individuals a message that acknowledges their loss and reaffirms their dignity. An apology is more than an expression of regret. It is an admission of wrong.[57]

However, at the political level, the process is more complicated than the individual act of apology. Normal models of compensation involve identifiable injured individuals and discrete and measurable harms as well as an identifiable aggressor who can be made responsible for compensating victims. In cases of political reparation, these elements may be ambiguous. Particularly with a historical injustice such as slavery in the USA, it is the descendents of slaves who are demanding reparations not only from the descendents of slave-owners but also a larger society that was divided over this issue among others. An act of apology and reparation may raise other political issues about entitlement, reminiscent of the affirmative action debates, where white applicants for jobs or study did not see why they should be penalized for the actions of their predecessors. The political apology is a rare act because with the apology comes a commitment to reparation with all the costs involved. More often one hears the language of regret, which is a partial acknowledgment of suffering, without the obligation to take responsibility for the past. In 2003, while in Africa, President Bush expressed regret for the history of slavery without taking the further step of acknowledging American responsibility.

Conclusion

Each of the therapeutic interventions was an experiment which represented an effort to address the trauma of war such that it would not be reproduced in the future. The weakness of each revolves around a tension between the individual and the political, which requires further theorization. Like political trauma, political therapy involves processes of making meaning. They are, however, quite opposite in the way that meaning is made. Political leaders may translate a collective experience of humiliation, fear, or other negative emotions into the construction of hard boundaries between self and the Other and the "deployment" of this humiliation outward. Political therapy by contrast shifts attention away from blaming to the articulation of suffering and listening to the other.

Acts of acknowledgment are central to the therapeutic dialogue, where the therapist acknowledges the pain and suffering of the client. Acknowledgment has also been a central element of various peace processes. For instance, the Palestinian acknowledgment of Israel's right to exist was key to starting the peace process.[58] But asymmetrical acknowledgment can also fuel conflict and bolster the power of one actor vis à vis another. The politics of the Middle East was historically, and again after September 11, shaped by unequal acknowledgment. Prior to the first Intifada, recognition of Jewish suffering in the Holocaust served to make Palestinian suffering invisible. Since the second Intifada and the re-escalation of force, this asymmetry has once again become pronounced, as was particularly evident in the Jenin massacre. The politics of acknowledgment can play a role in the reproduction of war or its transformation.

Suffering and acknowledgment are inseparable from larger issues of speaking and listening. It is often assumed that talk is unimportant at the international level. Yet "talk" does play an important role in shaping and sustaining power, particularly in defining who can and cannot speak and who should be listened to. The terrorist is, for instance, an actor who by definition does not deserve to be heard and with whom one should not engage in dialogue. The various peace processes of the post–Cold War period required that terrorists be transformed into partners in peace such that talking would be possible. Conflict is sustained by the absence of listening. A political dialogue that enhances the potential for listening to those who suffer from war and conflict is an essential element of political therapy.

Susan Bickford argues that political listening need not be motivated by compassion but rather by the necessity of recognizing others as fellow political actors because "no one is voluntarily going to go away."[59] Recognizing that the Other "is not going to go away" is to return from the isolation of trauma to a grief shared with others. It involves not only the acknowledgment of the Other, but an acknowledgment of the reality of loss and death. As in the South African TRC, speaking and listening can also be an important part of narrating the past as past rather than being confined to acting it out in the present.

The concept of therapeutic intervention places the problem of hypervigilance in a Hobbesian state of nature in a different framework. The legacy of IR theory derived from Hobbes concludes that we should consider war to be the normal state of affairs. This may have been more or less true of the international system in the past. Diplomacy, while relying on a language, a set of institutions and practices, has, as James DerDerian argues, assumed the isolation and alienation of states.[60] However, given processes of regional and global integration, and communication across state lines, by a wide range of actors, this is not necessarily the case at present. Bringing the human element of trauma and social suffering into the equation raises questions about the consequences of robbing people and societies of their dignity. From this perspective, war is less a normal state of affairs than one that distorts and creates the conditions for the reproduction of violence.

9
Critical Interventions

David Campbell has argued that undertaking a critique involves "an intervention or series of interventions in established modes of thought and action."[1] The purpose of an intervention of this kind is to disturb settled practices and to explore alternatives that may have been foreclosed or suppressed. A critical ethos begins with a logic of inquiry that differs from more conventional approaches to international relations in so far as its focus is on assumptions, their historical production, their social and political effects, and the possibility of going beyond them.[2]

This concluding chapter is an attempt to revisit the categories explored in this book in order to highlight the critical underpinning of the argument and its implications. The first section provides an overview of the argument thus far. The second explores how the critical intervention developed here relates to other traditions of critical theory in IR. The third places these practices in a theoretical framework, which reveals the critical dynamics of the larger analysis. The final section raises further questions about the possibilities this intervention might open up for rethinking practices of intervention and war.

Revisiting the categories

The previous eight chapters form four separate sections. The first section explores the significance of engaging in a constitutive analysis of intervention and war as distinct from a causal one. Rather than a single static conception of identity and practice, mirroring a "real" world across time, we see a changing constellation of identities, practices, and relationships, situated in historical and cultural context, yet transformed by agents who exercise some choice, more or less reflexively, as they "act as if" one set of assumptions or another prevails. This was illustrated in Chapter 2, which provided a historical sketch of various historical constellations that have defined the practices of war and diplomacy.

The second section explored the evolution of shared understandings regarding the conduct of war. The various moral and legal frameworks represent attempts to limit its worst effects. Just War theory accepts war as a necessary evil, but defines the limits within which it should be waged. The laws of war were a codification of many of these principles. International humanitarian law, a subset of the laws of war, attempts to ameliorate the conditions of those most affected by the practice of war, including soldiers, POWs, and vulnerable civilians. Human rights law, which has evolved as a separate category, but increasingly intersects with the latter, has addressed questions of abuse by a government of its own citizens. Each of these has emerged in response to unusual levels and new forms of barbarity.

That these rules have emerged in response to the increasing destructiveness of war, and particularly the emergence of total war, that they attempt to limit that which appears to have escaped control, may reinforce the idea that war is in fact part of a structural reality. However, specific policies related to these practices cannot be separated out from the moral and legal backdrop. This is the subject of section three, which explores the application of these principles in relation to specific military and economic interventions. The central tension running throughout these chapters is that between material or national interest and normative principle.

At least three things were clarified by placing changing policies in historical context. First, the concept of national interest, that is, the concern of a state for its material security, wealth, and the power, is no less dependent on the shared understanding of sovereignty than many norms are dependent on more recent shared understandings related to human rights. That they are often in conflict is less a function of the tension between an objective reality and a normative one than the way these have emerged historically in relation to each other. As stated in Chapter 4, human rights were tacked on to sovereignty rather than thinking through the relationship between the two concepts. State decisions are often shaped by both even when they are in conflict with each other. Second, the tension often manifests itself in the relationship between state and non-state actors, whether NGOs, seeking to uphold human rights principles, or terrorists, who act outside the laws of war. Both are dependent on a spatial division between state and non-state, even while these practices erode the sovereignty of the former. Third, the historical changes in policy revealed in these two chapters suggest that the key issue is often one of the unintended consequences of political choices rather than an absence of choice. For instance, the acceleration of the arms trade during the Cold War and the creation of a weapons surplus set the stage for present concerns about the proliferation of WMD and subsequent policies relating to economic sanctions and pre-emption.

The final section, focusing in particular on the post–Cold War period, looks at efforts to transform or reconstruct long-standing conflict. Chapters 7 and 8 juxtapose a distinction between practices, such as propaganda, or experiences, such as political trauma, that set the stage for the reproduction of conflict, on the one hand, and on the other hand, practices that attempt to introduce greater reflexivity, to the end of breaking down the assumptions that propel conflict. For instance, propaganda and dialogue represent two different communicative practices. Propaganda often reinforces the fixed distinct identity of the Other, as well as reinforcing the necessity of war. Dialogue is an attempt to break down static images of the Other such that through talk the language of force might be transformed. This opens a door to the re-description of conflict such that an integrative solution might be possible. Political trauma and therapy are two distinct but related experiences that grow out of past suffering and injustice in war. The former may result in a tendency to continuously re-enact the past in the present, in order to "do it differently," thereby reproducing the experience of war. The latter seeks to move beyond denial to the acknowledgment of suffering by individuals and communities in war, as well as the shades of complicity that constitute this practice.

To approach analysis in terms of constitution rather than causality is to engage with a much more messy reality than is often assumed by international relations theory. It involves a recognition that global politics does not reflect the pristine logic of Waltzian neorealism, where "reality" is pictured in an ideal model. The reality is more akin to the complexity of an ancient city. Rather than a picture, reflecting reality, we see the dependence of this reality on layers of language and practice. As the philosopher Ludwig Wittgenstein said: "Our language can be seen as an ancient city: a maze of little streets and squares, of old and new houses, and of houses with additions from various periods; and this surrounded by a multitude of new boroughs with straight regular streets and uniform houses."[3] The geography of the international landscape, juxtaposes the old and the new, sometimes in tension with each other, yet each a by-product of historical meaning and practice.

In juxtaposing the many different forms of intervention that have constituted global politics, I have sought to provide an overview, or what Wittgenstein refers to as a "perspicuous representation,"[4] of the range of practices that constitute this landscape and how they have developed over time. This could always be undertaken in more depth and has been limited by space constraints. The point is that there is no single foundational explanation for war. When we hit rock bottom, this is simply what we do. The practices have evolved in a particular way, although they could have evolved differently. The world in which we act, is the point of departure for greater reflexivity, for rethinking interventionary practices.

Theory and practice

Providing an "overview" of evolving practice and eschewing the search for foundations, pushes a step beyond existing approaches to theory in international relations. Robert Cox makes a distinction between problem-solving theory, which takes the world as it is, attempting to solve problems within it, and critical theory, which exposes the power relationships that underpin "what is," as well as the theories that represent it. He argues that "theory is always *for* someone and *for* some purpose."[5]

The work of Kenneth Waltz, particularly the *Theory of International Politics,* has been the most consistent object of criticism by critical theorists of different stripes.[6] Waltz uses the metaphor of a model plane to illustrate how theory works. A model, he argues can be used in two principal ways, that is, to represent a theory or to picture reality while simplifying it, through omission or reduction of scale. The model has explanatory power because it moves away from reality rather than staying close to it.[7] Its beauty is in its simplicity, in having captured the essence of the object in a parsimonious manner.

Waltz' model is based on a mechanical view of the universe which assumes balance to be the natural state. The model identifies states as the central features of this system and the balance of power as the fundamental dynamic by which equilibrium is maintained. Unlike some other theories of this kind, re-establishing the balance is a more or less automatic process for Waltz. The model provides an explanation for the conformity of states to the requirements of anarchy, that is, for their lack of choice. The urge to explain arises not from idle curiosity, but is produced by a "desire to control, or at least to know if control is possible."[8] This desire for control, from the perspective of critical theory, cannot be separated out from politics. Theory of this kind is presented as an objective and universal picture, when it in fact reinforces particular interests and power structures. It may become a model for problem-solving on the part of historically situated actors who seek to reproduce the existing order, justifying their policies on the basis of realist principles.

Critical theory has placed this model against the background of a larger and more complex reality, showing that the theory supports particular interests, and not least those of powerful states. It seeks to deepen the model by showing the relationship to other types of actors, and, in particular those positioned to engage in an imminent critique of the existing system. Those who benefit from the status quo seek to solve problems within its existing parameters; those outside this status quo, who seek change, identify the contradictions inherent in their historical context.

Critical theory with a capital C, that is, in the tradition of the Frankfurt School, has emphasized *emancipation*, in particular from the instrumental rationality that has come to govern human relations, a rationality that in its potential to dehumanize has made possible developments such as Auschwitz or Hiroshima. While the theory/praxis relationship is at the heart of Critical theory, Richard Wyn Jones, a sympathetic critic, argues that Critical theory has failed to provide a convincing account of the relationship between theoretical activity and political practice. While this failure was the impetus for a renewal of the Critical theory project by a second generation, including Habermas, the gap between theory and the struggles of the political world has not been sufficiently bridged. He argues that what is missing in Habermas "is any notion of struggle—of how ideals and interests intermingle and interact, of how movements take up, adapt, and utilize ideas as part of an interactive process within and between societies."[9] Jones states that if Critical theory is to have practical relevance it has to reflect on what emancipation means in terms of actual practices and institutions.[10] This in part means greater attention to how Critical theory can generate support for or sustain an emancipatory politics and a politics that places the experience of the disadvantaged, the voiceless, the unrepresented, and the powerless at the center of concern.[11]

Post-structuralists, who belong to a larger category of Critical theory with a small c, have been wary of the Frankfurt School's emphasis on emancipation, fearing it can in itself become a totalizing discourse. They instead focus on the act of unsettling existing assumptions and categories, or the act of *critique*. Both of these concerns are reflected in the contents of this book, which has revolved around a question about the potential to be emancipated from practices of war and unsettling the concept of intervention. However, the larger point, as regards the implications for practice, is somewhat different.

This project shifts away from an emphasis on theory to the construction of an overview of how existing practices have emerged over time, how human actors have responded to the historical contexts of war they have found themselves in and how these responses have set the stage for new constellations of practice, in part arising from the unintended consequences of earlier decisions. It seeks greater clarity, and an ability to look again from a new angle at the maze of intersecting social constructs. Rather than providing an interpretation, from either the position of the powerful or the weak, it is an attempt to stand outside and present an overview of the assumptions that have defined a world of mutual practice and interaction that is continuously being remade. The hope is to open space for greater reflexivity and choice.

The argument has emphasized war as a social construction. This is in part counterintuitive, in so far as war involves an obvious element of destruction, including the deconstruction of those more explicit social constructs that comprise culture and civilization. Deconstruction is a word that is associated theoretically with post-structuralism. In this theoretical discourse, deconstruction is a critical act that involves dismantling those social artifacts that have been imbued with power, which have become so much a part of the furniture that we take them for granted and which privilege some at the expense of others. In what follows, I explore the relationship between deconstruction and construction as it relates to war and intervention. This relates to the tension, discussed in Chapter 7, between the search for universal consent, by Critical theorists such as Linklater, and post-structuralists, who view this prospect as part of the problem. This involves two moves. First, I build on Anne Orford's deconstructive analysis of humanitarian intervention, to explore how dominant narratives limit the available choices in response to humanitarian disaster.[12] Second, I explore a broader notion of choice as it relates to consent, drawing on Elaine Scarry's work, *The Body in Pain*, which is an exploration of torture and war.[13] The goal is to think about the relationship between war and intervention, on the one hand, and construction and deconstruction, on the other hand.

A world of our making

A central point of the "perspicuous representation" provided in the previous chapters of this book was to show the constructedness of contemporary international politics and war. These practices have evolved in a particular way, although they could have evolved differently. The evolution was demonstrated in several narratives, each of which highlighted an interventionary practice that has shaped the experience of war. Constructivist (or deconstructivist) analyses are often criticized for focusing on language to the exclusion of a material reality. This narrative has highlighted the extent to which material reality is a product of categories defined by historically located actors, which have been passed on to future generations, who have introduced further additions and modifications. The current war on terrorism seems a departure from the past in so far as many have called for a rethinking of this inheritance, given its primary focus on states. One purpose of this concluding analysis is to contribute to bringing greater clarity and a critical stance to this process of rethinking.

Game theory, and other binary models of decision-making, revolve around two choices within a game where the rules are assumed. The question here regards the possibility of transforming the field within which choices are made, that is, of reconstructing the larger structure of rules or the "games" within which choices, and thus actions, are formed. The game metaphor has a long history in international relations.[14] While it may seem to trivialize life and death issues of war, my point in using the metaphor is simply to think about how choices are often constrained by the underlying assumptions which constitute them. Choices are made within the context of a game. The prior condition for choice is consent to play by the rules of a particular game, for instance, one cannot make choices related to chess in the context of monopoly.[15] These assumptions, which may be seen with more or less clarity, precede any specific choice.

In a political sense, consent may be manifest on two levels. The first, and most obvious, is consent to a particular action, for instance, the invasion of Iraq. The second, less obvious, is consent to the world within which choices are presented, which is the prior condition for any specific choice. It is at this level that choices seem limited precisely because the world appears as an objective reality, which constrains and circumscribes the possible. The first involves active consent to particular choices. The second is often a more passive consent where, as Frost suggests, agents uphold and endorse the ethics embodied in practices through their day to day participation in them.

The challenge, in regard to the second, is to develop distancing strategies that enable us to look as strangers upon the world in which we act, and thus to approach it from a different angle. From this distance, the single unchanging reality is replaced by an overview of a socially constructed world that has, over time, formed in response to a series of historically situated choices. A focus on the second level is a necessary condition for an agency that goes beyond the yes/no choice. The latter plays a role in making the world, but often as a result of the unintended consequences of choice. Greater reflexivity would arguably contribute to more deliberate acts of world-making and agency.

The deconstruction of choice

Anne Orford's book, *Reading Humanitarian Intervention*, is an interesting example of a narrative deconstruction that reveals how choices are circumscribed. She makes four points that are of particular relevance to this analysis. First, she highlights the sense of powerlessness which is often engendered by media images of humanitarian catastrophe. This powerlessness arises from the presentation of human suffering as a snapshot, which is a product of the conditions of photography itself.[16] The camera records and isolates a moment of agony which is violently isolated from the flow of time. The photograph sets up a relationship between viewer and viewed, which is communicated in a narrative that constitutes the meaning of humanitarian intervention.

Second, narratives of humanitarian intervention often constitute the need to protect people in "failed states," and rely on earlier colonial narratives about the benevolence of international governance over an uncivilized people who are as yet unable to govern themselves.[17] Narratives of intervention, codified in international law, focus on the ways in which violence could be used by good and righteous "men" to achieve the best for those against whom that violence was directed. The defense of military action by the "international community" in the name of peace, security, human rights, and democracy, she argues, has paved the way for the increasing willingness of citizens in industrialized states to support militaristic solutions to international conflicts, making intervention marketable to US citizens, in particular, in a way that it has not been since Vietnam.

Third, images of widespread suffering and genocide frequently give rise to demands that the international community "do something." The choice is presented in terms of either intervention or genocide, that is, of action or inaction. Orford argues that in fact, inactivity is not the alternative to intervention in so far as the international community is already profoundly engaged in shaping the structure of political, social, economic, and cultural life in many states through the activities of, among others, international economic institutions.[18] Cynthia Enloe similarly argues that the construction of the US military as a global police force since the end of the Cold War means that it is now "more thoroughly integrated into the social structure than it has been in the last two centuries."[19]

Fourth, the emphasis on the use of force to respond to security and humanitarian crises diverts attention away from questions about the extent to which policies of international institutions themselves, or a longer history of imperialism, have contributed to the conditions that gave rise to these crises. Intervention in the name of humanitarianism too readily provides an alibi for the continued involvement of those interested in exploiting and controlling the resources and people of target states. A central part of her argument is that post-conflict reconstruction in places like Bosnia-Herzegovina and East Timor replicates colonial practices by the international community in earlier periods. She states, "From its support for acquisition of territory belonging to uncivilized peoples through to the operation of the mandate system, the international community has systematically facilitated the enterprise of colonialism."[20] Orford provides a more specific example in the East Timor case. The policies of the Australian government and the international community supported the Indonesian government and the Indonesian military in their repression of the East Timorese for over 20 years. The Australian public was appalled by television images of the violence resulting from these policies. However, the ordering principles of the international political economy that supported the violence never became the object of interrogation.[21]

Narratives of humanitarian intervention, in Orford's argument, construct a particular kind of world, made up of a benevolent international community and a suffering "Third World." They fail to raise questions about the conditions which made these images possible or their relationship to a history of colonial domination by the West. Western publics view the monstrosities of war at home over dinner, but fail to think about the history that created the conditions for this violence. The liberal institutions of the international community are presented as protectors of contemporary victims rather than being implicated in their production. As Robert Cover argues, "No set of legal institutions or prescriptions exist apart from the narratives that locate it and give it meaning. ... Once understood in the context of narratives that give it meaning, law becomes not merely a system of rules to be observed, but a world in which we live."[22] Similar questions can be raised about more recent narratives relating to the "War on Terrorism." The images of September 11 or massacred school children in Breslan focus on the moment, and what should done, while precluding questions about prior policies or interactions on the part of the USA or USSR, respectively, that contributed to these outcomes.

Deconstruction and construction

Orfund's analysis reveals how narratives of humanitarian intervention restrict choice to the use of force or no force, action or no action. The yes/no choice is embedded in a larger global structure of rules and practices, which remain unquestioned. Deconstruction is an act of the analyst that involves exposing the latter as social constructs, which make particular acts of force possible. In this analysis, liberal practices that purportedly seek to protect and limit war are bound up in its continuation. This is one approach to the relationship between construction and deconstruction.

A second approach focuses more explicitly on the relationship between construction and deconstruction in the practice of war or intervention. While Orford focuses on narratives that make intervention possible, the following analysis shifts to the role of intervention in constituting the constructive and deconstructive elements of war, particularly as it relates to questions of consent. This book has emphasized the constructive elements of practice or the civilizing rules that have developed to constrain or limit the worst effects of war. There is an obvious paradox, however. While war is a social artifact, which rests on shared rules, it also involves the deconstruction of meaning and of civilization more generally. In this respect, the tension between construction and deconstruction are central to the act itself. This framework complicates the picture provided by Orford.

War as a contest

Elaine Scarry presents traditional war as a contest that involves mutual injury, and the consent of individuals within affected populations to give their physical bodies to this end. This aspect of mutual injury and pain tends to be written out of most historical, diplomatic, or strategic accounts of war but it is fundamental to the practice. As a *contest* for resolving differences, one might ask why war would be preferable to other forms of competition, such as a football match or a song contest, which are much more intimately associated with rules and with civilization in so far as they avoid the destruction of both, as well as human beings. One possible answer is that war carries the means of its own enforcement because it leaves one side out-injured and thus incapable of further struggle.

To a certain extent, this is true. The outcome, although arising from *mutual injury*, leaves the victor with more agency to impose their own self-description over what has transpired and what is to come in the future, while the loser has less of this agency. However, Scarry argues that in most wars the process of out-injuring does not completely debilitate the loser; it is rather the loss of *morale* and a changing perception that arises from this. In effect, what starts as a contest over an idea "worth dying for," ends with the perception by one side that the toll in human life outweighs the original ideal. Only in the case of total victory and defeat is this purely a matter of physical incapacity. More often wars end with a *perceptual change* that the equation between the level of acceptable physical injury and the social construct, over which the battle is waged, has shifted.

In this respect, there is always an "as if" function to the waging of war. Both sides are fighting over a construction that does not yet exist in material form. For instance, an image of an Ireland or Serbia or Europe "worth dying for" is necessitated by the absence or potential loss of this construction in fact. Traditionally, with the conclusion of war, a victor was able to realize their self-description. For instance, most of the island of Ireland became an independent Republic in 1921, following a civil war, and ceased to be a part of the United Kingdom. In this respect, the injuring contest is about determining which of two existing social constructs will be produced as an outcome.[23] While there is no difference between the physical bodies of soldiers on either side—the injured body of an Irish or a British soldier is simply an injured body—there is also no inherent relationship between these bodies and the self-description of either side. It is through the process of massive physical injury that the construct is substantiated as a material reality, that is, that the disembodied idea is embodied. According to Scarry, "the incontestable reality of the physical body to now become an attribute of an issue that at the moment has no independent reality of its own" becomes possible through the process of war.[24]

Normally we affirm the existence of objects through our direct experience of them, that is, by seeing or touching. In war, the observer sees and touches the hurt body of another person, which is juxtaposed to the disembodied idea, or issue over which the war is fought and, having seen the reality of the first, believes he or she has experienced the reality of the second.[25] The injury is thus not merely a means of deciding the contest. In the massive opening of human bodies, otherwise unanchored and disembodied beliefs are reconnected with the force and power of the material world.[26] In so far as war involves a contest over conflicting beliefs or constructs, the reaffirmation of one side's self-description contributes to the deconstruction of the competing construct. What is colliding in war is each population's right to generate their own forms of self-description.

In the contest of traditional warfare, intervention from outside may have been constitutive of a war or would primarily take the form of adding to the ability of one side to injure, in the form of economic or military support, thereby increasing the potential for one side to prevail over the other. There might be further moral and legal interventions to define the rules by which the contest was waged. In this respect, war is a game or contest like any other which has rules defining good play and that ends with a winner and a loser. The post–Cold War interventions, with the exception of the first Gulf War, have arguably changed this configuration. While the wars between Somalian warlords, or Serbs and Croats, or between paramilitaries in the North of Ireland were contests over disembodied ideas, as discussed here, subsequent international interventions, whether military or nonmilitary, have not been for the purpose of enhancing the ability of one side to realize their self-description at the expense of the other. They have instead attempted to bring an end to the contest, either by creating an incentive to stop fighting, through military intervention, or by assisting the parties to re-describe the conflict such that a *mutual* description of their past and future might be possible. The question is the desirability or limits of either of these options.

The contest of war rests on the relationship between the collective injury suffered in war and the reason for war (justified in terms of other social constructs, such as sovereignty, human rights, freedom, or democracy). Earlier interventions, such as Just War theory and the laws of war sought to specify the rules of the contest, that is, the way it was to be waged or the rights of occupiers and occupants in its aftermath. In response to the growing destructiveness of war, humanitarian laws were defined to shape how the injured should be treated. Human rights law has attempted to limit the injury done by a government to its own population. At the core of these social constructions is the brute reality of material, social, and human destruction.

The mutual injury which is central to the execution, process, and outcome of war ultimately brings the experience down to the most individual of levels, given pain is in and of itself an individual experience. Pain isolates. Scarry reveals how the pain of torture closes the suffering individual off from the civilized world, in a room, with no windows, no ability to extend the self to others, and no voices except that of the torturer. Torture is different than war because it is a relationship between two individuals, where one causes pain to the other without his or her consent. War, by contrast, is a relationship between two communities, involving mutual injury and the consent of populations.

Given the majority of victims of contemporary wars are civilian, the distinction between torture and war is potentially blurred.[27] Many of these conflicts take place within failed states where government actors, or actors supported by the government, as in Sudan, are the main source of civilian injury, or where public institutions lack the legitimacy or capacity to protect civilian populations, as in Somalia. From this perspective, the increasing emphasis on "human security," since the mid-nineties, makes sense. This represents an acknowledgment that the subjects of injury and of insecurity are primarily individuals rather than soldiers of the state.[28] The devolution of war from a practice of mutual injury by soldiers who have consented to their participation in a contest, to individual civilian victims, places contemporary war closer to the deconstructive end of the spectrum, and to Scarry's concept of torture.

There is an obvious sense in which war is simultaneously a social construction and the deconstruction of civilization. It rests on social rules. It makes possible the materialization of a victor's social construction. However, in the process it destroys those economic, social, and political frameworks within which everyday life is given meaning and material substance, replacing them with the physical pain and suffering of individuals. The brute reality of pain contrasts with the social construction. Torture is the extreme case of the former, and civilization the realization of the latter. Traditional war occupies a space between the two.

Torture and deconstruction

Social artifacts are not only imbued with meaning. They are forms that allow for the extension of the self to the world in service of particular functions. The chair, as a positive artifact, is a self-extension that increases the comfort of individuals and enables movement out of the boundaries of the body. Torture, as Scarry argues, is in many ways, the opposite. In inflicting extreme pain torture brings about a contraction and collapse of consciousness of a larger world. It transforms the room, which is normally a structure providing safety and connection to a larger world through its windows and doors, into a closed space, where all of its objects become potential weapons. In so far as pain is "produced," it becomes an artifact in itself, where the bodily condition becomes an attribute of the torturing regime's power.

The social artifact and torture represent two radically different models, that is, of social creation, on the one hand, and deconstruction of these creations, on the other. War occupies the same ground as torture in so far as it "produces" physical distress and bodily injury, as distinct from the artifact that enhances comfort. War also involves a contraction of social consciousness in so far as the minds of those involved become filled with events related to dying and killing. It also separates the attributes of the hurt body from the body, projecting them onto other constructs (such as sovereignty, freedom, etc.). But there is a critical difference between torture and war. In the one it is the body of the non-believer (the tortured) and in the other the believer (the population, soldiers) that is enlisted in the process of embodying power.[29] The victim of torture does not consent to his or her treatment. By contrast, war cannot be executed without consent. It cannot be carried out without the authorization of the population. The soldier gives consent, in agreeing to adopt the uniform, to make his body available for physical injury in the name of some larger collective ideal. Consent, in this view, can involve explicit choice; it also may also be reproduced in day to day participation in the practices of a militarized world.

War resides in the space between the deconstruction of civilization and its construction. Outside intervention may play a role in determining its location along this spectrum. At its worst, intervention may move the practice of war down the deconstructive path, where it comes closer to the practice of torture. At best, it may enhance the prospect for more civilizing constructions through a process of mutual re-description. The key factor in this distinction is the degree of consent and participation.

Scarry, writing in the mid-eighties, argued that nuclear war is a qualitatively different experience than conventional war because, among others, it eludes the practice of consent. Consent in this context is a structural impossibility given the one to millions ratio between the political and military persons involved in the decision and the number of people who would be the casualties. At no point does the population exercise any consent over their own participation. Prior to war, the existence of a nuclear arsenal may appear to be an implicit act of consent, in so far as it is paid for by taxpayer's money. However, taxpayers are not offered a choice of whether their tax money goes to social programs or the military. Even if there is some agreement to finance nuclear weapons, this is not a sanctioning of war itself. At the moment of war's outbreak, there would be no vote among the world's population, and, even if this were possible, the duration of a nuclear war would be so short as to make the continuous act of consent that exists in conventional war impossible. The war could be over in a day or a week, leaving millions of casualties, if not the destruction of the entire planet.

Individual soldiers or populations in a conventional war do not in a single act give or withdraw their participation. Consent is continuously renewed or may later be withdrawn as a war progresses, as was evident in wars from Vietnam to Iraq. Given the distance between the weapon of injury and the decision-maker, as well as the speed with which nuclear war would reap its destruction, it represents a building in of an unprecedented capacity to injure and the building out of consent, or "the shattering of the ratio of willed authorization to the willed risk by a factor of millions."[30] Nuclear war more closely approximates torture in so far as those experiencing the injury have not offered their consent and because the destruction of civilization would be total.[31]

The military intervention in Iraq in 2003, while conventional in its execution, can similarly be placed at the deconstructive end of the spectrum. In this respect, the powerful images of American soldiers and private contractors humiliating or torturing Iraqi prisoners can be seen as a metaphor for the war itself. The war was originally justified by the threat posed by Saddam's WMD. As it became apparent that no such weapons would be found, the humanitarian intent to liberate the Iraqi people from Saddam Hussein became more dominant in justifying the invasion. The images of torture again transformed the meaning of the war from one in defense of human rights and democracy into a war against Iraqis. The explicit sexual humiliation of prisoners, in contravention to the cultural taboos of Islam, reinforced a widespread perception in the Islamic world, a perception which has since added fuel to the "War on Terrorism," that the war was about the destruction of Islam, rather than the construction of democracy.

It was not only the Iraqi prisoners who did not consent to the injury they suffered from their torturers. The intervention, more than any other in the post–Cold War period, was lacking in consent. It went ahead without the approval of the UN Security Council and divided NATO. Those in Parliament or Congress who did explicitly consent thought they were consenting to a war whose just cause was the elimination of WMD. When it appeared no such weapons were to be found, the just cause became the removal of a tyrant from power, but this was not the act for which consent was granted. While the invasion was said to be a liberation of Iraq, it came to be perceived by Iraqis as an occupation, that is, the imposition of an outside regime without the consent of the population.[32] In its execution, the intervention and the war that followed had neither the consent of the international community, the populations of the intervening states, nor the Iraqi people. The loss of soldiers in a war whose rationale rested on shaky foundations, and the grief this has caused families who question whether their children died in vain, reveals the centrality of consent in the execution of war. Orfund's analysis emphasizes the important role of narratives of democracy and human rights in garnering the consent of populations behind acts of humanitarian intervention. This analysis of Iraq, by contrast, reinforces the importance of consent in a situation where it was largely absent.

The unequivocal moral rejection of war is more problematic than that of torture or of slavery, in so far as war rests on a calculation of the ratio between consent to physical injury and the fight for or surrender of belief. Waging war requires that the physical loss be viewed as an acceptable sacrifice to uphold the principles over which war is being fought. Consent may be withdrawn as a perception emerges that the costs in physical injury outweigh the beliefs that gave rise to war. Both nuclear weapons and aerial bombardment with conventional means create a greater distance between those deciding and executing war or intervention and those who suffer the injury. Terrorists also appropriate the right to engage in acts of violence without the consent of a population. As discussed in Chapter 6, the proliferation of highly sophisticated weapons, and the increasing role of terrorism are potentially related. The widespread proliferation of WMD is a byproduct of the Cold War. These weapons in and of themselves, and nuclear weapons as the most extreme expression, reflect the distancing of war from human participation in it. They move toward the deconstructive end of the spectrum. Interventions that move back toward the constructive and civilizing end, necessarily place more human practices of making meaning and the construction of social artifacts at the core.

Intervention and social construction

A case can be made that the international community as a whole, as distinct from the US Administration of George W. Bush, is moving toward practices of intervention that emphasise the positive social construction of meaning over the more destructive. Mark Duffield points to a change in international policy in the mid-nineties arising from a convergence of development and security discourses.[33] The change, he argues, is one of policy rather than in the nature of the conflict. The reason for the change of policy is the conclusion that underdevelopment is dangerous and is a source of conflict.[34] Unlike the earlier explanation of dependency theorists, who saw underdevelopment as a function of an unjust global system organized around a capitalist world economy, what Duffield refers to as the liberal governance model internalizes the causes of conflict and political instability. Conflict is a result of undeveloped and dysfunctional, war-torn societies.[35] The solution to underdevelopment is to be found in the transformation of individual societies rather than the global system. The policy of international organizations has thus shifted from an emphasis on humanitarian assistance and aid to the process of reconstructing post-conflict societies along liberal lines. This has lead to an increasingly complex array of UN agencies, donor governments, NGOs, and military establishments involved in working together to bring about a change in societies so that problems of the past do not re-emerge. This process rests on an argument that development is impossible without stability and that security is not sustainable without development.

Duffield argues that the nature of power and authority have changed radically. In contrast to Orford, he argues that this new power, expressed in the globalized structures of liberal peace, differs from old imperial structures. Rather than the brute imposition of power or the direct control of territory, we see partnership and participation, which implies a mutual acceptance of shared normative understandings. Inclusion in global structures means buying into the norms that underpin these structures. In sum, the intent is to replace the contest of mutual injury with the positive construction of meaning built on the consent and participation of affected populations.

However, while the practices referred to by Duffield are softer than those of old, what has been referred to as the new imperialism, in the late nineteenth century, was distinguished from earlier practices of Western intervention by precisely the attempt to transform entire societies.[36] Imperialism, as distinct from earlier practices of mercantalism and colonialism, penetrated the interior, of Africa in particular, moving inward from the coastal outposts, building warehouses, railroads, and entire infrastructure in support of Western wealth. Arguably, what has changed is the degree to which the interrelationships are institutionalized, as well as the degree of participation and cooperation by those who are exploited.

With the consolidation of liberal governance, soft power has become as important as hard power. Soft power relies on diplomatic resources, persuasion, the capacity to provide information, and the creative use of selective military tools rather than coercive force.[37] According to Joseph Nye, soft power is "getting others to want what you want."[38] Soft power rests more explicitly on consent than hard power. During the imperial period, societies outside Europe were transformed to enhance the wealth of European states. Present efforts, by contrast, seek to integrate societies into a liberal global order, with inclusion and exclusion defined in terms of compliance with the norms of that order.

Critics have argued that liberal governance is old power in new bottles, and perhaps all the more pernicious because it appears, on the surface, to be about saving lives.[39] In this line of thought the reproblematization of underdevelopment as dangerous is part of a moral rearming on the part of the "West." It locates the cause of conflict in the "Third World" and helps legitimate outside involvement. It is part of a process of global homogenization that, despite its humanitarian claims, is a site of power. In transforming societies to conform with Western constructs, alternative voices are silenced, indigenous practice curtailed and a set of power relations, built on a hierarchy between West and the rest, imposed. The process of self-description by societies involved in conflict is replaced by a re-description based on Western norms.

This analysis seems to come full circle, back to the narrative deconstruction presented by Orford. Consent remains at the level of the yes/no choice, offering few possibilities to question or look from a different angle at the assumed structures of meaning which constitute these choices. The problem, from a critical perspective, is that meaningful dialogue, or conflict transformation, requires real inclusiveness, and not just participation on the basis of rules established by Western elites. It requires a space to raise questions about the rules themselves, and the extent to which they favor some at the expense of others, or the extent to which they assume a particular set of values, excluding others. But the problem goes deeper. As discussed in Chapter 7, conflicts often revolve around fundamental questions of culture, which universal modes of intervention cannot possibly address if they silence the voices of those involved. The potential problem with the liberal governance model as a way of making meaning is that it involves the reconstruction, and thus the deconstruction, of societies on the basis of a blueprint imposed from outside.

In seeking to transform societies, rather than apply band-aids, the liberal governance model would, on one level, seem to be a positive development. If a society has for decades, or even centuries, been destroyed by war, then efforts to move beyond war would seem in principle to be welcomed. The question is whether partnership and cooperation are nice words for the imposition of rules and structures from outside, which ultimately contribute to the siphoning of resources from that society, or whether they involve a more mutual process of dialogue and exchange with communities that facilitates the process of self-description or mutual re-description without resort to war.

It may be inevitable that any act of intervention will combine idealism with powerful interests. The question is whether the framework of dialogue and participation can be made to mean just that, whether by its very nature dialogue opens the way to a transformation of both parties involved, or whether it inevitably devolves into the imposition on the weaker actors of a pre-given set of rules, which they can only accept or reject. To suggest that dialogue is a solution to a century of total war may sound idealist to the extreme. Dialogue is associated with "talking shops" as distinct from action. But this misses the point. In a crisis, for instance, involving genocide, action is essential and talking endlessly can represent little more than procrastination. In a conflict situation, talk has broken down to be replaced by a language and logic of force. However, approached reflexively, talk is a form of life that exists at the civilizing and constructive end of the spectrum. It is an essential part of building a global culture and not merely transferring a Western one. It is an essential ingredient in constructing a culture where democratic debate determines outcomes rather than force. It is at the heart of more deliberate acts of world making.

Michael Moore, in his award-winning film, *Bowling for Columbine*, asked why Canada, which has more guns than the USA, is less violent. His answer was that the Canadians have a different culture of dealing with conflict through negotiation rather than force. Intervention in Western Europe, during the Second World War, was complemented, after its end, not only by massive aid, but the development of the European Community, which was envisioned as an alternative to centuries of conflict, that would make the economies of Western Europe interdependent and created forums where small nations as well as large could have a voice. Global institutions such as the UN similarly create a forum, however imperfect, for dialogue. The peace processes of the 1990s involved a move away from an emphasis on force to the prospect of dialogue. The therapeutic experiments emphasize speaking of past trauma rather than projecting it onto future conflicts.

Talk with words stands in opposition to communication with force. It is the ability to speak and employ language that distinguishes human beings from animals. Language is a necessary condition for developing rules of war, which distinguish this practice from the pure violence of nature. It is the transition from violent force to mutual talk and re-description that has characterized societies moving out of conflict, whether in the West or outside. Critical Theorists, in the Frankfurt tradition, see dialogue as a path toward establishing universal consent. While emphasizing inclusiveness, this approach has been criticized by post-structuralists, who see any kind of universal consent as an expression of totalizing power. Implicit in both is the idea that effective dialogue assumes listening as well as talk. Listening begins with a recognition that "the other is not going to go away."[40] The liberal governance model assumes the primacy of talk, participation, and consent, in so far as it builds on a model of Western democracy. Listening has to be a part of that framework. A critical ethos is a requirement of a more ideal speech situation, where the force of the better argument is to have a chance. An effective global dialogue regarding an alternative way forward requires that hierarchies of power, maintained and reproduced by existing practice, be the object of critical intervention.

The choice

The last section presented a spectrum of practices beginning with deconstruction, represented by torture at one extreme, and social construction, represented by dialogue at the Other. The former is a one-way relationship between torturer and tortured, where injury is imposed, without the consent of the victim, and where the victim's voice, in confession, becomes a vehicle of self-betrayal, in the mock act of consent and participation. This reveals the absence of these in fact and contributes to the substantiation of the torturing regime's power. At the other extreme, dialogue is the opposite of torture, moving away from a practice of communication by force, and the injury this involves, toward language and processes of mutual re-description resulting in the materialization of social constructions that rest on consent and participation. Traditional warfare is located mid-way on this spectrum, sharing both positive and negative attributes. The context of contemporary warfare, as discussed in Chapters 7 and 8, more clearly presents a choice between the two extremes. Different forms of international intervention may push the practice of warfare in one direction along this spectrum or the other.

The two ends are distinguished less by real and ideal than the extent to which human language and choice have meaning and the extent to which agents are empowered to engage in the making of their social world. Indeed, the distinction is one between the absence or presence of a social world and the extent to which the objects in our midst are positive fabrications that enhance comfort or weapons of injury. The choice is between civilization, that is, the possibility of language, agency and choice itself, on the one hand, and on the other hand, the violence of the state of nature, where words lose their meaning and individual pain and insecurity closes the windows and doors to a wider world. The latter approximates the pure violence of nature; the former assumes that power is an inherently social phenomenon that rests on the human ability to act in concert.[41] Power is a property of groups rather than individuals.

Omer Bartov argues that the brute reality of two World Wars and the Holocaust went hand in hand with the search for ideal solutions that were a part of the modern quest to "unmake and remake humanity."[42] The tremendous destructive urge released by this project of remaking was part of a long and incomplete process of coming to terms with the disasters it had produced and is still producing in many parts of the world. In his view:

> ... neither the Final Solution, nor its subsequent analysis, can be understood without taking into account the wider historical framework in which reactions to the first collective trauma of the century, World War I, are of paramount importance. In trying to make sense of that initial instance of mass industrial killing in Europe, some viewed it, during the interwar period, as a mere aberration and hope against hope to return to what Stefan Zweig called the "world of yesterday." Among those who recognised immediately after the war that it embodied the terrifying destructive potential of modern society, some sought shelter in militant pacifism, others rushed to endorse a utopian (and increasingly violent) revolutionary communism, and others still embraced the nihilistic rhetoric of fascism or Nazism, which glorified and aestheticized war, death and destruction. The origins of the Holocaust cannot be grasped without understanding Europe's first attempts to draw lessons from the butchery of 1914–1918.[43]

The experience of total war gave rise to idealist and utopian visions of transcending the brute reality. This book has been an attempt to step outside this distinction between real and ideal, to see how it contributes to the construction of international politics, that is, how it has been the motor of the very brutality which it seeks to transcend. Rather than trying to establish one or the other as the underlying assumption of a theory, I have emphasized two different approaches to reality. In the one, reality is something "out there," to which human beings merely respond, as if propelled by larger forces outside themselves. In the other, choices made in historically specific circumstances contribute to the making and remaking of the world around us. These choices may be made more or less reflexively. They may be confined to the yes/no alternative or raise questions about the world in which yes and no are defined.

The real/ideal distinction is, from this perspective, a part of the problem. In Bartov's argument it is, on the one hand, an outgrowth of the mutual injury of total war, and the accompanying trauma, and, on the other hand, constitutive of future wars to the end of remaking identity on the basis of one ideal construction or another. This book is less about offering a solution than looking at the phenomenon from a different angle. I have sought to unsettle the meaning of categories, and most specifically that of intervention, whose meaning we tend to take for granted. This opens up a space for thinking about intervention not only as a coercive act between two states, whether for self-interested or humanitarian ends, but as a panoply of practices that through their presence shape or alter the experience of war and contribute to the making of the world. It contrasts the attempt to remake through the imposition of voice with processes of mutual re-description.

This is not to suggest an overly optimistic picture or that in willing "peace" we will bring it about. It is rather to unsettle the assumptions that hold us captive in order to see more clearly alternatives that may not have been considered. Wittgenstein said that when we hit rock bottom, explanations cease, this is merely what we do. In saying this, he takes distance from the idea that there is an objective explanation for phenomena in the world; rather over time cultural practice develops in one form rather than another, such that where we are going seems to be determined by where we have been. Instead of causes, we are concerned with the reasons for our action, and the degree to which these reasons are viewed with clarity. Causality, by contrast, assumes an "infinite chain and does not capture the notion of decision or choice."[44] It assumes something hidden which must be uncovered. In this case, things only appear hidden because they are familiar and simple and always before our eyes.[45] What is sought is to render clear the relationships in a tangle, making transparent the foundation of construction. Standing outside this real/ideal distinction and getting an overview, we recognize it as a construction over time, which releases us from captivity to it. Approaching the study of war from the intersection of various social interventions provides a point of departure for a more reflexive approach to analysis and action.

Notes

Preface

1. L. Oppenheim, *International Law*, vol. 1 (London: Longmans, 1905).
2. R. J. Vincent, *Nonintervention and International Order* (Princeton: Princeton University Press, 1974), p. 13.
3. Hedley Bull, ed., *Intervention in World Politics* (Oxford: Clarendon Press, 1984), p. 1.
4. Stanley Hoffmann, "The Problem of Intervention," in Bull, ed., *Intervention in World Politics*, p. 8. Remembering the effects of British and French noninterventions in the Spanish Civil War, Hoffman goes a step further to claim that even non-acts can constitute an intervention.
5. Many scholars have recognized the potential broadness of the term, although in the context of trying to find a more succinct definition. Richard Little pointed out that intervention is an ubiquitous social phenomena. At the individual level, parents intervene in the lives of their children or social workers intervene in the family. Domestically, states intervene in the economy, providing financial support to private industry or introducing wage restraints. Internationally, intervention can range from foreign aid to the use of military force. Richard Little, *Intervention: External Involvement in Civil Wars* (London: Martin Robinson, 1975), p. 1. Vincent similarly recognizes the potential broadness of the concept, pointing to various types of international intervention. In addition to military coercion, economic interventions may take the form of attaching strings to aid or denying contracts to an underdeveloped state. Political interventions may take the form of hostile propaganda disseminated abroad. The support extended to or withheld from a revolutionary struggle, or the recognition or refusal of recognition to an established government may represent moral interventions. Vincent, *Nonintervention and International Order*, pp. 9–10.

1 Cause or Constitution?

1. John G. Stoessinger, *Why Nations Go to War* (Bedford: St Martin's Press, 2001), p. 205. Neta Crawford provides the positive example of the League of the Iroquois who in precolonial North America prevented warfare between the indigenous nations for over 300 years. Neta C. Crawford, "Cooperation Among Iroquois Nations," *International Organization*, 48, 3 (1994).
2. On the debate surrounding Democratic Peace Theory, see: Alan Gilbert, *Must Global Politics Constrain Democracy?: Great-Power Realism, Democratic Peace and Democratic Internationalism* (Princeton, NJ: Princeton University Press, 1999); Michael E. Brown *et al.*, eds, *Debating the Democratic Peace* (Cambridge, MA: MIT Press, 1996); James L. Ray, *Democracy and International Conflict: An Evolution of the Democratic Peace Proposition* (Columbia, SC: University of South

Carolina Press, 1998); Tarak Barkawi and Mark Laffey, eds, *Democracy, Liberalism and War: Rethinking the Democratic Peace Debates* (Boulder, CO: Lynne Rienner, 2001).

3. Adam Roberts and Richard Guelff, *Documents on the Laws of War* (Oxford: Oxford University Press, 2000), p. 3.

4. These two sections clarify the reason for presenting the central contrast, in the introduction and the rest of the book, as that between realism and constructivism.

5. Hobbes, *Leviathan* (New York: Penguin Books, [1651] 1980), part I, ch. 13.

6. Hobbes, *Leviathan*, part I, ch. 13.

7. Hobbes, *Leviathan*, part II, ch. 21.

8. The most famous realist theories of international relations, include the classic by Edward Hallett Carr, *The Twenty Years' Crisis, 1919–1939: An Introduction to the Study of International Relations* (London: Macmillan, 1939), and Hans Morgenthau, *Politics Among Nations*, 6th edn (New York: Knopf, 1948, rev. by K. W. Thompson, 1985). Kenneth Waltz, *Theory of International Politics* (Reading, MA: Addison-Wesley, 1979) is the foremost proponent of neorealism. See: Robert Keohane, ed., *Neorealism and Its Critics* (New York: Columbia University Press, 1986) for a collection of articles that critique his theory.

9. For a discussion of the security dilemma, see: John Herz, "Idealist Internationalism and the Security Dilemma," *World Politics*, 2 (1950), 157; H. Butterfield, *History and Human Relations* (London: Collins, 1951), p. 20; Robert Jervis, "Cooperation under the Security Dilemma," *World Politics*, 30 (1978), 167–214; Nicholas Wheeler and Ken Booth, "The Security Dilemma," in John Baylis and N. J. Rengger, eds, *Dilemmas of World Politics: International Issues in a Changing World* (Oxford: Oxford University Press, 1991), pp. 29–31, and Charles L. Glaser, "The Security Dilemma Revisited," *World Politics*, 50 (1997), 171–201.

10. Hugo Grotius, *De Jure Belli ac Pacis* (Cambridge: Cambridge University Press, [1625] 1853).

11. Scott Burchill, "Liberalism," in Scott Burchill *et al.*, eds, *Theories of International Relations* (Basingstoke: Palgrave, 2001), p. 33. See also: I. Kant, *Kant's Political Writings*, edited by H. Reiss and translated by H. Nisbet (Cambridge: Cambridge University Press, 1970). For an indepth analysis of Republican thought, see: Nicholas Onuf, *The Republican Legacy in International Thought* (Cambridge: Cambridge University Press, 1998).

12. C. B. Macpherson, *Democratic Theory* (Oxford: Oxford University Press, 1972), p. 24.

13. For a discussion of the liberal challenge to realism, see: Charles W. Kegley, ed., *Controversies in International Relations Theory: Realism and the Neoliberal Challenge* (New York: St Martin's, 1995), and D. Baldwin, ed., *Neorealism and Neoliberalism: The Contemporary Debate* (New York: Columbia University Press, 1993).

14. Francis Fukuyama, *The End of History and the Last Man* (London: Free Press, 1992), p. xx.

15. See: Inis Claude, *Power and International Relations* (New York: Random House, 1962); Waltz, *Theory of International Politics*.

16. See: Nicholas Onuf, "Institutions, Intentions and International Relations," *Review of International Studies*, 28 (2002), 211–28. Also, for a survey of liberal

internationalism, see: M. W. Zacher and R. A. Matthew, "Liberal International Theory: Common Threads, Divergent Strands," in Kegley, Jr., ed., *Controversies in International Relations Theory*, pp. 107–50; R. N. Gardner, "The Comeback of Liberal Internationalism," *The Washington Quarterly*, 13, 3 (1990), pp. 23–39; Stanley Hoffmann, "The Crisis of Liberal Internationalism," *Foreign Policy*, 98 (1995), pp. 159–77.

17. The International Society theorists, such as Martin Wight and Hedley Bull, stand at the intersection of these two traditions, emphasizing, on the one hand, the importance of rules in the construction of a "society" of states and, on the other hand, highlighting realist themes of power and order. See: Martin Wight, *International Theory: The Three Traditions* (London: Leicester University Press, 1991), and Hedley Bull, *The Anarchical Society* (London: Macmillan, 1977).

18. Immanuel Kant, for instance, saw peace, rather than war, as the normal state of affairs. War is both unnatural and irrational. Faith in the power of human reason and the capacity of human beings to realize their inner potential relates to a confidence that the stain of war can be removed. Kant, *Kant's Political Writings*.

19. Michael Nicholson, *Causes and Consequences in International Relations: A Conceptual Study* (London: Pinter, 1996), p. 188.

20. Indeed, the word methodology is used in different ways. Many scholars use it interchangeably with method as the particular steps involved in setting up an experiment. I am using it more broadly to refer to the underlying assumptions about the world or the philosophy of social science that underpin either specific theories or methods.

21. For a discussion of the controversy surrounding the meaning of contructivism, see: K. M. Fierke and Knud Erik Jorgensen, *Constructing International Relations: The Next Generation* (Armonk, NY: M. E. Sharpe, 2001).

22. For a discussion of the scientific approach and causation in international relations, see: Nicholson, *Causes and Consequences in International Relations*; K. Knorr and J. N. Rosenau, eds, *Contending Approaches to International Relations* (Princeton: Princeton University Press, 1969). On its relation to other approaches, see: Steve Smith, Ken Booth, and Marysia Zalewski, eds, *International Theory: Positivism and Beyond* (Cambridge: Cambridge University Press, 1996), and David Dessler, "Constructivism within Positivist Social Science," *Review of International Studies*, 25 (1999), 123–37.

23. See: C. W. Kegley, "How Did the Cold War Die? Principles for an Autopsy," *International Studies Review*, 38, 1 (1994), 11–42.

24. Popper's principle of falsification was a critique of the logical positivist emphasis on verification. He rejected the idea that statements can be supported inductively by positive evidence and attempted to articulate a scientific methodology based on deduction. See: Sir Karl Popper, *Conjectures and Refutations* (London: Routledge and Kegan Paul, 1963), pp. 33–9.

25. Robert Keohane and Joseph Nye, *Power and Interdependence: World Politics in Transition* (Boston: Little, Brown, 1977).

26. Fukuyama, *The End of History and the Last Man*, pp. xi–xii and 48.

27. Jack S. Levy, "Domestic Politics and War," *Journal of Interdisciplinary History*, 18 (1988), 662. See also: Bruce Russett, *Grasping the Democratic Peace: Principles for a Post–Cold War World* (Princeton: Princeton University Press, 1993), and Michael W. Doyle, "Kant, Liberal Legacies and Foreign Affairs," *Philosophy and Public Affairs*, 12 (1983), 205–35.

28. On constructivism and related debates, see: Alexander Wendt, "Anarchy is What States Make of It," *International Organization*, 46, 2 (1992); Nicholas Onuf, *World of Our Making: Rules and Rule in Social Theory and International Relations* (Columbia, SC: University of South Carolina Press, 1989); Fierke and Jorgensen, *Constructing International Relation*, and Emmanuel Adler, "Seizing the Middle Ground: Constructivism in World Politics," *European Journal of International Relations*, 3, 3 (1997), 319–63. For a sympathetic critique of constructivism, see: Ronan Palan, "A World of Our Making: An Evaluation of the Constructivist Critique in International Relations," *Review of International Studies*, 26, 4 (2000). Hayward Alker's book, *Rediscoveries and Reformulations: Humanistic Methodologies for International Studies* (Cambridge: Cambridge University Press, 1996), is an exploration of methodological issues compatible with a constructivist approach.

29. This is reflected in the titles of the seminal works on constructivism in IR, for instance, Onuf's *World of our Making* or Wendt's "Anarchy is What States Make of It."

30. See: Thomas Biersteker and Cynthia Weber, eds, *State Sovereignty as Social Construct* (Cambridge: Cambridge University Press, 1996).

31. For more depth on the problem of cause vs. constitution, see: Alexander Wendt, "Constitution and Causation in IR," *Review of International Studies*, 24, Special Issue (1998), 101–18. Hollis and Smith analyze a similar problem in the contrast between explaining and understanding. Martin Hollis and Steve Smith, *Explaining and Understanding International Relations* (Oxford: Clarendon Press, 1991).

32. Kenneth N. Waltz, *Man, the State and War: A Theoretical Analysis* (New York: Columbia University Press, 1954).

33. On the levels of analysis problems, see: J. David Singer, "The Level-of-Analysis Problem in International Relations," in Klaus Knorr and Sydney Verba, eds, *The International System: Theoretical Essays* (Princeton, NJ: Princeton University Press, 1961). Waltz, *Man, the State and War*, refers to images of international relations rather than levels of analysis. For a critique, see William B. Moul, "The Levels of Analysis Problem Revisited," *Canadian Journal of Political Science*, 6 (1973), 494–513.

34. Examples of studies dealing with the causes of war include: Stoessinger, *Why Nations Go to War*; Hidemi Suganami, *On the Causes of War* (Oxford: Clarendon, 1996); Stephen Van Evera, *Causes of War: Power and the Roots of Conflict* (Ithaca, NY: Cornell University Press, 1999); John Burton, *Violence Explained* (Manchester: Manchester University Press, 1997); Franco Fornari, *The Psychoanalysis of War* (New York: Anchor Books, 1974); David A. Welch, *Justice and the Genesis of War* (Cambridge: Cambridge University Press, 1993); Waltz, *Man, the State and War*; Jack Levy, "The Causes of War: A Review of Theories and Evidence," in P. Tetlock *et al.*, eds, *Behavior, Science and Nuclear War* (Oxford: Oxford University Press, 1990), pp. 209–23.

35. See for instance: Stoessinger, *Why Nations Go to War*.

36. The best example of an inductive analysis is David Singer's Correlates of War project. See: David J. Singer and Melvin Small, *Correlates of War Project: International and Civil War Data, 1816–1992* (Ann Arbor, MI: Inter-University Consortium for Political and Social Research, 1994).

37. This argument is made by Waltz, *Theory of International Politics*.

38. Welch, *Justice and the Genesis of War*.

39. See: John Lewis Gaddis, "International Relations Theory and the End of the Cold War," *International Security*, 17, 3 (1992–93), 5–58; C. W. Kegley, "How Did the Cold War Die? Principles for an Autopsy," *International Studies Review* 38, 1 (1994), 11–42; Ellen Schrecker, ed., *Cold War Triumphalism: The Misuse of History after the Fall of Communism* (New York: New Press, 2004), and Richard Ned Lebow and Janice Stein, *We All Lost the Cold War* (Princeton, NJ: Princeton University Press, 1995).
40. Wendt, "Anarchy is What States Make of It."
41. See: Roxanne Doty, "Aporia: A Critical Exploration of the Agent-Structure Problematique in International Relations Theory," *European Journal of International Relations*, 3, 3 (1997), 365–92.
42. See: K. M. Fierke, *Changing Games, Changing Strategies: Critical Investigations in Security* (Manchester: Manchester University Press, 1998).
43. For more depth on the concept of abduction, see: K. M. Fierke, "Logics of Force and Dialogue: The Iraq/UNSCOM Crisis as Social Interaction," *European Journal of International Studies*, 6, 3 (2000), 335–71. This use of abduction builds on the work of Charles Peirce. See: Justus Buchler, ed., *The Philosophy of Peirce: Selected Writings* (London: Routledge and Kegan Paul, 1956); Justus Buchler, *Charles Peirce's Empiricism* (New York: Octagon Books, 1966).
44. Some examples that could be put in the category of constitutive analyses of war, intervention or conflict transformation, include: Julie Mertus, *Kosovo: How Myths and Truths Started a War* (Berkeley, CA: University of California Press, 1999); David Campbell, *Politics before Principle: Sovereignty, Ethics and Narratives of the Gulf War* (Boulder, CO: Lynne Rienner, 1993); Jennifer Milliken and David Sylvan, "Soft Bodies, Hard Targets and Chic Theories: U.S. Bombing Policy in Indochina," *Millennium: Journal of International Studies*, 25, 2 (1996), 321–60, and Fierke, *Changing Games, Changing Strategies*.
45. See: Mertus, *Kosovo*.
46. Campbell, *Politics before Principle*.
47. For a discussion of the distinction between "why necessary" and "how possible" questions, see: Roxanne Lynne Doty, "Foreign Policy as Social Construction: A Post-Positivist Analysis of U.S. Counterinsurgency Policy in the Philippines," *International Studies Quarterly*, 37, 3 (1993), 297–320; Daniel Little, *Varieties of Social Explanation: An Introduction to the Philosophy of Social Science* (Boulder, CO: Westview Press, 1991), and Alexander E. Wendt, "The Agent-Structure Problem in International Relations Theory," *International Organization*, 14, 3 (1987), 335–70.

2   War and Diplomacy

1. Michael Walzer, *Just and Unjust Wars* (New York: Basic Books, 1977), p. 24.
2. Mary Kaldor, *New and Old Wars: Organized Violence in a Global Era* (Oxford: Polity Press, 1999), p. 17.
3. W. E. Hall as quoted in R. J. Vincent, *Nonintervention and International Order* (Princeton: Princeton University Press, 1974), p. 9.
4. Brian White, "Diplomacy," in John Baylis and Steve Smith, eds, *The Globalization of World Politics: An Introduction to International Relations* (Oxford: Oxford University Press, 1997), p. 250.

5. James DerDerian, *On Diplomacy: A Genealogy of Western Estrangement* (Oxford: Blackwell, 1987).
6. White, "Diplomacy," p. 250.
7. Keith Hamilton and Richard Langhorne, *The Practice of Diplomacy: Its Evolution, Theory and Administration* (London: Routledge, 1995), p. 7.
8. White, "Diplomacy," p. 251. Other works on diplomacy include: R. P. Barston, *Modern Diplomacy* (London: Longmans, 1988); G. R. Berridge, *Diplomacy: Theory and Practice* (Hemel Hempstead: Harvester Wheatsheaf, 1995); Hamilton and Longhorne, *The Practice of Diplomacy*; J. L. Richardson, *Crisis Diplomacy: The Great Powers since the Mid-Nineteenth Century* (Cambridge: Cambridge University Press, 1994), and Adam Watson, *Diplomacy: The Dialogue Between States* (London: Methuen, 1982).
9. Hamilton and Langhorne, *The Practice of Diplomacy*, p. 9.
10. Hamilton and Langhorne, *The Practice of Diplomacy*, p. 9.
11. Torbjorn L. Knutsen, *A History of International Relations Theory* (Manchester: Manchester University Press, 1992), p. 11.
12. Knutsen, *A History of International Relations Theory*, p. 14.
13. Augustine, *The City of God* (New York: Fathers of the Church, Inc. [VIII] 1954).
14. Books that discuss these factors include: Knutsen, *A History of International Relations Theory*; Charles Tilly, ed., *The Formation of Nation States in Western Europe* (Princeton, NJ: Princeton University Press, 1975) and *Coercion, Capital and European States, A.D. 990–1992* (Oxford: Blackwell, 1992); N. Elias, *The Civilising Process* (Oxford: Blackwell, 2000), and William McNeill, *The Pursuit of Power: Technology, Armed Force and Society since A.D. 1000* (Chicago: University of Chicago Press, 1982).
15. This emphasis on the individual and historical consciousness influenced thought about relations between the Italian city-states. Niccolo Machiavelli (1469–1527) was one major thinker, whose work continues to influence thought about international relations. His famous book, *The Prince*, was part of a tradition of advice books that prescribed rules for the successful prince. For a discussion of Machiavelli's place in the tradition of princely advice books, see: Quentin Skinner, *The Foundations of Modern Political Thought: Volume One, The Renaissance* (Cambridge: Cambridge University Press, 1978), pp. 113–38. While the old guidebooks emphasized moral questions about how a good Christian prince should act, Machiavelli raised questions about what an individual prince needed to do to be successful. He thus shifted from a focus on ethics and the distinction between just and unjust acts to a focus on rules, self-interest, and calculations about how to realize the latter. Machiavelli was responding to issues of the time. Spain and France were emerging as states on Italy's border. Italy was the place where they competed for power and influence. See: Niccolo Machiavelli, *The Prince and the Discourses* (New York: The Modern Library, 1950). Machiavelli's concern was Italy's position and its survival. He appealed to the Prince to raise an army, unify Italy, and chase foreign invaders from Italian soil.
16. The Catholic Church had become wealthy and corrupt. A monk named Martin Luther (1483–1546) began to question this corruption, and particularly the practice of selling indulgences, which was a way for parishioners to buy their way to heaven. Luther articulated a new theology in which individuals

had a direct relationship to God and didn't need to rely on the churches for interpretation of the Bible. Faith was an individual matter. This gave rise to a conflict between Catholics and Protestants that spread across Europe.

17. See: McNeill, *The Pursuit of Power*.

18. J. Bodin, *Six Books on the Commonwealth* (Oxford: Basil Blackwell, [1576] 1967).

19. This was personified by Louis the XIV of France, who called himself the Sun King. Everything in his palace had suns on it. The symbolism was that Louis was like the sun. Everything revolved around him. The king was absolute. This model was widely copied by other monarchs. For a more in-depth discussion of Louis the XIV, see: David Kaiser, *Politics and War: European Conflict from Philip II to Hitler* (Cambridge, MA: Harvard University Press, 1990), pp. 139–202.

20. For a discussion of mercantilism, see: B. J. Cohen, *The Question of Imperialism* (Basingstoke: Macmillan, 1973).

21. E. de Vatell, *The Law of Nations or the Principles of Natural Law Applied to the Conduct and to the Affairs of Nations and of Sovereigns* (Philadelphia: T & J. W. Johnson, [1758] 1916).

22. DerDerian, *On Diplomacy*.

23. See: Knutsen, *A History of International Theory*, for a more in-depth discussion of these revolutions, pp. 163–70.

24. On the subject of imperialism, see: J. A. Hobson, *Imperialism* (Boston: Unwin Hyman, 1902); V. I. Lenin, *Imperialism: The Highest Form of Capitalism* (New York: International Publishers, 1939); Geoffrey Barraclough, "Industrialism and Imperialism as Catalysts of a New World," pp. 43–64, in *An Introduction to Contemporary History* (New York: Penguin Books, 1967); Cohen, *The Question of Imperialism*; Ronald Robinson and John Gallagher, *Africa and the Victorians: The Official Mind of Imperialism* (Basingstoke: Macmillan, 1961).

25. Each country had a term for their role in helping the people they conquered. The British referred to the White Man's Burden while the French talked of a Civilizing Mission. Both were means to justify exploitative policies. This took place during an era of scientific theories about the inferiority of nonwhites, Slavs, and southern Europeans. They were understood to be incompetent to govern themselves and had to be educated like children. It was the duty of Europeans to civilize them. The aura of science provided legitimacy to these theories, making them appear to be objective truths.

26. In contrast to Rousseau, Hobbes saw war as a natural state of affairs. His book *Leviathan* argued that in the absence of this central authority, there would be perpetual insecurity. Reason provided escape from perpetual war, but in the creation of the commonwealth, the problem of insecurity in the state of nature was transferred to the international level. The book provided a justification for absolute monarchy. Thomas Hobbes, *Leviathan* (New York: Penguin Books, [1651] 1980). During the most destructive phase of the Thirty Years' War on the European continent, Hugo Grotius came to a different conclusion, that states can interact peacefully, according to rules that benefit all. He was commissioned by the Dutch East India Company to deal with a legal dispute with a Portuguese company and in the process established international law as an independent area of learning. He argued that humans could use reason to devise a set of positive laws, that is, laws made by states,

which would reflect this natural order. These laws would guarantee peaceful interactions among sovereign states that would benefit everyone. Once rulers realized that they would benefit from cooperation, they would devise rules and legal institutions to arbitrate conflict between states.

27. Karma Nabulsi, *Traditions of War: Occupation, Resistance and the Law* (Oxford: Oxford University Press, 1999), pp. 183–90. Hugo Grotius, *De Jure Belli ac Pacis* (Cambridge: Cambridge University Press, [1625] 1853).

28. *Columbia Electronic Encyclopedia*, 6th edn (New York: Columbia University Press, 2004). Http://www.infoplease.com/ce6/history/A0813286.html

29. Karma Nabulsi provides an in-depth analysis of the various traditions of war that developed during this process in *Traditions of War: Occupation, Resistance and the Law*, especially chapters 4–6.

30. While states had previously met after wars to sign peace treaties, this represented a commitment to meet in times of peace to prevent war. The Congress system eventually gave rise to the looser format of the Concert of Europe, with the great powers consulting together on problems as they arose. Clive Archer, *International Organizations*, 3rd edn (London: Routledge, 2001), pp. 6–7.

31. Some important debates about the permissible limits of intervention characterized Concert diplomacy in the period 1815–56. For a discussion of these, see: Ian Clark, *The Hierarchy of States: Reform and Resistance in the International Order* (Cambridge: Cambridge University Press, 1989), and Henry Kissinger, *A World Restored: Metternich, Castlereagh and the Problems of Peace 1812–22* (Boston, MA: Houghton Mifflin, 1957).

32. See: C. von Clausewitz, *On War* (Princeton, NJ: Princeton University Press, [1832] 1976).

33. Kaldor, *New and Old Wars*, pp. 22–3.

34. Kaldor, *New and Old Wars*, p. 19.

35. For a discussion of total war, and the influence of Clauswitz' thought on the First and the Second World Wars, see: J. F. C. Fuller, *The Conduct of War 1789–1961* (London: Eyre and Spottiswoode, 1969). See also Michael Handel, "Clausewitz in the Age of Technology," in Michael Handel, ed., *Clauswitz and Modern Strategy* (London: Frank Cass, 1986), pp. 51–92.

36. For a discussion of the distinction between the old and the new diplomacy, see: White, "Diplomacy," and Hamilton and Langhorne, *The Practice of Diplomacy*.

37. Terry Terriff, Stuart Croft, Lucy James, and Patrick M. Morgan, *Security Studies Today* (Oxford: Polity Press, 1999), p. 67.

38. Hamilton and Langhorne, *The Practice of Diplomacy*, pp. 189–92.

39. On the consequences of nuclear winter, see: Lester Grinspoon, ed., *The Long Darkness: Psychological and Moral Perspectives on Nuclear Winter* (New Haven: Yale University Press, 1986); Owen Green *et al.*, *Nuclear Winter* (Oxford: Policy, 1985); Carl Sagan, *A Path Where No Man Thought: Nuclear Winter and its Implications* (New York: Random House, 1995).

40. See: John Lewis Gaddis, "International Relations Theory and the End of the Cold War," *International Security*, 17, 3 (1992–93), 5–58; C. W. Kegley, "How did the Cold War Die? Principles for an Autopsy," *International Studies Review* 38, 1 (1994), 11–42.

41. See, for instance: K. M. Fierke, *Changing Games, Changing Strategies: Critical Investigations in Security* (Manchester: Manchester University Press, 1998); Mary Kaldor, *Global Civil Society: An Answer to War* (Oxford: Polity, 2003);

Matthew Evangelista, *Unarmed Forces: The Transnational Movement to End the Cold War* (Ithaca, NY: Cornell University Press, 1999), and Dan Thomas, *The Helsinki Effect: International Norms, Human Rights and the Demise of Communism* (Princeton: Princeton University Press, 2001).

42. There is a vast literature on globalization. See, for instance: John Baylis and Steve Smith, *The Globalization of World Politics: An Introduction to International Relations*, 2nd edn (Oxford: Oxford University Press, 2001); Jan Aart Scholte, *Globalization: A Critical Introduction* (Basingstoke: Palgrave, 2000); Patrick O'Meara, Howard D. Mehhlinger, and Mathew Krain, eds, *Globalization and the Challenges of the New Century: A Reader* (Bloomington: Indiana University Press, 2000), and David Held and Anthony McGrew, eds, *Global Transformation Reader* (Oxford: Blackwell, 2000).

43. Kaldor, *New and Old Wars*.

44. On ethnicity and war, see also: Hakan Wiberg and Christian P. Scherrer, *Ethnicity and Intra-State Conflict: Types, Causes and Peace Strategies* (Aldershot: Ashgate, 1999); David Turton, ed., *War and Ethnicity: Global Connections and Local Violence* (Rochester, NY: University of Rochester Press, 1997).

45. For a discussion of playing with a weak hand, see: K. M. Fierke, "Besting the West: Russia's Machiavella Strategy," *International Feminist Journal of Politics*, 1, 3 (1999), 403–34.

46. Michael Walzer, *Just and Unjust Wars*, pp. 329–35.

47. Gene Sharpe, *The Politics of Nonviolent Action* (Boston, MA: Porter Sargent Publishers, 1973).

48. Anonymous contributor, "Talk of the Town," *The New Yorker* (April 13, 1981), as quoted in: Lawrence Weschler, *Solidarity: Poland in the Season of its Passion* (New York: Simon and Schuster, 1982), p. 56.

49. For a discussion of acting as if, see: K. M. Fierke "Logics of Force and Dialogue: The Iraq/UNSCOM Crisis as Social Interaction," *European Journal of International Relations*, 6, 3 (2000), 335–71; K. M. Fierke, "Constructing an Ethical Foreign Policy: Analysis and Practice from Below," in Margot Light and Karen E. Smith, eds, *Ethics and Foreign Policy* (Cambridge: Cambridge University Press, 2001).

50. Walzer, *Just and Unjust Wars*, p. 177.

51. Walzer, *Just and Unjust Wars*, p. 180.

52. For further reading on terrorism, see: Walter Laqueur, *The New Terrorism: Fanaticism and the Arms of Mass Destruction* (London: Phoenix Press, 1999); Nadine Gurr and Benjamin Cole, *The New Face of Terrorism: Threats from Weapons of Mass Destruction* (New York: IB Taurus, 2000), and Bruce Berkowitz, *The New Face of War: How War will be Fought in the 21st Century* (New York: Simon and Schuster International, 2003).

53. Bruce Hoffman, "Defining Terrorism," *Inside Terrorism* (New York: Columbia University Press, 1998). For a history of terrorism, see also: Jessica Stern, *The Ultimate Terrorists* (Cambridge, MA: Harvard University Press, 2000).

54. Russell D. Howard and Reid L. Sawyer, *Terrorism and Counterterrorism: Understanding the New Security Environments* (Guildford, CT: McGraw Hill, 2003), p. 13.

55. Some, such as Coker, have argued that we have entered a period of "humane warfare" since the end of the Cold War, with attempts to once again limit warfare. See: Christopher Coker, *Humane Warfare* (London: Routledge, 2001).

3 Moral Interventions

1. For the latter argument, see: Michael N. Barnett, "The UN and Global Security: The Norm is Mightier than the Sword," *Ethics and International Affairs* 9 (1995), 50; John Keegan, *A History of Warfare* (London: Hutchinson, 1993); Martin van Creveld, "The Persian Gulf Crisis of 1990–1991 and the Future of Morally Constrained War," *Parameters*, 22, 2 (1992), 37–8; Neta Crawford, *Argument and Change in World Politics: Ethics, Decolonization and Humanitarian Intervention* (Cambridge: Cambridge University Press, 2002). See: Jutta Weldes, *Constructing the National Interest* (Minneapolis: University of Minnesota Press, 1999), for an argument that the national interest is itself a social construct.
2. Attempts to outlaw war actually began in the 1890s at the Hague Conferences, although without success.
3. Terry Nardin and David R. Mapel, eds, *Traditions of International Ethics* (Cambridge: Cambridge University Press, 1992), p. 2. Nardin and Mapel's edited volume provides an excellent overview of various traditions of international ethics. See also: Charles R. Beitz, Marshall Cohen, Thomas Scanlon and A. John Simmons, eds, *International Ethics* (Princeton, NJ: Princeton University Press, 1985); Ward Thomas, *The Ethics of Destruction* (Ithaca, NY: Cornell University Press, 2001); Stanley Hoffman *et al.*, *The Ethics and Politics of Humanitarian Intervention* (Notre Dame, IN: University of Notre Dame Press, 1996); Jonathan Moore, ed., *Hard Choices: Moral Dilemmas in Humanitarian Intervention* (New York: Rowman and Littlefield, 1999); David Campbell, *Politics before Principle: Sovereignty, Ethics and Narratives of the Gulf War* (Boulder, CO.: Lynne Rienner, 1993); Karen E. Smith and Margot Light, eds, *Ethics and Foreign Policy* (Cambridge: Cambridge University Press, 2001).
4. Thomas Donaldson, "Kant's Global Rationalism," in Nardin and Mapel, *Traditions of International Ethics*, pp. 136–7. See also: Immanuel Kant, *Groundwork of the Metaphysics of Morals* (New York: Liberal Arts Press, 1964), and *Critique of Practical Reason and Other Writings in Moral Philosophy* (Chicago: University of Chicago Press, 1949). For a discussion of agent-centered deontological theory, see: Thomas Nagel, *The View from Nowhere* (New York: Oxford University Press, 1986), pp. 164–85.
5. Consequentialism is one of the basic premises of utilitarianism, a British tradition most often associated Jeremy Bentham, but which also had an influence on Berkeley and Hume, among others. The other basic premise of utilitarianism is that the only thing that is intrinsically good, or good in itself, is well-being.
6. Anthony Ellis, "Utilitarianism and International Ethics," Nardin and Mapel, *Traditions of International Ethics*, p. 158.
7. Max Weber, *Politics as Vocation* (Philadelphia: Fortress Press, 1965).
8. Thucydides, *History of the Peloponnesian War* (New York: Penguin Books, 1954), Book I, para. 76. The realist description of Thucydides is an incomplete reading of the role of morality in the *History*. See: Hayward Alker, *Rediscoveries and Reformulations: Humanistic Methodologies for International Studies* (Cambridge: Cambridge University Press, 1996), pp. 59–60, APRS; Crawford, *Argument and Change*.
9. He contrasted the actions of Cesare Borgia, who created order in his state with ruthlessness, to the Florentines, who, in avoiding cruelty, allowed the

development of such disorder that their acquisition was "destroyed." Niccolo Machiavelli, *The Prince and the Discourses* (New York: The Modern Library, 1950), chs 17, 65.

10. Thomas Hobbes, *Leviathan* (New York: Penguin Books, ([1651] 1980), ch. 13.

11. Another angle is that morality is a private not a public concern, inappropriate for policy. From the perspective of the practitioner theorist, morality should not enter into international discourse, although it is possible for it to do so. The classical perspective denies the possibility of moral considerations in an anarchical system. There are broadly descriptive and prescriptive accounts of the absence of morality in international relations. G. Graham, *Ethics and International Relations* (Oxford: Blackwell, 1997).

12. Reinhold Neibuhr, *Moral Man and Immoral Society: A Study in Ethics and Politics* (New York: Charles Scribner's Sons, 1932), p. 91.

13. Nicholas John Spykman, *America's Strategy in World Politics: The United States and the Balance of Power* (New York: Harcourt, Brace, 1942), p. 18.

14. Henry Kissinger, *American Foreign Policy*, 2nd edn (New York: W. W. Norton, 1977); Hans Morgenthau, *Politics Among Nations*, 6th edn (New York: Knopf, 1948, rev. by K. W. Thompson, 1985).

15. Neta Crawford, "Just War Theory and the U.S. Counterterror War," *Perspectives on Politics*, 1, 1 (2003).

16. See the discussion in Chapter 5.

17. Michael Walzer, *Just and Unjust Wars: A Moral Argument with Historical Illustrations* (New York: Basic Books, 1977).

18. Thomas, *The Ethics of Destruction*, p. 9.

19. Mervyn Frost, "The Ethics of Humanitarian Intervention: Protecting Civilians to Make Democratic Citizenship Possible," in Karen E. Smith and Margot Light, eds, *Ethics and Foreign Policy* (Cambridge: Cambridge University Press, 2001), p. 26.

20. Janice A. Thomson, "Norms in International Relations: A Conceptual Analysis," *International Journal of Group Tensions*, 23 (1993), p. 73.

21. Crawford, *Argument and Change*.

22. Crawford, "Just War Theory and the U.S. Counterterror War," p. 3.

23. Although justness was still linked to a cause ordained by God. For a discussion of the Islamic Just War tradition, see: Terry Nardin, ed., *The Ethics of War and Peace: Religious and Secular Perspectives* (Princeton, NJ: Princeton University Press, 1996).

24. Torbjorn L. Knutsen, *A History of International Relations Theory* (Manchester: Manchester University Press, 1992), p. 18.

25. St Augustine, *City of God* (New York: Image Books, 1958), book 19, chapter 7.

26. Knutsen, *A History of International Relations Theory*, p. 18. See Thomas Aquinas, *Summa Theologiae* (New York: Benzinger Brother, [1266–1273] 1947).

27. The concept of natural law goes back much further to the Greek Stoics. Cicero, the Roman orator and statesman, who had a huge impact on later scholars of international law such as Grotius and Pufendorf was also an especially important promoter of natural law ideas.

28. James Turner Johnson, *Morality and Contemporary Warfare* (New Haven, CT: Yale University Press, 1999), pp. 42–4.

29. Johnson, *Morality and Contemporary Warfare*; Walzer, *Just and Unjust War*.

30. Punishment is no longer considered a just cause.

31. Prior to the Second World War, this meant that non-state actors, for instance, those resisting occupation, had no just cause for war. On the contrary, occupying powers were justified in employing force against persons or groups that had no political superior. This was at the core of Rousseau's critique of the laws of war as formulated by Grotius. For an in-depth discussion of historical debates regarding the relationship between occupation and resistance, see: Karma Nabulsi, "Occupying Armies and Civilian Populations," in *Traditions of War: Occupation, Resistance and the Law* (Oxford: Oxford University Press, 1999), pp. 19–65.

32. A. J. Coates, *The Ethics of War* (Manchester: Manchester University Press, 1997), p. 2.

33. Johnson, *Morality and Contemporary Warfare*, pp. 46–8.

34. Adam Roberts and Richard Guelff, eds, *Documents on the Laws of War* (Oxford: Oxford University Press, 2000), p. 2.

35. For a more detailed discussion of this particular issue, see: Thomas, *The Ethics of Destruction*, pp. 87–146.

36. Geoffrey Best, *War and Law since 1945* (Oxford: Clarendon Press, 1994), p. 45. See also the discussion of the role of peace movements in William C. Olson and A. J. R. Groom, *International Relations Then and Now: Origins and Trends in Interpretation* (London: HarperCollins, 1991).

37. Best, *War and Law since 1945*, p. 40.

38. This work, which was titled "Instructions for the Government of Armies of the United States in the Field," was followed by the Brussels Declaration (1874) regarding the Laws and Customs of War on Land, established by the leading states of Europe.

39. It also arose out of a belief that different more acceptable practices were needed in a battle with southern gentlemen as distinct from Indians and Mexicans. See: Best, *War and Law in 1945*, p. 41.

40. C. I. A. D. Draper, *The Red Cross Conventions* (London, Stevens and Sons Ltd, 1958), p. 2. The numbers appear to be contested since Draper puts the number of deaths at 38,000 while the Encyclopedia of Britannica states the more conservative estimate of 29,000. See http://concise.britannica.com/ebc/article?tocId=9379057

41. For further background on Dunant's experience and the pamphlet, see: Pierre Boissier, *From Solferino to Tsushima: History of the International Committee of the Red Cross* (Geneva: Henry Dunant Institute, 1978).

42. Draper, *The Red Cross Conventions*, p. 3.

43. Best, *War and Law since 1945*, p. 42.

44. Best, *War and Law since 1945*, p. 43.

45. In the wake of the Napoleonic War, as European and American elites formed local peace societies, peace activism became less religious and more secularized and institutionalized. These activists eventually organized Peace Congresses (1843, 1848–53, and 1889–91) in various European cities to promote their work. These congresses laid the groundwork for the formation of the International Peace Bureau (IPB) in 1892. The IPB then organized Universal Peace Congresses (1893, 1894, and 1896) which culminated in the first Hague Conference in 1899. Although it failed to promote general disarmament, the resulting Hague Convention did codify and regulate conduct in war.

46. Roberts notes that the Hague rules of Aerial Bombardment (1923) specifically relate to the indiscriminate bombing of noncombatant civilians in the First World War. Also the Geneva Protocol for the prohibition of the Use in War of Asphyxiating Poisonous and other Gases and of Bacteriological Methods of Warfare (1925) was also directly related to the experience of the First World War. Roberts and Guelff, *Documents on the Laws of War*, pp. 139, 155.
47. Best, *War and Law since 1945*, pp. 50–51.
48. Best, *War and Law since 1945*, p. 52.
49. Michael Burleigh, *The Third Reich: A New History* (Basingstoke: Macmillan, 2001), p. 32.
50. They also had the dual task of making a settlement between the victors and the defeated and of establishing a functioning international system after the disturbance of the First World War.
51. Collective Security was not a new idea but one as old as the Westphalian System. Adam Roberts and Benedict Kingsbury, *United Nations, Divided World: The UN's Role in International Relations*, 2nd edn (Oxford: Clarendon Press, 1993), p. 30.
52. Articles 12–15 took up South African Jan Smut's idea for a breathing space, during which war would be precluded as countries attempted to settle their disputes peacefully and public opinion would thus be allowed time to restrain any rush to war. Clive Archer, *International Organizations* (London: Routledge, 2001), p. 16.
53. See: Olson and Groom, *International Relations Then and Now*.
54. E. H. Carr, "The Beginning of a Science," *The Twenty Years' Crisis: 1919–1939* (London: Papermac, [1939] 1964), p. 34.
55. As late as 1936 the pact was referred to as the most far-reaching agreement ever entered into by sovereign states.
56. Archer, *International Organizations*, p. 20.
57. The conference had as its stated purpose the revision of the 1929 Geneva Convention for the Relief of Wounded and Sick in Armies in the Field, the 1907 Hague Convention for the Adaptation to Maritime Warfare, the Principles of the 1906 Geneva Convention and the 1929 Geneva Convention Relative to the Treatment of Prisoners of War. The conference was also to establish a convention for the Protection of Civilian Persons in time of war. Roberts and Guelff, *Documents on the Laws of War*, p. 195.
58. Best, *War and Law since 1945*, p. 80.
59. Best, *War and Law since 1945*, p. 102.
60. AM RC: 041.IRC, Prelim. Conf. 1946, in Best, *War and Law since 1945*, p. 103.
61. Best, *War and Law since 1945*, p. 106.
62. Roberts and Guelff, *Documents on the Laws of War*, p. 195.
63. Best, *War and Law since 1945*, pp. 130–1. As he states, "The biggest change (in the 1949 conventions) was the legitimization of armed resistance *in occupied territory*. The Hague Regulations' phraseology had implied, and all regular military doctrine had asserted, that once an occupation existed *de facto*, guerrilla resistance to it was impermissible *de jure*. There was indeed room for argument about what constituted an occupation but no benefit of the doubt was allowed to the resister. Now, the question was definitely settled. So long as a properly organized resistance movement could fulfill the military conditions it could lawfully operate in no matter how thoroughly

occupied a territory." The problem, which reflects the continuing controversy surrounding this change, is that the "military conditions" mirror the criteria of the lawful combatant, that is, being commanded by a person responsible for subordinates, having a fixed distinctive sign recognizable at a distance, carrying arms openly, and conducting operations in accordance with the laws and customs of war. One can question whether it is possible in a situation of occupation for resisters or guerillas to follow the rules of lawful combatants. Guerilla war is defined by the absence of some of these criteria, as discussed in Chapter 2.

64. Draper, *The Red Cross Conventions*, p. 9.
65. Draper, *The Red Cross Conventions*, p. 10. See also: Roberts and Guelff, *Documents on the Laws of War*, p. 2.
66. Thomas Weiss and Cindy Collins, *Humanitarian Challenges and Intervention: World Politics and the Dilemmas of Help* (Boulder, CO: Westview Press, 1996), p. 3.
67. For instance, the US government in 1985 labeled the food, telecommunications equipment and uniforms sent to Nicaraguan Contras as "humanitarian." In 1986, the International Court of Justice had an opportunity to define the word in legal terms, in the context of the 1986 ruling in favor of Nicaragua against the USA, but declined to do so. It instead pointed to the principles held by one humanitarian actor, the International Committee of the Red Cross. Weiss and Collins, *Humanitarian Challenges and Intervention*, p. 7.
68. Weiss and Collins, *Humanitarian Challenges and Intervention*.
69. Larry Minear, *The Humanitarian Enterprise: Dilemmas and Discoveries* (Bloomfield, CT: Kumarian Press, 2002), p. 2.
70. As Minear notes, this statistic applies to the past century and not to the past decade alone. Minear, *The Humanitarian Enterprise*, p. 3. It should be noted that this statistic is contested.
71. Emergency and distress relief increased from $766 million in 1989 to 4.365 billion in 1999, OECD/DAC, *Development Cooperation 2000 Report* (Paris), table 2, 180–1.
72. For an analysis of UN powers under chapter VII, see: Danesh Sarooshi, *The United Nations and the Development of Collective Security: The Delegation by the UN Security Council of its Chapter VII Powers* (Oxford: Oxford University Press, 1999).
73. Rights of due process, under the Third and Fourth Geneva Conventions of 1949, deal with prisoners of war and civilians respectively. The defendant has the right to be told—early on and in a language he understands—what he is accused of; to be presumed innocent until proven guilty; to be tried without undue delay; to be heard before an impartial decision-maker; to be tried in a "regularly constituted court" (if the accused is a PoW, it may be a military court); to prepare and present a defense; to present witnesses; not to be required to testify against himself or to confess guilt; to be tried in his presence; to be convicted only of a crime that he himself committed; not to be punished more than once for the same act; to be convicted only for what was a crime at the time of the act in question; to have a sentence no more severe than the law allowed at the time of the act in question; to be told of his rights of appeal and what time limits there are; to appeal and ask for pardon or reprieve; and to have any death sentence stayed until six months after

notification of the protecting power. For a more detailed discussion, see: Gideon Levy, "Due Process," in Roy Gutman and David Rieff, eds, *Crimes of War: What the Public Should Know* (London: W. W. Norton, 1999), pp. 127–30.

74. In 1977 the requirement that these be "distinctively recognizable at a distance was scrapped," due to difficulties raised by the discussion of guerrilla war. Best, *War and Law since 1945*, pp. 335–6.

75. White House, Office of the Press Secretary, "Fact Sheet: Status of Detainees at Guantanamo," February 7, 2002.

76. Adam Roberts, "Counter-Terrorism, Armed Force and the Laws of War," *Survival*, 44, 1 (2002), p. 24. See also: Adam Roberts, "The Laws of War in the War on Terror," *Israeli Yearbook on Human Rights*, vol. 32 (The Hague: Martinus Nijhoff, 2002).

4   Legal Interventions

1. Geoffrey Best, *War and Law since 1945* (Oxford: Clarendon, 2001), p. 5.

2. According to Shaw, the essence of custom, according to Article 38, is that it should constitute "evidence of a general principle accepted as law." Thus, two possible elements constitute custom. First, the actual behavior of states and second the belief that such behavior is law. In 1950 the International Court of Justice declared that a customary rule must be "in accordance with a constant and uniform usage practiced by the states in question." In a later case, the court ruled that it was not necessary that a practice be "in absolutely rigorous conformity" with purported customary rules. The court continued "In order to deduce the existence of customary rules, the Court deems it sufficient that the conduct of states should, in general, be consistent with such rules, and that instances of state conduct inconsistent with a given rule should generally have been treated as breaches of that rule, not as indications of the recognition of a new rule." M. N. Shaw, *Theory of International Law*, 3rd edn (Cambridge: Cambridge University Press, 1991), pp. 62–5.

3. Adam Roberts and Richard Guelff, *Documents on the Laws of War* (Oxford: Oxford University Press, 2000), p. 9.

4. According to Roberts and Guelff, the term "international humanitarian law" focuses attention on the central issue of the treatment of the individual, whether civilian or military. In some views, in addition to being used more or less synonymously with the term "laws of war," international humanitarian law can also encompass relevant parts of the international law of human rights. A possible disadvantage of the term is that it could be thought to exclude some parts of the laws of war (such as the law on neutrality) whose primary purpose is not humanitarian. Indeed, the term "international humanitarian law" could be seen as implying that the laws of war have an exclusively humanitarian purpose, when their evolution has in fact reflected various practical concerns of states and their armed forces on grounds other than those which may be considered humanitarian. Roberts and Guelff, *Documents on the Laws of War*, p. 2.

5. Best, *War and Law since 1945*, p. 247.

6. Hersch Lauterpacht, "General Rules of the Law and Peace," in Elihu Lauterpacht, ed., *International Law: Collected Papers of Hersch Lauterpacht*,

Vol 1 (Cambridge: Cambridge University Press, 1970), p. 279. See also: Richard Bilder, "An Overview of Human Rights Law," in Hurst Hannum, ed., *Guide to International Human Rights Practice* (Philadelphia: University of Pennsylvania Press, 1984), pp. 4–5.

7. Tom J. Farer and Felice Gaer, "The UN and Human Rights: At the End of the Beginning," in Adam Roberts and Benedict Kingsbury, eds, *United Nations, Divided World: The UN's Role in International Relations*, 2nd edn (Oxford: Clarendon Press, 1993), p. 240.

8. William A. Schabas, *Genocide in International Law* (Cambridge: Cambridge University Press, 2000), p. 2.

9. Some international legal scholars resist this division.

10. In this respect, as Adam Roberts notes, "Despite the many on-going attempts to strengthen the means of formal international legal redress against major war crimes committed by a state, there remains a strong case for viewing the laws of war as having thus far consisted principally of a set of internationally approved national professional military standards, backed up by national military and civil legal systems, rather than as a system of international criminal justice." Adam Roberts, "Implementation of the Laws of War in Late 20th Century Conflicts," Part II, *Security Dialogue*, 29 (1998), 265–80.

11. The tension between the duty to respect sovereignty and the duty to protect human rights is not only one of a conflict between specific norms but a problem of which laws have primacy when a conflict arises.

12. Paul Gordon Lauren, *The Evolution of International Human Rights: Visions Seen* (Philadelphia, PA: University of Pennsylvania Press, 1998).

13. Vincent further says that all human rights contain three duties: to avoid depriving, to protect from deprivation of and to aid the deprived. R. J. Vincent, *Human Rights and International Relations* (Cambridge: Cambridge University Press, 1986), pp. 8, 11, 13. For further reading on human rights at the international level, see: Thomas Risse, Stephen Ropp, and Kathryn Sikkink, eds, *The Power of Human Rights: International Norms and Domestic Change* (Cambridge: Cambridge University Press, 1999); Lauren, *The Evolution of International Human Rights*; Tim Dunne and Nicholas Wheeler, *Human Rights in Global Politics* (Cambridge: Cambridge University Press, 1999); Ann Marie Clark, *Diplomacy and Conscience: Amnesty International and Changing Human Rights Norms* (Princeton, NJ: Princeton University Press, 2001); David Forsyth, *Human Rights in International Relations* (Cambridge: Cambridge University Press, 2000); Carla Hesse and Robert Post, *Human Rights in Political Transitions: Gettysburg to Bosnia* (New York: Zone Books, 1999); Tony Evans, ed., *Human Rights Fifty Years On: A Reappraisal* (Manchester: Manchester University Press, 1998).

14. John Locke's *Second Treatise of Government*, published in 1689, was an important theoretical articulation of the argument that human rights are inalienable. John Locke, *Two Treatises of Government* (Cambridge: Cambridge University Press, [1689] 1960).

15. Schabas, *Genocide in International Law*, p. 15f.

16. Maximilien Robespierre, Oeuvres, IX (Paris: Presses universitaires de France, 1952), p. 130.

17. Adam Hochschild, *King Leopold's Ghost* (Boston and New York: Houghton Mifflin, 1998), p. 112.

18. Schabas, *Genocide in International Law*, p. 17.
19. Richard G. Hovannisian, "Etiology and Sequelae of the Armenian Genocide," in George J. Andreopoulous, ed., *Genocide: Conceptual and Historical Dimensions* (Philadelphia: University of Pennsylvania Press, 1994).
20. For a discussion of the specific agreements, see: Shaw, *International Law*, p. 193.
21. William Korey, *NGOs and the Universal Declaration of Human Rights* (Basingstoke: Palgrave, 1998).
22. Korey, *NGOs and the Universal Declaration of Human Rights*, p. 206.
23. Among others here refers to crimes against peace, war crimes, and conspiracy. Prosecution for crimes against humanity and crimes against peace was itself a focus of controversy given these had not been clearly recognized as criminal in existing international law, and, it was argued, thereby violated the legal principle that subjects should not be tried under law enacted ex-post facto. David Cohen, "Beyond Nuremberg: Individual Responsibility for War Crimes," in Carla Hesse and Robert Post, eds, *Human Rights in Political Transitions: Gettysburg to Bosnia* (New York: Zone Books, 1999), p. 56.
24. Schabas, *Genocide in International Law*, p. 10.
25. Schabas, *Genocide in International Law*, p. 154.
26. Although technically Nuremberg only addressed atrocities committed in war, its attempt to address a state's treatment of its own nationals, through inclusion of crimes against humanity, made it a springboard for the development of international human rights law. S. R. Ratner and J. S. Abrams, *Accountability for Human Rights Atrocities in International Law: Beyond the Nuremberg Legacy* (Oxford: Clarendon Press, 1997), p. 6.
27. Shaw, *Theory of International Law*, p. 196.
28. For a more detailed discussion of the various covenants, see: Farer and Gaer, "The UN and Human Rights."
29. For a discussion of the concept, Alan James, *Sovereign Statehood: The Basis of International Society* (London: Allen and Unwin, 1986).
30. As cited in Michael Howard, "The Historical Development of the UN's Role in International Security," in Adam Roberts and Benedict Kingsbury, *United Nations, Divided World*, 2nd edn (Oxford: Clarendon Press, 1993), p. 64.
31. Farer and Gaer, "The UN and Human Rights," pp. 245–6.
32. In any case, the right of states to use force in self-defense can itself be a source of human rights violations. This is particularly problematic in relation to the process of decolonization after the Second World War. The doctrine of *uti possidetis* maintained the colonial boundaries of new states and legitimated the effort of states to resist threats to their territorial integrity. This allowed states to derogate human rights law in times of national emergency, particularly in regard to intra-state groups seeking self-determination.
33. Best, *War and Law since 1945*, p. 68.
34. Schabas, *Genocide in International Law*, p. 7.
35. For a discussion of the distinction between political or civil rights vs. economic or social rights, as they relate to West, East, North, and South, see Vincent, *Human Rights and International Relations*.
36. The Helsinki Final Act was the outcome of the Conference on Security and Cooperation in Europe, held in 1975 between the USA, Canada, the USSR, and the countries of Europe, including Turkey, but not Albania. The document was signed by 35 nations and was at the time considered a milestone

of détente between East and West. Both East and West viewed themselves as winners, with the West focusing on the acknowledgment by the East of the validity of human rights issues and the Eastern bloc countries on the confirmation of existing borders. The civil rights portion of the agreement provided the basis for the work of Human Rights Watch and the monitoring of the application of human right's provisions in the Eastern bloc.

37. The USSR entered into many international agreements on human rights on the basis that only a state obligation was indicated, without a direct link to the individual and that a country might interpret this obligation in light of its own socio-economic system. Shaw, *Theory of International Law*, p. 191.

38. Indeed, as Vincent notes, "a person deprived of subsistence, it has often been said, is insulted rather than dignified by a right to vote." Vincent, *Human Rights and International Relations*, p. 78.

39. The International Court of Justice is an organ of the UN. Its status was adopted in 1945 at the same time as the UN Charter. All UN Member states are parties. The court can issue binding decisions in cases between states that have in some way consented to its jurisdiction. It has no jurisdiction over individuals who wish to pursue claims against their state or regarding individual criminal responsibility. Its function is to act and decide over disputes brought to it by consenting states.

40. This is expressed in Chapter VII, which is the core of the Charter: Action with Respect to Threats to the Peace, Breaches of the Peace and Actions of Aggression. The Security Council was empowered to call on the members of the UN to apply sanctions, short of war, and, in case these failed, to "take such action by air, sea, or land forces as may be necessary to maintain or restore international peace and security."

41. Between 1945 and 1992, the USSR cast 114 vetoes, the USA 69, the UK 30, France 18, and China 3. Roberts and Kingsbury, "The UN's Role in International Society since 1945," in Adam Roberts and Benedict Kingsbury, eds, *United Nations, Divided World: The UN's Role in International Relations*, 2nd edn (Oxford: Clarendon Press, 1993), p. 10.

42. See: Nicholas Wheeler, *Saving Strangers* (Oxford: Oxford University Press, 2000), pp. 100–5, for a discussion of this case. Also: B. Kiernan, *The Pol Pot Regime: Genocide in Cambodia under the Khmer Rouge, 1975–1979* (New Haven, CT: Yale University Press, 1996).

43. By this, I mean interventions that were explicitly defined in humanitarian terms, as distinct from those that were otherwise defined but may have had a humanitarian outcome.

44. Korey, *NGOs and the Universal Declaration of Human Rights*, p. 2; Clark, *Diplomacy and Conscience*.

45. The Security Council avoided the word in its resolution on Rwanda (UN Doc., S/RCS/955), which, as Schabas states, betrayed "the concerns of several members that use of the 'g-word' might have onerous legal consequences in terms of their obligations under the Convention." Eventually, the Security Council set up an ad hoc tribunal with jurisdiction over the Rwandan genocide. Schabas, *Genocide in International Law*, p. 8.

46. Wheeler, *Saving Strangers*, p. 41.

47. Anne Orford, *Reading Humanitarian Intervention: Human Rights and the Use of Force in International Law* (Cambridge: Cambridge University Press, 2003), p. 3.

48. A further concern, which is indirectly relevant here, is whether it is legal to move governments to act if doing so is in conflict with their own interests. As Kuper has argued, in responding to genocide the UN has tended to evade responsibility, protect offending governments, as well as be preoccupied with state interests, and regional alliances. Leo Kuper, *The Prevention of Genocide* (New Haven, CT: Yale University Press, 1986), p. 160. See also: S. Totten, W. Parsons, and I. W. Charney, eds, *Century of Genocide: Eyewitness Accounts and Critical Views* (New York: Garland Publishing, Inc., 1997), p. 22.

49. "The Responsibility to Protect, Report of the International Commission on International and State Sovereignty," 2001, http://www.dfait-maeci.gc.ca/iciss-ciise/report-en.asp

50. For a more lengthy discussion of pluralist and solidarist approaches to intervention, see Wheeler, *Saving Strangers*, pp. 27–51.

51. See: Wheeler, *Saving Strangers*, pp. 31–2.

52. Yves Bergbeider, *Judging War Criminals: The Politics of International Justice* (Basingstoke: Macmillan, 1999), p. 27.

53. Sharf notes two further criticisms of the Nuremberg Trials, that is, that the defendants were prosecuted and punished for crimes that were defined by the victors following a war and that the Nuremberg Tribunal utilized limited procedural rules that didn't adequately protect the rights of the accused. Michael P. Scharf, *Balkan Justice: The Story Behind the First International War Crimes Trial since Nuremberg* (Durham, NC: Carolina Academic Press, 1997), p. 11.

54. Bergbeider, *Judging War Criminals*, p. 27.

55. Bergbeider, *Judging War Criminals*, p. 150.

56. Spyros Economides, "The International Criminal Court," in Karen E. Smith and Margot Light, eds, *Ethics and Foreign Policy* (Cambridge: Cambridge University Press, 2001), p. 114.

57. Samantha King, "Locating Moral Responsibility for War Crimes: The New Justiciability of 'System Criminality' and its Implications for the Development of an International Polity" (PhD Dissertation, University of Plymouth, 2003), p. 152.

58. Scharf, *Balkan Justice*, p. 6.

59. Cited in Coalition for an International Criminal Court, Press Overview, 1998; see Economides, "The International Criminal Court," p. 115.

60. For a discussion of the issues surrounding the International Criminal Court, see: Howard Ball, *Prosecuting War Crimes and Genocide: The Twentieth Century Experience* (Lawrence, KS: University of Kansas, 1999). Other books on war crimes tribunals include: Mark Osiel, *Mass Atrocity, Collective Memory and the Law* (Transaction Publishers, 1997), and Gary Jonathan Bass, *Stay the Hand of Vengeance: The Politics of War Crimes Tribunals* (Princeton: Princeton University Press, 2002).

61. This term was a product of the war in the former Yugoslavia, and was not previously a category of crime. The UN Commission of Experts defined ethnic cleansing in a January 1993 report to the Security Council, as "rendering an area ethnically homogenous by using force or intimidation to remove persons of given groups from the area." For further detail regarding the criminal offences subsumed by this category, see: Roy Gutman and David Reiff,

Crimes of War: What the Public Should Know (New York: W. W. Norton and Company, 1999), p. 136.

62. Economides, "The International Criminal Court," p. 118.
63. Economides, "The International Criminal Court," p. 118.
64. For a more lengthy discussion of these objections, see Ball, *Prosecuting War Crimes and Genocide*, p. 188.
65. Historically the USA has given primacy to national sovereignty, from its refusal to join the League of Nations to the crises over US membership in the UN (1948) and acceptance of the World Court's jurisdiction. Ball, *Prosecuting War Crimes and Genocide*, p. 200.
66. This concern has a longer history, however. As Ball states, it led the USA to reject the call for an international tribunal to try the Kaiser after the First World War to defeat President Wilson's efforts to get the USA to join the League, and to take four decades to ratify the Genocide Convention. Ball, *Prosecuting War Crimes and Genocide*, pp. 203–4.
67. Martha Minow, *Between Vengeance and Forgiveness* (Boston, CA: Beacon Press, 1998); Mark Osiel, *Mass Atrocity, Collective Memory and Law.*

5   Military Interventions

1. G. F. Hudson, "Threats of Force in International Relations," in Herbert Butterfield and Martin Wight, eds, *Diplomatic Investigations: Essays in the Theory of International Politics* (London: Allen and Unwin, 1966), p. 201.
2. Thomas C. Schelling, *Arms and Influence* (New Haven, CT: Yale University Press, 1966), pp. 69–72.
3. See: Schelling, *Arms and Influence.*
4. Peter Viggo Jakobsen, *Western Use of Coercive Diplomacy after the Cold War: A Challenge for Theory and Practice* (St Martin's Press, 1998), p. 14.
5. Jackobsen, *Western Use of Coercive Diplomacy*; Schelling, *Arms and Influence*; Alexander George and William Simons, *The Limits of Coercive Diplomacy*, 2nd edn (Boulder, CO: Westview Press, 1994).
6. Schultz argues that democratic governments are at a disadvantage when it comes to coercive diplomacy. Internal divisions in democratic states make the state's threat of force appear weak, which is a problem that auto-cratic regimes, where opposition is silenced, do not face. Democratic governments are susceptible to criticism from domestic opposition which can raise doubts about their willingness and ability to act. Kenneth Schultz, *Democracy and Coercive Diplomacy* (Cambridge: Cambridge University Press, 2001).
7. For a discussion of Cold War nuclear strategy, see: Lawrence Freedman, *The Evolution of Nuclear Strategy* (Basingstoke: Palgrave, 2003); J. L. Gaddis, *Cold War Statesmen Confront the Bomb: Nuclear Diplomacy since 1945* (Oxford: Oxford University Press, 1999); Thomas Schelling, *Arms and Influence*; J. L. Gaddis, *Strategies of Containment* (Oxford: Oxford University Press, 1982).
8. However, as Graham Allison notes, the Turkish missiles were less than 3 percent of US capability to deliver a nuclear first strike on Soviet territory and were largely useless for a second strike because of their extreme vulnerability.

Graham T. Allison, *Essence of Decision: Explaining the Cuban Missile Crisis* (Boston, CA: Little, Brown, 1971), p. 44.

9. For further background on the Gulf War, see: Ian Johnstone, *Aftermath of the Gulf War: An Assessment of UN Action* (Boulder, CO: Lynne Rienner, 1994); Lawrence Freedman, *The Gulf Conflict, 1990–1991: Diplomacy and War in the New World Order* (London: Faber and Faber, 1993); James Gow, ed., *Iraq, the Gulf Conflict and the World Community* (London: Brassey's, 1993); and Amatzia Baram and Barry Rubin, *Iraq's Road to War* (Basingstoke: Macmillan, 1994).

10. See: James Gow, *Triumph of the Lack of Will: International Diplomacy and the Yugoslav War* (London: Hurst, 1997). For a discussion of why, despite its superior power, the USA found it so difficult in the post–Cold War period to achieve their objectives by threat alone, see: Barry Blechman and Tamara Cofman Wittes, "Defining Moment: The Threat and Use of Force in American Foreign Policy," in Demetrios James Caraley, ed., *The New American Interventionism* (New York: Columbia University Press, 2000).

11. Indeed, as Keohane and Hozgreffe note, humanitarian intervention is a difficult concept because people often don't believe that violence and war can be humanitarian on any grounds. There is an underlying suspicion that only self-interest motivates a country to action. J. Hozgreffe and R. Keohane, "Introduction," *Humanitarian Intervention: Ethical, Legal and Political Dilemmas* (Cambridge: Cambridge University Press, 2003).

12. Adam Roberts, *Humanitarian Action in War*, Adelphi Paper, 305 (Oxford: Oxford University Press, 1997), p. 19.

13. Gow, *Triumph of the Lack of Will*, p. 127.

14. Stanley Hoffman *et al.*, *The Ethics and Politics of Humanitarian Intervention* (Notre Dame, IN: University of Notre Dame Press, 1996), p. 7.

15. Boutros-Boutros Ghali, *Agenda for Peace*, June 1992. The Agenda put forward the idea that the UN Security Council make forces available on a permanent basis, in accord with Article 43.

16. For a more in-depth discussion of problems related to the overloading of the UN after the Cold War, see: Adam Roberts, "The United Nations and International Security," in Michael E. Brown, ed., *Ethnic Conflict and International Security* (Princeton: Princeton University Press, 1993), pp. 207–35, and Thomas G. Weiss, "Introduction," *Military–Civilian Interactions: Intervening in Humanitarian Crises* (Oxford: Rowman and Littlefield, 1999).

17. See: Brian Urquhart, "The UN and International Security after the Cold War," in Adam Roberts and Benedict Kingsbury, *United Nations, Divided World*, 2nd edn (Oxford: Clarendon Press, 1993), p. 82.

18. www.preventgenocide.org/prevent/UNdocs/KofiAnnansActionPlanto PreventGenocide7April2004.htm

19. Urquhart, "The UN and International Security after the Cold War," p. 82.

20. See: Nicholas Wheeler, *Saving Strangers: Humanitarian Intervention in International Society* (Oxford: Oxford University Press, 2000); O'Hanlan and O'Hanlan, who have defined more explicit military criteria, state that intervention should "mitigate suffering where that can be done with high confidence, modest cost and limited duration but should avoid open-ended commitments and high casualties." Michele O'Hanlon and Michael O'Hanlon, *Saving Lives with Force: Military Criteria for Humanitarian Intervention* (Washington, DC: Brookings Institute, 1997), p. 3.

21. For further reading on the Somalia case, see: John L. Hirsh and Robert B. Oakley, *Somalia and Operation Restore Hope: Reflections on Peacemaking and Peacekeeping* (Washington, DC: US Institute for Peace, 1995); John Prendergast, *Crisis Response: Humanitarian Band-Aids in Sudan and Somalia* (London: Pluto Press, 1997); James Mayall, ed., *The New Interventionism, 1991–1994: UN Experience in Cambodia, the Former Yugoslavia and Somalia* (Cambridge: Cambridge University Press, 1996); Walter Clarke and Jeffrey Herbst, eds, *Learning from Somalia: Lessons of Armed Humanitarian Intervention* (Boulder, CO: Westview Press, 1997); Thomas H. Henriksen, *Clinton's Foreign Policy in Somalia, Bosnia, Haiti and North Korea* (Stanford, CA: Hoover Institution Press, 1996); Lester H. Brune, *The United States and Post–Cold War Interventions: Bush and Clinton in Somalia, Haiti and Bosnia, 1992–1998* (Claremont, CA: Regina Books, 1999).

22. "Ambush in Mogadishu, Chronology: The US/UN in Somalia," *Frontline,* http://www.pbs.org/wgbh/pages/frontline/shows/ambush/etc/cron.html

23. For further reading on the Kosovo case, see: Martin Smit and Paul Latawski, *The Kosovo Crisis: And the Evolution of a Post–Cold War European Security* (Manchester: Manchester University Press, 2003); Tim Judah, *Kosovo: War and Revenge* (Hartford, CT: Yale University Press, 2000); Stephen D. Wrage, ed., *Immaculate Warfare: Participants Reflect on the Air Campaigns over Kosovo, Afghanistan and Iraq* (New York: Praeger, 2003); Wesley Clark, *Waging Modern War: Bosnia, Kosovo and the Future of Combat* (New York: Public Affairs Press, 2002); Independent International Commission on Kosovo, *The Kosovo Report: Conflict, International Response, Lessons Learned* (Oxford: Oxford University Press, 2000); Andrew J. Bacevich and Eliot A. Cohen, eds, *War over Kosovo: Politics and Strategy in a Global Age* (New York: Columbia University Press, 2001), and Robert C. DiPrizio, *Armed Humanitarians: US Interventions from Northern Iraq to Kosovo* (Baltimore, MD: Johns Hopkins University Press, 2002).

24. Howard Clark, *Civil Resistance in Kosovo* (London: Pluto Press, 2000), pp. 115–17.

25. Although it has been argued that if Kosovo had been on the table in Dayton it would not have been possible to secure the agreement. See Richard Holbrooke, *To End a War* (New York: The Modern Library, 1998).

26. Wheeler, *Saving Strangers,* p. 258.

27. Wheeler, *Saving Strangers,* p. 269.

28. Michael Malvesti, "Explaining the United States' Decision to Strike Back at Terrorists," *Terrorism and Violence,* 13, 2 (2001).

29. Richard K. Betts, "The Soft Underbelly of American Primacy Tactical Advantages of Terror," *Political Science Quarterly* (2002).

30. Richard H. Schultz and Andreas Vogt, "The Real Intelligence Failure on 9/11 and the Case for a Doctrine of Striking First," in Russell D. Howard and Reid L. Sawyer, *Terrorism and Counterterrorism: Understanding the New Security Environment* (Guildford, CT: McGraw Hill, 2003), p. 377.

31. These trends were based on a declassified summary, *Patterns of Global Terrorism,* released annually by the US State Department's Office of the Coordinator for Counterterrorism, as well as intelligence community testimony at congressional hearings, studies, and reports by contractors that support the intelligence community such as RAND, and publications by

intelligence officers such as the former deputy chief of CIA's Counterterrorism Center, Paul Pillar, as summarized in Schultz and Vogt, "The Real Intelligence Failure on 9/11 and the Case for a Doctrine of Striking First," p. 369.

32. See: Bruce Berkowitz, *The New Face of War: How War will be Fought in the 21st Century* (New York: Simon and Schuster International, 2003).

33. Schultz and Vogt, "The Real Intelligence Failure on 9/11," p. 372.

34. Foreign Policy Association, "In Focus—Al Qaeda," available from http://www.fpa.org/newsletter_info2478/newsletter_info.htm; accessed May 8, 2002; Peter L. Bergen, *Holy War, Inc.: Inside the Secret World of Osama Bin Laden* (New York: The Free Press, 2001), p. 222.

35. Schultz and Vogt, "The Real Intelligence Failure of 9/11," p. 374.

36. Remarks by President Bush at 2002 Graduation Exercise of the United States Military Academy; http://www.whithouse.gov/news/releases/2002/06/200206013.html

37. National Security Strategy, September 2002, http://www.whitehouse.gov/nsc/nss5.html

38. National Security Strategy, 2002, p. 2, para. 2.

39. National Security Strategy, 2002, p. 6, para. 5.

40. Neil C. Livingstone, "Proactive Responses to Terrorism: Reprisals, Preemption and Retribution," in Charles W. Kegley, Jr., ed., *International Terrorism: Characteristics, Causes, Controls* (Basingstoke: Macmillan, 1990), pp. 219–27.

41. Livingstone, "Proactive Responses to Terrorism," p. 219.

42. Livingstone, "Proactive Responses to Terrorism," p. 224.

43. Neta Crawford, "Just War Theory and the U.S. Counterterror War," *Perspectives on Politics*, 1, 1 (2003).

44. Donald Rumsfeld, Department of Defense news briefing, with General Richard Myers, October 22, 2001. Available at:www.defenselink.mil/news/Oct2001/t10222001_t1022sd.html

45. Crawford, "Just War Theory and the U.S. Counterterror War," p. 11.

46. Jean Beth Elshtain, *Just War Against Terror: Ethics and the Burden of American Power in a Violent World* (New York: Basic Books, 2003), and Crawford, "Just War Theory and the U.S. Counterterror War."

47. Further, some have claimed that the US Central Intelligence Agency was under intensive political pressure to provide information that would back the administration's case. Julian Borger, "Senate Fingers CIA for 'sloppy' analysis of Iraq: Battle over who is to Blame for Misleading Public," *The Guardian*, October 25, 2003, 20.

6 Economic Interventions

1. Meghan L. O'Sullivan, *Shrewd Sanctions: Economic Statecraft in an Age of Global Terrorism* (Washington, DC: The Brookings Institution, 2003), p. 18.

2. Michael Brzoska and Frederic Pearson, *Arms and Warfare: Escalation, De-escalation and Negotiations* (New York: Columbia University Press, 1994); Frederic Pearson, Michael Brzoska, and Christopher Crantz, "The Effect of Arms Transfers on Wars and Peace Negotiations," in Stockholm International Peace Research Institute, *SIPRI Yearbook 1992: Armaments and Disarmament* (Oxford: Oxford University Press, 1992).

3. Cassady B. Craft, *Weapons for Peace, Weapons for War* (London: Routledge, 1999), p. 1.
4. Miles Wolpin, *America Insecure: Arms Transfers, Global Interventionism and the Erosion of National Security* (London: McFarland and Company, 1991); William Hartung, *And Weapons for All: How America's Multibillion Dollar Arms Trade Warps our Foreign Policy and Subverts Democracy at Home* (New York: Harper and Collins, 1994); Craft, *Weapons for Peace*, p. 153.
5. Wolpin, *America Insecure*; Hartung, *And Weapons for All*; David Louscher and Michael Salamone, "The Imperative for a New Look at Arms Sales," in David Louscher and Michael Salamone, eds, *Marketing Security Assistance: New Perspectives on Arms Sales* (Lexington, MA: Lexington Books, 1987).
6. Lora Lumpe, ed., *Running Guns: The Global Black Market in Small Arms* (London: Zed Books, 2000), p. 3. See also: Graduate Institute of International Studies, *Small Arms Survey 2001: Profiling the Problem* (Oxford: Oxford University Press, 2001); John Sislen and Frederic S. Pearson, *Arms and Ethnic Conflict* (Lanham, MD: Rowman and Littlefield Publishers, 2001); and Mary Kaldor, *New and Old Wars*, chapter 5, "The Globalised War Economy."
7. Mark Phythian, *The Politics of British Arms Sales since 1964* (Manchester: Manchester University Press, 2000), p. 3.
8. Pythian, *The Politics of British Arms Sales*, p. 10.
9. Pythian, *The Politics of British Arms Sales*, p. 21.
10. Lumpe, *Running Guns*, p. 3.
11. Geoff Simons, *Imposing Economic Sanctions* (London: Pluto Press, 1999).
12. Stephan Chan and A. Cooper Drury, ed., *Sanctions as Economic Statecart: Theory and Practice* (Basingstoke: Palgrave, 2000), p. 2. For further reading on economic sanctions, see: Gary Clyde Hufbauer, Jeffrey J. Schott, and Kimberly Ann Elliot, *Reforming Economic Sanctions* (Washington, DC: The Institute for International Economics, 2000); Richard N. Haass and Meghan L. O'Sullivan, eds, *Honey and Vinegar: Incentives, Sanctions and Foreign Policy* (Washington, DC: Brookings Institution Press, 2001); Sarah Graham Brown, *Sanctioning Saddam* (New York: IB Taurus, 1999); Richard Haas, *Economic Sanctions and American Diplomacy* (New York: Council on Foreign Relations Press, 1998); Thomas Weiss *et al.*, eds, *Political Gain and Civilian Pain: Humanitarian Impacts of Economic Sanctions* (Lanham, MD: Rowman and Littlefield, 1997).
13. The actual quote was "We shut their doors and lock them in ... they are absolutely boycotted by the rest of mankind. I do not think that after that remedy it will be necessary to do any fighting at all." As quoted in David Hunt Miller, *Drafting of the Covenant* (New York: GP Putnam's Sons, 1928), p. 570.
14. David Cortright and George Lopez, eds, *Smart Sanctions: Targeting Economic Statecraft* (Lanham, MD: Rowman and Littlefield, 2002), p. 5.
15. O'Sullivan, *Shrewd Sanctions*, p. 15.
16. For further reading on economic sanctions against Rhodesia, see: David M. Row, *Manipulating the Market: Understanding Economic Sanctions, Institutional Change and the Political Unity of White Rhodesia* (Ann Arbor, MI: University of Michigan Press, 2001); Leonard T. Kapunga, *United Nations and Economic Sanctions against Rhodesia* (Lanham, MD: Lexington Books, 1973); Donald L. Losman, *International Economic Sanctions: The Cases of Cuba, Israel and Rhodesia* (Albuqerque, NM: University of New Mexico Press, 1979); and

Robert Baldwin Sutcliffe, *Sanctions against Rhodesia: The Economic Background* (London: Africa Bureau, 1966).

17. Simons, *Imposing Economic Sanctions*, p. 84.
18. "Applicability of International Law Standards to UN Economic Sanctions Programmes," *European Journal of International Law*, http://www.ejil.org/journal/Vol9,No1/art4-03.html
19. Margaret P. Doxey, *International Sanctions in Contemporary Perspective* (London: Macmillan, 1987), p. 46.
20. Gary Clyde Hufbauer, Jeffrey J. Schott, and Kimberly Ann Elliott, *Economic Sanctions Reconsidered, Volume II, Supplemental Case Histories* (Washington, DC: Institute for Economic Sanctions, 1990), p. 292.
21. For further reading on economic sanctions against South Africa, see: Richard Moorsom, *Scope for Sanctions: Economic Measures against South Africa* (London: Catholic Institute for International Relations, 1986); Mark Orken, *Sanctions against Apartheid* (Basingstoke: Macmillan, 1990); Audie Klotz *et al.*, eds, *How Sanctions Work: Lessons from South Africa* (New York: St Martin's Press, 1999); Robert R. Edgar, *Sanctioning Apartheid* (Trenton, NJ: Africa World Press, 1990); Joe Hanlon, ed., *South Africa: The Sanctions Report* (London: Commonwealth Secretariat in Association with James Currey, 1990), and George W. Shepherd, *Effective Sanctions on South Africa: The Cutting Edge of Economic Intervention* (New York: Greenwood Press, 1991).
22. Simons, *Imposing Economic Sanctions*, p. 80.
23. For a discussion of the disinvestment campaign, see: Jennifer Davis, "Sanctions and Apartheid: The Economic Challenge to Discrimination," in David Cortright and George A. Lopez, *Economic Sanctions: Panacea or Peacebuilding in a Post–Cold War World?* (Boulder, CO: Westview Press, 1995).
24. *Washington Post*, July 23, 1986, A14.
25. http://www.australianpolitics.com/executive/howard/pre-2002/991112 howard-mandela.shtml. See also: Nelson Mandela's Statement to the UN, New York, September 24, 1993.
26. O'Sullivan, *Shrewd Sanctions*, p. 14.
27. The political movements include the Khmer Rouge in Cambodia, UNITA in Angola, the Revolutionary United Front in Sierra Leone, and the Taliban in Afghanistan. See: David Cortright and George A. Lopez, *The Sanctions Decade: Assessing UN Strategies in the 1990s* (Boulder, CO: Lynne Rienner, 2000).
28. O'Sullivan, *Shrewd Sanctions*, p. 17.
29. For a discussion of the broader context of sanctions against Serbia, see: S. Licht, "The Use of Sanctions in the Former Yugoslavia: Can they Assist in Conflict Resolution?" in Cortright and Lopez, *Economic Sanctions*; J. Stedman, "The Former Yugoslavia," in Richard Haass, ed., *Economic Sanctions and American Diplomacy* (New York: Council on Foreign Relations Press, 1998); and S. L. Woodward, "The Use of Sanctions in Former Yugoslavia: Misunderstanding Political Realities," in Cortright and Lopez, eds, *Economic Sanctions*.
30. Simons, *Imposing Economic Sanctions*, p. 102.
31. For further readings on economic sanctions against Haiti, see: Elizabeth D. Gibbons, *Sanctions in Haiti: Human Rights and Democracy under Assault* (New York: Greenwood Press, 1999); Weiss, Cortright, Lopez and Minear, *Political Gain and Civilian Pain*; Cortright and Lopez, eds., *Economic Sanctions*.

32. "Applicability of International Law Standards to UN Economic Sanctions Programmes," *European Journal of International Law*, http://www.ejil.org/journal/Vol9,No1/art4-03.html
33. "Sanctions: Children Hard Hit in Haiti," *Children In War: The State of the World's Children 1996*, http://www.unicef.org/sowc96/dsanctions.htm
34. Simons, *Imposing Economic Sanctions*, p. 107.
35. For further reading on economic sanctions against Iraq, see: R. Thomas Naylor, *Economic Warfare: Sanctions, Embargo Busing and their Human Cost* (Boston, MA: Northeastern University Press, 2001); Tim Niblock, *Pariah States and Sanctions in the Middle East: Iraq, Libya and Sudan* (Boulder, CO: Lynne Rienner, 2002); Abbas Alnasrawi, *Iraq's Burdens: Oil, Sanctions and Underdevelopment* (New York: Greenwood Press, 2002); Simons, *Imposing Economic Sanctions*; Anthony Arnove, *Iraq Under Siege*; and Brown, *Sanctioning Saddam*.
36. Many accusations, particularly from the USA and the UK, have been leveled at Saddam Hussein in this regard. For instance, he has been accused of building presidential palaces, a stadium, and a lavish safari park while his people were suffering. The US government claimed that, under the Oil for Food program, he failed to order adequate baby foods, to order pulses—a main ingredient of Iraqi diets—and even of exporting food. UK Minister of Defense George Robertson accused Iraq of preventing medical supplies in Iraqi warehouses from reaching the population. See, respectively: Patrick Laws, "A Look at Sanctioning Iraq: The Numbers Don't Lie, Saddam Does," *The Washington Post*, February 27, 2000; US Department of State, "Saddam Hussein's Iraq," September 13, 1999, http://usinfo.state.govregional/neairaqiraq99.htm and George Robertson, "Bombing Iraq, Letter," *The Times*, (*London*), March 6, 1999. It has been argued that many of these allegations proved to be unfounded or were based on misrepresentation and part of a campaign of vilification. See, for instance, Global Policy Forum "Iraq Sanctions: Humanitarian Implications and Options for the Future," August 6, 2002, http://www.globalpolicy.org/securitysanction/iraq1/ 2002/paper.htm
37. Simons, *Imposing Economic Sanctions*, p. 173.
38. Peter Pellett, "Sanctions, Food, Nutrition and Health in Iraq," in A. Arnove, *Iraq Under Seige* (London: Pluto Press, 2000), p. 151.
39. Simons, *Imposing Economic Sanctions*, p. 175.
40. G. Capaccio, "Sanctions: Killing a Country and a People," in A. Arnove, *Iraq Under Seige*, p. 141.
41. For a discussion of the effects of sanctions on Iraqi children, see: G. Simons, *The Scourging of Iraq: Sanctions, Law and Natural Justice*, 2nd edn (Basingstoke: Macmillan, 1998), pp. 127–8.
42. Madeleine Albright, interviewed by Lesley Stahl, *60 Minutes*, CBS, May 12, 1996.
43. Cortright and Lopez, *Smart Sanctions*, p. ix.
44. For an overview of issues raised by the Ethical Foreign Policy, see: Karen E. Smith and Margot Light, eds, *Ethics and Foreign Policy* (Cambridge: Cambridge University Press, 2001).
45. Foreign and Commonwealth Office, "Speech by the Foreign Secretary: Human Rights into a New Century," *Daily Bulletin*, July 17, 1997.
46. Pythian, *The Politics of British Arms Sales*, pp. 5–7.
47. United Nations Mission in East Timor Press Release, September 9, 1999.
48. Foreign and Commonwealth Office News, September 7, 1999.

49. Tim Dunne and Nicholas J. Wheeler, "Blair's Britain: A Force for Good in the World," in Smith and Light, *Ethics and Foreign Policy*, p. 175.
50. Robin Cook, "Britain is Ready to Pursue Justice in East Timor," *The Observer*, September 19, 1999.
51. Dunne and Wheeler, "Blair's Britain," p. 175.

7 Cultural Interventions

1. On the debate between communitarian and cosmopolitan positions, see: Chris Brown, "Cosmopolitan and Communitarian International Relations Theory," *International Relations Theory: New Normative Approaches* (New York: Harvester/Wheatsheaf, 1992), pp. 21–106; Molly Cohrane, *Normative Theory in International Relations: A Pragmatic Approach*, chapters 1 and 2 (Cambridge: Cambridge University Press, 1999); Charles Bietz, "Cosmopolitan Ideals and National Sentiment," *Journal of Philosophy*, 80 (1983), 591–600; Molly Cochrane, "Cosmopolitanism and Communitarianism, in a Post–Cold War World," in J. Macmillan and A. Linklater, eds, *Boundaries in Questions: New Directions in International Relations* (London: Pinter, 1995), pp. 40–53; D. Morice, "The Liberal-Communitarian Debate in Contemporary Political Philosophy and its Significance for International Relations," *Review of International Studies*, 26 (2000), 233–51; C. F. Delaney, ed., *The Liberalism-Communitarianism Debate* (Boston, MA: Rowman and Littlefield, 1994); E. Frazer, *The Problems of Communitarian Politics: Unity and Conflict* (Oxford: Oxford University Press, 1999); and D. Rasmussen, ed., *Universalism vs. Communitarianism: Continuing Debates in Ethics* (Boston, MA: MIT Press, 1995).
2. Richard Shapcott, *Justice, Community and Dialogue in International Relations* (Cambridge: Cambridge University Press, 2001), pp. 11–12.
3. Valerie M. Hudson, "Culture and Foreign Policy: Developing a Research Agenda," *Culture and Foreign Policy* (Boulder, CO: Lynne Rienner, 1997), p. 2.
4. For a discussion of thick and thin culture, see: Michael Walzer, *Thick and Thin: Moral Argument at Home and Abroad* (Notre Dame, IN: University of Notre Dame Press, 1994).
5. The phrase has been attributed to the English diplomat, Henry Wotton (1568–1639).
6. John Vincent, *Human Rights and International Relations* (Cambridge: Cambridge University Press, 1986), pp. 121–2.
7. Adam Watson, *Diplomacy: The Dialogue Between States* (London: Methuen, 1982).
8. For a discussion of threats as promises, see: K. M. Fierke and Michael Nicholson, "Divided by a Common Language: Formal and Constructivist Approaches to Games," *Global Society* (2000).
9. Herbert Butterfield, "The New Diplomacy and Historical Diplomacy," in Herbert Butterfield and Martin Wight, eds, *Diplomatic Investigations: Essays in the Theory of International Politics* (London: Allen and Unwin, 1966), pp. 187–8.
10. Butterfield, "The New Diplomacy and Historical Diplomacy," p. 189.
11. See, in particular: Andrew Linklater, *The Transformation of Political Community: Ethical Foundations of the Post-Westphalian Era* (Cambridge: Polity Press, 1997).

12. Shapcott, *Justice, Community and Dialogue in International Relations*, p. 84.
13. Andrew Linklater, "Citizenship and Sovereignty in the Post-Westphalian State," *European Journal of International Relations*, 2, 1 (1996), 86.
14. Shapcott, *Justice, Community and Dialogue in International Relations*, p. 83.
15. Linklater, "Citizenship and Sovereignty," 85–7.
16. Shapcott, *Justice, Community and Dialogue in International Relations*, p. 78.
17. Richard Ashley and R. B. J. Walker, "Reading Dissidence/Writing the Discipline: Crisis and the Question of Sovereignty in International Studies," *International Studies Quarterly*, 34 (1990), 391.
18. Ashley and Walker, "Reading Dissidence/Writing the Discipline," 395.
19. Ashley and Walker, "Reading Dissidence/Writing the Discipline," as quoted in Shapcott, *Justice, Community and Dialogue in International Relations*, p. 71.
20. This argument is made by David Campbell in particular. See: David Campbell, "The Deterritorialisation of Responsibility: Levinas, Derrida and Ethics after the End of Philosophy," *Alternatives* 19 (1994), 455–85; David Campbell, *National Deconstruction: Violence, Identity and Justice in Bosnia* (Minneapolis, MN: University of Minnesota Press, 1998).
21. Shapcott, *Justice, Community and Dialogue in International Relations*, p. 78.
22. For an analysis of this question, see: K. M. Fierke, "Logics of Dialogue and Force: The Iraq/UNSCOM Crisis as Social Interaction," *European Journal of International Relations*, 6, 3 (2000), 335–71.
23. Philip M. Taylor, *Munitions of the Mind: A History of Propaganda from the Ancient World to the Present Day* (Manchester: Manchester University Press, 1995), p. 15.
24. Taylor, *Munitions of the Mind*, p. 3.
25. Adolph Hitler, *Mein Kampf* (London: Pimlico, [1948] 1992).
26. Taylor, *Munitions of the Mind*, p. 4.
27. Taylor, *Munitions of the Mind*, p. 11.
28. Benedict Anderson, *Imagined Communities: Reflections on the Origin and Spread of Nationalism* (London: Verso, 1983).
29. On nationalism and culture, see: Ernest Gellner, *Nations and Nationalism* (Oxford: Basil Blackwell, 1983); and E. J. Hobsbawm, *Nations and Nationalism since 1780: Programme, Myth, Reality* (Cambridge: Cambridge University Press, 1992).
30. Alternatively, some have argued that bombardment with media images of mass suffering can either lead to compassion fatigue or to trivialization as it comes to be viewed as an unreal form of entertainment or voyeurism. See, for instance: Susan Moeller, *Compassion Fatigue: How the Media Sells Disease, Famine, War and Death* (London: Routledge, 1999).
31. See: Mitchell Stevens, ed., *Covering Catastrophe: How Broadcast Journals Covered September 11* (New York: Bonus Books, 2002).
32. For further reading on the role of the media in conflict areas, see: Larry Minear *et al.*, *The New Media: Civil War and Humanitarian Action* (Boulder, CO: Lynne Rienner, 1996); Robert I. Rothberg *et al.*, *From Massacres to Genocide: The Media, Public Policy and Humanitarian Crises* (Washington, DC: Brookings Institute, 1996); Susan Carruthers, *The Media at War: Communication and Conflict in the 20th Century* (Basingstoke: Palgrave, 1999); Bradley Greenberg, ed., *Communication and Terrorism: Public and Media Responses to 9/11* (Cresskill, NJ: Hampton Press, 2002); Danny Schechter, *Media Wars: News at*

a Time of Terror (Lanham, MD: Rowman and Littlefield, 2003); Moeller, *Compassion Fatigue*; Tim Allen and Jean Seaton, eds, *The Media in Conflict* (London: Zed Books, 1999); Philip M. Taylor, *War and Media: Propaganda and Persuasion in the Gulf War* (Manchester: Manchester University Press, 1998); and David D. Perlmutter, *Photojournalism and Foreign Policy: Icons of Outrage in International Crises* (New York: Praeger, 1998).

33. The Croat government was actually the first to hire a public relations firm, the Ruuder Finn, to portray the conflict. Aleksandar Pavkovic, "Wars for Independence, 1991–1995," *The Fragmentation of Yugoslavia: Nationalism and the War in the Balkans*, 2nd edn (London: Macmillan, 2000), p. 147. See also: Spyros A. Sofos, "Culture, Media and the Politics of Disintegration and Ethnic Division in Former Yugoslavia," in Allen and Seaton, *The Media in Conflict*, chapter 8.

34. Tim Judah, *Kosovo: War and Revenge* (New Haven: Yale University Press, 2000), p. 57.

35. Misha Glenny, *The Fall of Yugoslavia* (New York: Penguin Books, 1992), p. 44; Misha Glenny, *The Balkans, 1804–1999: Nationalism, War and the Great Powers* (London: Granta Books, 1999), p. 629.

36. Howard Clark, *Civil Resistance in Kosovo* (London: Pluto Press, 2000), p. 18.

37. Julie Mertus, *How Myths and Truths Started a War* (Berkeley, CA: University of California Press, 1999), p. 8.

38. Mel McNulty, "Media Ethnicization and the International Response to War and Genocide in Rwanda," in Allen and Seaton, *The Media of Conflict*, p. 270.

39. For a discussion about the role of Holocaust images in post–Cold War conflicts, see: Susan D. Moeller, "Covering War: Getting Graphic about Genocide," *Compassion Fatigue*.

40. McNulty, "Media Ethnicization and the International Response to War and Genocide in Rwanda," p. 274.

41. Moeller, *Compassion Fatigue*, p. 229.

42. Moeller, *Compassion Fatigue*, p. 223.

43. See: Terrell Northrup, "The Dynamics of Identity in Personal and Social Conflict," in Louis Kriesberg, Terrell Northrup, and Stuart Thorson, *Intractable Conflicts and their Transformation* (Syracuse, NY: Syracuse University Press, 1989). See also: Herbert C. Kelman, "Social-Psychological Dimensions of International Conflict," in I. William Zartman and J. Lewis Rasmussen, eds, *Peacemaking in International Conflict: Methods and Techniques* (Washington, DC: US Institute of Peace Press, 1997), pp. 191–238.

44. Ball notes that ideological indoctrination and propaganda, with its corollary concept of distancing, are central to any explanation of genocide. He points to phrasing for victims in different contexts of genocide, for example, as undesirable parasites (Bosnia), dog food (Turkey), a creature not of this world with horns and tails (Rwanda-Hutu Power), less valuable than a pig because a pig is edible (Japan). Howard Ball, *Prosecuting War Crimes and Genocide: The Twentieth Century Experience* (Lawrence, KS: University of Kansas, 1999), p. 220.

45. See: Yuen Fhong Kong, *Analogies at War: Korea, Munich, Dien Bien Phu, and the Vietnam Decisions of 1965* (Princeton: Princeton University Press, 1992).

46. Herbert C. Kelman and V. Lee Hamilton, *Crimes of Obedience: Toward a Social Psychology of Authority and Responsibility* (New Haven: Yale University Press, 1989).

47. Edward Albee, *Who's Afraid of Virginia Woolff?* (New York: Penguin, 1962).

48. Kenneth Waltz, *Theory of International Politics* (Reading, MA: Addison-Wesley, 1979).

49. See: Fred Dallmayr and T. A. McCarthy, eds, *Understanding and Social Inquiry* (Notre Dame, IN: University of Notre Dame Press, 1977), p. 116; and Hannah Pitkin, *Wittgenstein and Justice: On the Significance of Ludwig Wittgenstein for Social and Political Thought* (Berkeley: University of California Press, 1972).

50. Pitkin, *Wittgenstein and Justice*, pp. 150–2.

51. For a discussion of the Adversarial model, see: Jay Rothman, *From Confrontation to Cooperation: Resolving Ethnic and Regional Conflict* (London: Sage, 1992).

52. For a discussion of the significance of asymmetry, see: Kumar Rupesinghe, *Civil Wars, Civil Peace: An Introduction to Conflict Resolution* (London: Pluto, 1998); and William Zartman, *Elusive Peace: Negotiating an End to Civil War* (Washington, DC: Brookings Institute, 1995).

53. John Burton, *Conflict Resolution: Its Language and Process* (Scarecrow, 1996); Jay Rothman, *From Conflict to Cooperation: Resolving Ethnic and Regional Conflict* (Boulder, CO: Sage, 1992).

54. Raymond Cohen, *Negotiating Across Cultures: International Communication in an Interdependent World* (Washington, DC: US Institute for Peace, 1997).

55. Richard Holbrooke, *To End a War* (New York: The Modern Library, 1998).

56. For an overview of the theory and practice of mediation, see: Jacob Bercovitch, "Mediation in International Conflict: An Overview of Theory, A Review of Practice," in Zartman and Rasmussen, *Peacemaking in International Conflict*, pp. 125–54.

57. Rothman, *From Conflict to Cooperation*.

58. The High Commissioner seeks early resolution of ethnic tensions that might endanger peace, stability, or friendly relations between OSCE and participating states.

59. The concept of ripeness was developed by Zartman. See: I. William Zartman, *Ripe for Resolution* (New York: Oxford University Press, 1985/1989).

8 Therapeutic Interventions

1. Stanley Cavell, "Comments on Veena Das's Essay 'Language and Body: Transactions in the Construction of Pain,' " in Arthur Kleinman, Veena Das, and Margaret Lock, eds, *Social Suffering* (Berkeley, CA: University of California Press, 1997), p. 94.

2. Ian Hacking, *Rewriting the Soul: Multiple Personality and the Sciences of Memory* (Princeton: Princeton University Press, 1995); see also: Elizabeth Fischer-Homberg, *Die Traumatische Neurose: vom Samtischen zum sozialen Leiden* (Bern: Huber, 1975); and Ruth Leys, *Trauma: A Genealogy* (Chicago: University of Chicago Press, 2000).

3. Leys, *Trauma: A Genealogy*.

4. For a discussion of the diagnostic criteria of PTSD, see: Judith Herman, *Trauma and Recovery* (New York: Basic Books, 1997); Bessel van der Kolk, A. McFarland, and L. Weisaeth, eds, *Traumatic Stress: The Effects of Overwhelming*

Experience on the Mind, Body and Society (New York: Guildford, 1996); J. P. Wilson, "The Historical Evolution of PTSD Diagnostic Criteria," in J. P. Wilson and B. Raphael, eds, *International Handbook of Traumatic Stress Syndromes* (New York: Plenum Press, 1993).

5. AllenYoung, *Harmony of Illusions: Inventing Post-Traumatic Stress Disorder* (Princeton: Princeton University Press, 1997), p. 5. Young also points out that the desire for compensation also played a role in the manifestation of symptoms. Judith Herman has emphasized the importance of political movements, also relating to child abuse and the women's movement in gaining recognition for the existence of trauma. Herman, *Trauma and Recovery*. Diagnostic criteria for "Gross Stress Reaction" were formulated in 1952, and codified as PTSD in 1987. *The Diagnostic and Statistical Manual of Mental Disorders*, which is the clinical handbook of the American Psychiatric Association, has specified and revised the concept of trauma in several stages (DSM-I, 1952; DSM-II, 1968; DSM-III, 1987; DSM-IV, 1994).

6. Young, *Harmony of Illusions*; DSM-IV, 1994.

7. Thomas Hobbes, *Leviathan* (New York: Penguin Books, [1651] 1980).

8. Rena Moses-Hrushovski, *Grief and Grievance: The Assassination of Yitzak Rabin* (London: Minerva Press, 2000), p. xv.

9. See, for instance: Saul Friedlander, ed., *Probing the Limits of Representation: Nazism and the "Final Solution"* (Cambridge, MA: Harvard University Press, 1992); Julie Kristeva, *Black Sun. Depression and Melancholia,* translated by L. S. Roudiez (New York: Columbia University Press, 1989); and Jenny Edkins, *Trauma Time and the Memory of Politics* (Cambridge: Cambridge University Press, 2003). Patrick Bracken argues that trauma is a expression of the post-modern condition and the collapse of meta-narratives of meaning. Patrick Bracken, *Trauma: Culture, Meaning and Philosophy* (London: Whurr Publishers, 2002).

10. Derek Summerfield, "The Social Experience of War and Some Issues for the Humanitarian Field," in Patrick J. Bracken and Celia Petty, eds, *Rethinking the Trauma of War* (London: Free Association Books, 1998), pp. 9–37.

11. The view that trauma has a destablizing effect on the meaningfulness of a victim's world is widespread among practitioners of PTSD. See: R. J. Lifton, "Understanding the Traumatized Self: Imagery, Symbolization, and Transformation," in J. P. Wilson, ed., *Human Adaptation to Extreme Stress* (New York: Plenum, 1988); S. Epstein, "The Self-Concept, the Traumatic Neurosis, and the Structure of Personality," in D. Ozer, J. M. Healy, and A. J. Steward, eds, *Perspectives on Personality*, vol. 3 (London: Jessica Kingsley, 1991); D. Meichenbaum, *Treating Traumatic Stress Disorder: A Handbook and Practice Manual for Therapy* (Chichester: John Wiley and Sons, 1997); R. Janoff-Bulman, *Shattered Assumptions: Towards a New Psychology of Trauma* (New York: The Free Press, 1992); and I. L. McCann and L. A. Pearlman, *Psychological Trauma and the Adult Survivor: Theory, Therapy and Transformation* (New York: Brunner/Mazel, 1990).

12. Edkins, *Trauma Time*.

13. For a very thorough analysis of this absence and several propositions about the relationship, see Neta C. Crawford, "The Passion of World Politics: Propositions on Emotion and Emotional Relationships," *International Security*, 24, 4 (2000).

14. See: Edkins, *Trauma Time*.

15. Vamik Volkan, *Bloodlines: From Ethnic Pride to Ethnic Terror* (Boulder, CO: Westerview Press, 1997).

16. Volkan, *Bloodlines*, p. 40.

17. Volkan presents the example of the Navajo for whom time stopped in 1864 when Kit Carson and his men destroyed their way of life. The population was decimated by the three-hundred mile march to Fort Sumner, often referred to as the "Long Walk." Those who survived passed down the memory of the tragedy to descendents, as if the later generation could carry out the mourning and adaptation that their ancestors could not (Volkan, *Bloodlines*, p. 41).

18. Volkan, *Bloodlines*, p. 42.

19. Zahava Solomon, "From Denial to Recognition: Attitudes Toward Holocaust Survivors from World War II to the Present," *Journal of Traumatic Stress*, 8, 2 (1995).

20. Moses-Hrushovski, *Grief and Grievance*.

21. Volkan, *Bloodlines*, p. 46.

22. For a discussion of the problem of the relationship between the unconscious and trauma for social memory, see: K. M. Fierke, "Bewitched by the Past: Social Memory, Trauma and International Relations," in Duncan Bell, ed., *Memory, Trauma and World Politics* (forthcoming).

23. Fergus Kerr, *Theology After Wittgenstein* (Oxford: Blackwell, 1996), p. 76.

24. "Inside the mind of a terrorist," *The Observer*, March 9 (2003), 24–5.

25. For instance, he states: "The people in their overwhelming majority are so feminine by nature and attitude that sober reasoning determines their thoughts and actions far less than emotion and feeling." Adolf Hitler, *Mein Kampf* (London: Pimlico [translation 1969] 2001), pp. 164–9.

26. For a more in-depth discussion of the idea that political trauma is based in language, and of this particular case, see: K. M. Fierke, "Whereof We Can Speak, Thereof We Must Not be Silent: Trauma, Political Solipsism and War," *Review of International Studies*, 30, 4 (2004).

27. As cited in Thomas J. Scheff and Suzanne M. Rezinger, *Emotion and Violence: Shame and Rage in Destructive Conflicts* (Lexington, MA: Lexington Books, 1991), p. 158.

28. Hitler, *Mein Kampf*, p. 577.

29. Patricia Hayner, *Unspeakable Truths: Confronting State Terror and Atrocity* (London: Routledge, 2001), p. 134.

30. Michael Cox, "Bringing in the 'International': The IRA Ceasefire and the end of the Cold War," *International Affairs*, 73, 4 (1997), 671–93; Michael Cox, Adrian Guelke, and Fiona Stephen, eds, *Farewell to Arms? From "Long War" to Long Peace in Northern Ireland* (Manchester: Manchester University Press, 2000); Andrew Wilson, "From the Beltway to Belfast: The Clinton Administration, Sinn Fein, and the Northern Ireland Peace Process," *New Hibernia Review*, 1, 3 (1997), 23–39; Roger MacGinty, "Bill Clinton and the Northern Ireland Peace Process," *Aussenpolitik*, 111 (1997), 237–44.

31. Kenneth Waltz, *Theory of International Politics* (Reading, MA: Addison-Wesley, 1979). See, in particular, his discussion of socialization into conflict which relies on an analogy to George and Martha in Edward Albee's play, *Who's Afraid of Virginia Woolf?*

32. George Mitchell, *Making Peace* (Berkeley, CA: University of California Press, 1999), p. 37.

33. George Mitchell, " 'There will be Peace'—But First, Violence and Intransigence in Northern Ireland Must End," Editorial, *The Boston Herald*, March 16, 1997, 25.

34. Mitchell, *Making Peace*, pp. 32–3.

35. John Burton, *Conflict Resolution: Its Language and Process* (Lanham, MD: Scarecrow, 1996); Chris Mitchell and Michael Banks, *Handbook of Conflict Resolution* (London: Pinter, 1996); Jay Rothman, *From Confrontation to Cooperation: Resolving Ethnic and Regional Conflict* (Boulder, CO: Sage, 1992); Deioniol Lloyd Jones, *Cosmopolitan Mediation?—Conflict Resolution and the Oslo Accords* (Manchester: Manchester University Press, 1999).

36. Rothman, *From Confrontation to Cooperation.*

37. In the Northern Ireland context, the first hurdle was to get actors to speak face to face. Gerry Adams voice had been censored from the media for close to two decades, given a conviction that allowing "terrorists" to speak would grant them legitimacy. This stigma haunted the process until after the Belfast Agreement was signed, when the first face-to-face meeting between Adams and Trimble finally began.

38. Holland, *Hope against History*, pp. 318–19.

39. William C. Wohlforth, ed., *Witnesses to the End of the Cold War* (Baltimore, MD: The Johns Hopkins University Press, 1996); K. M. Fierke, *Changing Games, Changing Strategies: Critical Investigations in Security* (Manchester: Manchester University Press, 1998).

40. Tutu further emphasizes the African approach to justice is more restorative, in contrast to the Western emphasis on retribution. The goal is to redress or restore a balance rather than punish. He stated, "The justice we hope for is restorative of the dignity of the people." See: Tina Rosenberg, "A Reporter at Large: Recovering from Apartheid," *New Yorker*, November 18, 1996.

41. Analysts of the TRCs have contrasted the ends of vengeance and forgiveness. While both War Crimes Tribunals and TRCs seek to accumulate an accurate record of the past, in order to move beyond it, the former focuses more on punishment and vengeance, and latter on forgiveness. Martha Minow, *Between Vengeance and Forgiveness* (Boston, MA: Beacon Press, 1998); Hayner, *Unspeakable Truths.*

42. Minow, *Between Vengeance and Forgiveness*, p. 61.

43. Father Hehir, *Truth Commissions: A Comparative Assessment*, 24, as cited in Minow, *Between Vengeance and Forgiveness*, p. 79.

44. Rosenberg, "Reporter at Large," 86, 95.

45. Hayner, *Unspeakable Truths*, p. 139.

46. Hayner, *Unspeakable Truths*, p. 141.

47. Bracken and Petty, *Rethinking the Trauma of War.*

48. Daniel Hallock, *Hell, Healing and Resistance: Veterans Speak* (Farmington, PA: The Plough Publishing House, 1998). British soldiers from the Falklands War have also recently taken action against the British government for lack of support in dealing with the trauma of war.

49. Bracken and Petty, *Rethinking the Trauma of War*, p. 50.

50. Bracken and Petty, *Rethinking the Trauma of War*, p. 53.

51. Summerfield, "The Social Experience of War."

52. N. Higgenbotham and A. Marsella, "International Consultation and the Homogenization of Psychiatry in Southeast Asia," *Social Science and Medicine*, 27 (1988), 553–61.

53. Vanessa Pupavac, "Therapeutic Governance: Psycho-Social Intervention and Trauma Risk Management," *Disasters*, 25, 4 (2001), 358–72.

54. Sharon Lamb, *The Trouble with Blame: Victims, Perpetrators and Responsibility* (Boston, MA: Harvard University Press, 1999), p. 150.

55. For further reading on reparations, see: David Horowitz, *Uncivil Wars: The Controversy Over Reparations for Slavery* (San Francisco, CA: Encounter Books, 2002); Raymond A. Winbush, ed., *Should America Pay? Slavery and the Raging Debate on Reparations* (New York: Amistad, 2003); Ellis Cose, *Bone to Pick: Of Forgiveness, Reconciliation, Reparation, and Revenge* (New York: Atria Books, 2004); Roy L. Brooks, eds., *When Sorry Isn't Enough: The Controversy Over Apologies and Reparations for Human Injustice* (New York: New York University Press, 1999).

56. Martha Minow, *Breaking the Cycles of Hatred: Memory, Law and Repair* (Princeton, NJ: Princeton University Press, 2002), p. 23.

57. Minow, *Breaking the Cycles of Hatred*, p. 9.

58. Structured dialogues, in the conflict resolution tradition, created a space for both sides in a conflict to tell their story, to the end of creating "analytic empathy" such that each could understand that the other has suffered as much as they. See: Rothman, *From Conflict to Cooperation*.

59. Susan Bickford, *The Dissonance of Democracy: Listening, Conflict and Citizenship* (Ithaca, NY: Cornell University Press, 1996).

60. James DerDerian, *On Diplomacy* (Oxford: Blackwell, 1987).

9 Critical Interventions

1. David Campbell, *National Deconstruction: Violence, Identity and Justice in Bosnia* (Minneapolis: University of Minnesota Press, 1998), p. 4.

2. Campbell, *National Deconstruction*, p. 5.

3. Ludwig Wittgenstein, *Philosophical Investigations* (Oxford: Basil Blackwell, 1958), para. 18.

4. He said, "A main source of our failure to understand is that we do not *command a clear view* of our use of words—Our grammar is lacking in this sort of perspicuity. A perspicuous representation produces just that understanding which consists in 'seeing connexions'. Hence the importance of finding and inventing *intermediate cases*. The concept of a perspicuous representation is of fundamental significance for us. It earmarks the form of account we give, the way we look at this ..." Wittgenstein, *Philosophical Investigations*, para. 122.

5. Robert W. Cox, "Social Forces, States and World Orders: Beyond International Relations Theory," *Millennium*, 10, 2 (1981), 128.

6. Kenneth Waltz, *Theory of International Politics* (Reading, MA: Addison-Wesley, 1979). See, for instance: Robert Keohane, ed., *Neorealism and its Critics* (New York: Columbia University Press, 1986).

7. Waltz, *Theory of International Politics*, p. 34.

8. Waltz, *Theory of International Politics*, p. 33.

9. Richard Wyn Jones, *Security, Strategy and Critical Theory* (Boulder, CO: Lynne Rienner, 1999), p. 85.
10. Jones, *Security, Strategy and Critical Theory*, p. 76.
11. Edward Said, *Representations of the Intellectual* (London: Vintage, 1994), p. 84.
12. Anne Orford, *Reading Humanitarian Intervention: Human Rights and the Use of Force in International Law* (Cambridge: Cambridge University Press, 2003).
13. Elaine Scarry, *The Body in Pain: The Making and Unmaking of the World* (Oxford: Oxford University Press, 1985).
14. For a discussion of this history, see: K. M. Fierke and Michael Nicholson, "Divided by a Common Language: Formal and Constructivist Approaches to Games," *Global Society*, 15, 1 (2001), 7–26.
15. For a more in-depth discussion of these ideas, see: K. M. Fierke, *Changing Games, Changing Strategies: Critical Investigations in Security* (Manchester: Manchester University Press, 1998).
16. Orford, *Reading Humanitarian Intervention*, p. 31. In making this point she draws on John Berger's work. See John Berger, *About Looking* (New York: Random House, 1988).
17. Orford, *Reading Humanitarian Intervention*, p. 11.
18. Orford, *Reading Humanitarian Intervention*, pp. 17–18.
19. Cynthia Enloe, *The Morning After: Sexual Politics at the End of the Cold War* (Berkeley, CA: University of California Press, 1993), p. 184.
20. Orford, *Reading Humanitarian Intervention*, p. 26.
21. Orford, *Reading Humanitarian Intervention*, p. 31.
22. Robert M. Cover, "Forward: Norms and Narrative, *Harvard Law Review*," 97 (1983), 54.
23. Scarry, *The Body in Pain*, p. 132.
24. Scarry, *The Body in Pain*, p. 125.
25. Scarry, *The Body in Pain*, p. 125.
26. Scarry, *The Body in Pain*, p. 128.
27. As the distinction between combatant and civilian has dissolved, the number of civilian casualties and wounded in war has outstripped that of combatant casualties. Arguably, forms of "humane" warfare that allow the targeting of strategic assets from a great distance, while intending to reduce "collateral" damage, that is, of civilians, have been more successful in protecting soldiers on the side of the intervenor. For an in-depth discussion of the concept of "humane warfare," see: Christopher Coker, *Humane Warfare* (London: Routledge, 2001). The landscape of war has thus altered. Forms of military intervention often originate outside of the central contest of war to which they are responding. Forms of aerial bombardment from a distance keep the intervenors out of harm's way. The task of peacekeeping has been expanded to include the protection or assistance of civilians in war, while the precipitating contest continues in the background. The two are not easily combined in so far as the threat of aerial bombardment may turn peacekeepers on the ground into the targets of war, like those they are attempting to protect. The question is whether these acts, intended to alter the shape of the contest, in so doing provide scope for addressing the subject over which the contest is being fought, that is, two competing self-descriptions of reality.
28. The concept has been criticized for its emphasis on the individual rather than state or societal security. See, for instance: Barry Buzan, "A Reductionist,

Idealistic Notion that Adds Little Analytical Value," *Security Dialogue* 35, 3 (2004).

29. Scarry, *The Body in Pain*, p. 50.
30. Scarry, *The Body in Pain*, p. 155.
31. This absence is revealed in the difficulty of withdrawing consent from nuclear weapons; the whole notion of "acting as if," so powerfully mobilized in nonviolent campaigns against an oppressor, is virtually impossible with nuclear weapons except as an act of imagination. It is possible to "act as if" Europe were whole and free, as many independent movements in East and West did in the decade prior to the end of the Cold War. It is virtually impossible to act as if nuclear weapons do not exist.
32. It is not surprising, within this framework, that the transfer of power from the occupiers to an interim Iraqi government happened soon after the exposure of the treatment of Iraqi prisoners.
33. Mark Duffield, *Global Governance and the New Wars* (London: Zed Books, 2001).
34. Duffield, *Global Governance and the New Wars*, p. 22.
35. Duffield, *Global Governance and the New Wars*, p. 17.
36. Benjamin Cohen, *The Question of Imperialism: The Political Economy of Dominance and Dependence* (Basingstoke: Macmillan, 1973).
37. Lloyd Axworthy, "Introduction," in Rob McRae and Don Hubert, eds, *Human Security and the New Diplomacy: Protecting People, Promoting Peace* (Montreal and Kingston: McGill-Queen's University Press, 2001), p. 9.
38. Joseph S. Nye, Jr., *The Paradox of American Power* (Oxford: Oxford University Press, 2000), p. 9.
39. See, for instance: Frank Furedi, *The New Ideology of Imperialism* (London: Junius Publications Ltd, 1994) and Noam Chomsky, *The New Military Humanism: Lessons from Kosovo* (London: Pluto Press, 1999).
40. Susan Bickford, *The Dissonance of Democracy: Listening, Conflict and Citizenship* (Ithaca, NY: Cornell University Press, 1996).
41. Indeed, as Hannah Arendt argues, violence and power can be seen as opposites. While opposites, the two usually appear together. However, where one rules absolutely the other is absent. Hannah Arendt, "Communicative Power," in S. Lukes, ed., *Power* (New York: New York University Press, 1986), pp. 64–5, 71.
42. Omer Bartov, *Mirrors of Destruction: War, Genocide and Modern Identity* (Oxford: Oxford University Press, 2000), p. 5.
43. Bartov, *Mirrors of Destruction*, p. 166.
44. John M. Heaton, *Wittgenstein and Psychoanalysis* (Cambridge: Icon Books, 2000), p. 54.
45. Ludwig Wittgenstein, *Philosophical Investigations* (Oxford: Basil Blackwell, 1958), para. 129.

Index

Page numbers in bold indicate tables.